SYNOC: 17th Grade Level Reading

Religious Education
Ministry with Youth

Religious Education Ministry with Youth

Edited by

D. Campbell Wyckoff and Don Richter

Religious Education Press
Birmingham, Alabama

Copyright © 1982 by Religious Education Press
All rights reserved

Library of Congress Cataloging in Publication Data

Main entry under title:

Religious education ministry with youth.

    Includes bibliographical references and index.
    1. Christian education of young people—
Addresses, essays, lectures.   I. Wyckoff, D.
Campbell.   II. Richter, Don.
BV1485.R43   261.8'3423   81-19239
ISBN 0-89135-030-6   AACR2

Religious Education Press, Inc.
1531 Wellington Road
Birmingham, Alabama 35209
10 9 8 7 6 5 4

Religious Education Press publishes books exclusively in religious education and in areas closely related to religious education. It is committed to enhancing and professionalizing religious education through the publication of serious, significant, and scholarly works.

PUBLISHER TO THE PROFESSION

Contents

Preface   vii

1. A Bibliographical Survey of Youth and Youth Ministry   1
   Don Richter
2. Questions the Church Needs to Answer About Youth   54
   Freda A. Gardner
3. Culture, Youth, and Socialization in American
   Protestantism   75
   Gwen Kennedy Neville
4. Problems, Predicaments, and Gravity   100
   Roger W. Paine III
5. Desired Outcomes of Religious Education and
   Youth Ministry in Six Denominations   132
   Dean R. Hoge et al.
6. Youth and Church Renewal   149
   Lawrence O. Richards
7. *Kairos* and Youth: A Call for Community   166
   Jackie M. Smith
8. The Creative Process in Adolescent Development   208
   Don Richter
   Afterword   242
   D. Campbell Wyckoff
   Index of Names   250
   Index of Subjects   254

Preface

For all the efforts that the churches have made to work with youth, what is being done currently remains rather ineffective in reaching youth at their points of need, in engaging them responsibly in the life and work of the church, and in getting at the vital contribution that they must make to its present and future.

Denominational youth organizations have largely been dismantled in recent years. Responsibility now rests largely with local congregations not only for the quality of youth work, but indeed for its very existence. There are great differences from congregation to congregation in what is being done. The churches are, for the most part, ineffective in reaching a significant number of youth. Youth leaders flounder.

To some extent the churches have been thrown off base by the demographic changes in our population. Increased attention has been given to the older elements. While this is good in itself, it has tended to be detrimental to the claims of ministry with youth.

There is little agreement on what church youth work is to be or the future direction it is to take. Important projects have been undertaken to serve particular groups like black youth and inner-city youth, and out of this has grown the conviction that the problems of adolescents in our society, for all their differences, transcend racial lines and class divisions.

But how is this conviction to be translated into action?

The need is for the churches to recommit themselves to a ministry with youth. This need may be addressed by engaging representatives of the churches, including clergy, professionals, youth, and adult volunteers in:

—A critical reassessment of ministry with youth, including recent efforts in this work.

—Thinking about youth work in the coming days in ways that are appropriate to the challenges of the 1980s.

—Developing new forms of ministry with youth, exploring promising models now in use.

—Assessing all the resources for leadership: clergy, professional Christian educators, youth, and adult volunteers.

Considerations such as the following emerge as necessary in recommitment of the churches to youth ministry:

—The basic dynamics in youth ministry need clarifying: the dynamics of self-esteem, authority, and peer relationships, as well as the dynamics of working with youth and families with emphasis on the intergenerational.

—Parents are the key to youth ministry, and are to be approached as persons with their own problems, needs, and aspirations, not merely in their role as parents.

—Youth ministry is to be conceived as integral to the ministry of the church and its educational work, not as separate from the church.

—The unit of mission is now the local congregation. In addition, it can be the judicatory (a presbytery, conference, diocese, or association). Judicatories are now treated as units of administration rather than units of mission.

—Training events are to be experiences of youth ministry in themselves ("Let's experience these things together; let's come together and *do* ministry,") as over against administrative events ("Let's think of how it can be done").

—The development of a theology of youth ministry, a working theological context for youth ministry, is crucial in the face of the value crisis in the culture. Then perhaps programs may be developed that local people can operate.

These were hypotheses for a two-year project, sponsored by Princeton Theological Seminary and funded by the Lilly Endowment, Inc., of which this book is a substantial, if partial, report. Two basic stages of the project are reported here. The first stage was the assembling of the preliminary survey of what is known about today's youth, the condition of youth work in the churches, and existing youth programs of promise. Chapter 1 consists of the survey and concludes with a summary of findings and the presentation of a list of questions still requiring investigation.

The second stage of the project was a study conference, held at Princeton Theological Seminary's Center of Continuing Education, at which a representative group of scholars and youth workers met to consider a series of papers designed to lift up essential elements in the future of youth ministry.

Freda A. Gardner's paper, chapter 2, sets the problems of youth ministry in perspective, and sorts out the basic elements requiring study.

Gwen Kennedy Neville, in the paper included here as chapter 3, brings to the project the skills and findings of a social scientist who is at the same time keenly interested in youth ministry. Her challenge is that youth be seen deliberately and analytically in the cultural setting of the family and community.

In chapter 4, Roger W. Paine III, contributes the insights of the psychological analyst and counselor. But more, his very style of presentation and his insights born of long personal and professional experience make youth and their families live for us, communicate something of the depth of his insight to us, and motivate strongly toward youth ministry.

Sober and challenging realities on church youth are reviewed by Dean R. Hoge and his Boys Town Research Center colleagues in chapter 5.

Lawrence O. Richards, who thinks and works in the framework of evangelical church renewal, explores in chapter 6 the dynamics and implications for youth ministry of the recovery of the community of faith as family.

In chapter 7, Jackie M. Smith calls for orientation of our thinking in youth ministry to the threats, crises, and challenges of the contemporary world. Christ's call is to a ministry of justice, and Smith's vision of youth ministry is that it will answer that call courageously and without flinching.

Community, personal faith, creativity, and mission are blended in the acts of youth ministry reported by Don Richter in chapter 8. Those acts of ministry stem from his own experience and testify to the fact that fruitful youth ministry is a contemporary reality.

These papers (chapters 2–4 and 6–8, Hoge's being excepted), before being analyzed and discussed by the conference participants, were systematically reflected on by Andrew P. Grannell, then of Bangor Theological Seminary, and now of St. John's University, Collegeville, Minnesota. Grannell's reflections provide the continuity by which the elements in youth ministry included in the papers are clarified, their relationship to each other established, and points for further discussion identified.

The Afterword reports the summary of insights with which the study conference concluded and the subsequent work of the project's steering committee in determining the elements to be included in an experimental model for youth ministry.

Many persons were responsible for bringing the youth ministry study to completion and thereby making this book possible. Robert W. Lynn, vice president for religion at the Lilly Endowment, has shown consistent interest in the project, and has provided suggestions and encouragement. He has made available the services of an evaluator, in the person of Sara Little. In the process, Sara Little became one of the major guides in determining the character and the direction of the project.

The original design of the youth ministry project was worked out by a steering committee appointed by James I. McCord, president of Princeton Theological Seminary. The steering committee developed, in addition to the original design, every aspect of the work, and has been careful both to redesign when necessary and to refuse to let the project "get ahead of itself." Don Richter served as project director. The other members were Freda A. Gardner, James E. Loder, Jr., Stephen F. Boehlke, William N. Kight, and Roger W. Uittenbogaard. Freda Gardner chaired the committee during the months in which the plans for the consultation were taking definitive shape. James F. Armstrong assisted in drawing up the project proposal.

When Don Richter took in the task of project director, he was a middler at Princeton Theological Seminary. As the project is coming to its conclusion, he is a graduating senior, and has accepted a call to join the staff of the Second Presbyterian Church of Louisville, Kentucky.

D. CAMPBELL WYCKOFF

Chapter 1

A Bibliographical Survey of Youth and Youth Ministry

DON RICHTER

This chapter surveys what is known about today's youth and the condition of youth in the churches.

There are five sections. Section I explores resources that consider youth from a sociological perspective. Section II is divided into subsection A—Behavioral Studies of Youth, and subsection B—Behavioral Studies of the Religious Experience of Youth. This section evaluates in particular the insights to be gained from developmental psychology. Section III presents those works that are most helpful in developing a theological and practical framework for doing youth ministry. Section IV is a summary of findings. Section V, based on these findings, is a list of questions for further inquiry.

The materials analyzed here were selected as representative from a comprehensive list of available books and articles. They were chosen for the significance of their ideas and findings, and for their coverage of the field.

YOUTH FROM A SOCIOLOGICAL PERSPECTIVE

In this first section, it is appropriate to consider the situation of youth within the larger context of culture and society. Six books that offer insightful resource material in this area are Smith

1

(1962), Sherif and Sherif (1964), Manning and Truzzi (1972), Havighurst and Dreyer (1975), Westerhoff and Neville (1979), and Paine (1975).

The structural-functionalist adolescence presented by Ernest Smith in *American Youth Culture* is not outdated, for it provides a sound sociological framework for defining youth in addition to listing the characteristics of a particular generation of young people (the 1950s). His approach is to shift attention away from the formal institutions of adult culture (church, school, family), and to examine, instead, the *informal* institutions of youth (clique, crowd, dating) that satisfy the young person's basic socialization needs.

Young persons tend to progress through these different levels of informal groups as they strive for adult status. Ironically, dating (single male with single female), which should be a natural and desirable relationship for young people, may often be dysfunctional because of disapproval and discouragement by adults. Conflict between youth and adult culture is mitigated by the withdrawal of youth from adult institutions (e.g., the church). In this way, young people find the freedom to develop and to reinforce the autonomy, norms, and behavior of their own culture.

Thus, youth culture has evolved to fulfill the essential socialization functions of adolescents. The degree of unity and organization of youth culture varies inversely with the degree of its integration with adult culture. Smith's observations were validated by the prominence of youth movements during the 1960s.

Group formation's basic concepts and significance for adolescent behavior are demonstrated in the empirical research done by Sherif and Sherif for *Reference Groups*. Groups, whether formal or informal, have identifiable characteristics. A group delineates those who are "in" from those who are "out" and restricts ingroup conversation to certain topics. Group members are related to one another through definitive role expectations that involve status and role differentiation. A code of values or set of norms is formed internally by the group to regulate the relationships and behavior of its members.

The "reference group" is that association of people with which an individual identifies and to which he or she aspires to belong. The reference group has a formative influence on the attitudes of its individual members. Because of the uncertain self-image and the great need for acceptance experienced by most adolescents, their reference groups (usually peer groups) become more important, influential, and predictive factors of their current behavior than are parents, school, or church.

There are two particularly pertinent articles in Manning and Truzzi's *Youth and Sociology*. In "Archetypal Patterns of Youth" (1961), S.N. Eisenstadt claims that we must consider youth not only in biological and chronological terms, but also in cultural terms. He maintains that an archetype of youth is exemplified by the universal phenomenon of the rite of passage, which has these cross-cultural characteristics:

1) The adolescent is symbolically divested of the characteristics of childhood and invested with those of the adult.

2) There is sometimes a symbolic separation of males from their mothers and females from their fathers.

3) There is a dramatization of intergenerational conflict expressing the discontinuity between adolescent and adult.

4) Tribal lore and instructions for behavior are transmitted.

5) There is a relaxation of adults' external authority, replaced by an assumption of internal authority and responsibility on the adolescents' part.

Eisenstadt holds that adolescence may be the only age in which full identification with the ultimate symbols and values of a society is obtained. This is problematic for youth, people striving for adulthood, for they sense the discontinuity between the idealistic social values that are presented to them and the reality of contradictory values manifest in adult lifestyles.

Eisenstadt points to youth culture as the main socializing unit for young people in a pluralistic society, whereas kinship patterns perform this function in traditional societies.

The second particularly insightful article in *Youth and Sociology* is Robert Jay Lifton's "Protean Man" (1970). There are three characteristics of the "Protean Man," who is the prototype of the modern individual: psychohistorical dislocation, a fragmented ideology, and the search for a new immortality.

Psychohistorical dislocation is the result of a lack of perceived continuity in experience. Ironically, historical forces play an increasing role in the emergence of a universally shared style of ahistorical self-process. "Self-process" is more resonant with the Protean Man's experience of self than is "personality" or "character." Only the moment of here and now is valuable, and there is no celebration of the past nor hope in the future; the individual is a passive victim of process.

There is a shift from a fixed form of ideology to more fluid ideological fragments. Like Proteus, the Protean Man can assume many shapes (a polymorphous personality) but cannot become committed to any one. Therefore, a life of inconsistent values and behavior is not problematic, because life itself is perceived as ambiguous. Flexibility and noncommitment are exalted, especially during adolescence. Truth is viewed as relative and ethics are situational. Above all, experiences sought are those that give a meaning to life.

With Protean Man, the traditional modes of immortality, such as heaven, the kingdom of God, resurrection, reincarnation, or living on through one's children, have lost their power to connect a person with all of human history. Yet there is a compelling urge for the Protean Man to establish a means of symbolic immortality, which is done by projecting self over against nature (time and space) and by experimenting with self-transcendence.

Whether any of these characteristics of Protean Man may be applied to youth, Lifton does not explicitly say. However, if the existential awareness of "Protean Man" is made possible by the formal-operational stage of cognitive development, then we should reserve this question until the discussion of adolescent development in section II.

The 1974 Yearbook of the National Society for the Study of Education is a valuable compendium of studies concerning middle through late adolescence. *Youth*, edited by Robert Havighurst and Philip Dreyer, deals with youth as a stage of life, youth and social institutions, and youth in a pluralistic society.

In "Prologue: Youth as a Stage of Life" (1970), Kenneth Keniston claims that the unprecedented prolongation of education in American society has extended the opportunity for psychological development and created a "new" stage of life: youth. Keniston defines youth as the stage between adolescence and adulthood, yet the themes he considers are useful for describing those in the transitional years of high school as well.

The central emerging issue for youth is the tension between self and society. Youth is the time when one first experiences the conflict between the need to develop autonomous selfhood and the necessity of social involvement. This ambivalence is explored by a testing and probing of societal values, and produces alternating feelings of omnipotentiality and estrangement for the young person. There is usually a peer-oriented rejection of the traditional socialization processes, which are replaced by the adoption of youth-specific identities and roles on a temporary basis. Youth are characterized by their need for *movement* in three ways: They have a need to be moved, a need to move others, and a need to move through the world without being "stuck in a rut." There is an abhorrence of *stasis*, for this signifies the loss of vitality associated with the "older generation" that leads inevitably to death.

There is also a positive aspect in a young person's relationship to adults, Keniston claims. Throughout adolescence, there is a transition from *hero worship* to *role-model imitation* to *sponsorship*, as the older person becomes progressively more real and three-dimensional to the younger one, whose individuality is appreciated and confirmed by the elder. A youth in late adolescence is more likely to view significant adults as sponsors who do not require their own behavior to be emulated or imitated. This is occurring at the same time that young people are compelled to live out a "telescoped reenactment" of their parents' lives, testing to see how their parents have shaped and influenced their own identities.

In her article, "Sex Differences in the Opportunities, Demands, and Development of Youth" (1974), Elizabeth Douvan explains how sexuality influences the development of identity in youth. A young male achieves identity by separating himself from others and defining his *self* in relation to a vocational choice. Then he is ready to confront the problems of intimacy (relationship). For the young female, the identity and intimacy tasks are entwined: she develops her *self* through her connection with others. Most women then go through life with an identity based primarily on their relationship to others. Douvan suggests three factors that are presently having the most significant impact on the socialization of females: 1) education, 2) birth control technology, and 3) the women's movement. As we are witnessing, the changing role of women demands even greater changes in the role of men (as, for example, in the motion picture *Kramer vs. Kramer*).

The discussion of "Youth and Experiential Learning" (1974), by Richard Graham, is a sound application of Kohlberg's stages of moral development to the public education system. Graham maintains that 75 percent of American high school graduates leave school at the stage three or stage four level of *conventional* moral judgment. This is below the stage five (*postconventional* level) principled judgment, upon which the morality of the American government and the Constitution are based. Therefore, our schools are not adequately preparing young people to be competent citizens of this country. Graham suggests the institution of action-learning programs and jobs to help youth progress through the successive stages of cognitive development, social role perspectives, and moral judgment in their transition to adulthood.

Vern Bengtson and Jerold Starr, in "Contrast and Consensus: A Generational Analysis of Youth in the 1970s" (1974), provide a comprehensive framework for analyzing the continuously emerging groups of youth interacting with structural changes and historical events, which alter the course of societies over time. They suggest five variables that must be considered when comparing age groups: age strata, lineages, aging or life-cycle stages, historical periods, and generation units (a unit is distinguished by its specific historical consciousness and ideology).

A chief contribution of this book is "Youth and Cultural Pluralism" (1974), by Robert Havighurst and Philip Dreyer. The term "cultural pluralism" conveys an understanding of many separate groups co-existing with respect for their differences. This description runs counter to the earlier "melting pot" theory of American enculturation, the ideal that was to have all of the various national groups fuse into a single, large cultural group and conform to the "American Way."

The 1970s have been termed "the Decade of the Ethnics" (Michael Novak), for there has been a marked rise in ethnic consciousness during this period. Ethnic consciousness is described by Novak in relation to Jung's theory of the collective unconscious, which transmits an historical memory and a sense of reality by archetypes. This is well-illustrated by the impact of the book and subsequent film *Roots* on our culture. This television movie represented the collective black experience in America for millions.

There are two main requirements for youth growing up in a pluralistic society. The first is that they must view their parents as their normative reference group, and they must identify with the positive attributes of the "significant others" in that group. The second requirement is that youth must understand and tolerate the right of other, differing groups to exist. This is often difficult, for in-group solidarity is commonly promoted by pointing to the faults of the out-groups. One of the few elements that oppose ethnic solidarity among youth is political-economic ideology, although this probably affects only a small percentage of youth in a convictional way.

According to Douvan, the *family* is the best paradigm for understanding pluralism on the level of social organization. The family itself is a social organization, including people with various roles, goals, needs, and interests, yet functioning as a unity within this diversity. When this system is applied on a contract (societal) rather than a kinship basis, it is highly ambitious and may lie beyond human capability.

At the individual level, a pluralistic society requires:

1. The capacity to maintain simultaneous commitment and loyalty to two or more groups.

2. A capacity for empathy or "taking the role of the other" to soften the sting of an adverse judgment when conflict arises, to ease envy and allow pleasure in the good fortune of others.

3. The capacity to integrate a self out of a variety of roles and committed identifications (p. 284).

In "Young Women and Their Roles" (1974), Helen Astin explores what kinds of early experience for girls facilitate the development of problem-solving behavior, mathematical aptitude, and ultimately a career orientation. She also summarizes the effects of sex-role identification for young men. Girls have greater latitude in achieving an appropriate gender identity than do boys, who are more vulnerable to physical and mental illness because of the pressure put upon them to achieve a well-defined male identity. "Male" traits and characteristics are nevertheless more highly valued by our society than are those associated with femininity.

According to Astin, it is not the mother's own achievement that affects her children's need of achievement, but how she deals with her children and the standards she sets for them. Boys in father-absent homes tend to develop higher verbal aptitude because the mother feels compelled to interact with her son to compensate. Girls tend to develop a higher mathematical aptitude when they are confronted early by more problem situations that they have to solve on their own. This higher mathematical aptitude seems to be the differentiating factor in a girl being career-oriented rather than developing a homemaking orientation.

Generation to Generation, by Westerhoff and Neville (1979), is a collection of essays that examine the relations between religion and culture, especially the dynamics of how both are transmitted from parent to child within religious-cultural communities. Westerhoff, as a religious educator, looks at catechesis as a process of *intentional socialization*, which aims to initiate persons into the faith community by understanding, internalizing, and transmitting its ways and values. He understands the life-long process of nurture and transformation as mediated through symbolic narrative (myth) and symbolic action (ritual). Neville, as an anthropologist, explores the structure and design of human symbolic life and the patterned regularity of recurrence of certain design features within a culture. She views these ritual assemblies as important "encapsulators" of culture that must be taught and learned for the continuation of a cultural community.

In chapter 1, Westerhoff states that the foundation of religious education must no longer be viewed as teaching of beliefs and morals or learning about scripture. The primary concern must be the life and work of the community of faith. Churches have created a bifurcation between the worship experience and the religious education program. Authentic catechesis will involve a person in the *total* life and work of the church, from liturgy to making moral decisions. The early church focused on the religious education of adults, but the contemporary church has limited catechesis to children. *Maturity* of faith must be reestablished as the goal of catechesis, as adults learn how to communicate their lives of faith more effectively to others.

Because the terms that we use to describe a process influence how it is carried out, Westerhoff (chapter 2) maintains that we should now think in terms of religious *socialization* rather than *education*. Religious education is "those deliberate, systematic, and sustained efforts of a community of faith which intentionally aim at enabling persons and groups to evolve particular ways of thinking, feeling and acting." Religious socialization is "a process consisting of lifelong formal and informal mechanisms, through which persons sustain and transmit their faith (world view, value system) and lifestyle" (p. 41). Socialization is more inclusive, involving both the intentional and the unintentional. Westerhoff bids us become more aware of the influences of "hidden curricula," the roles played by various members of the congregation, family, and peer groups, and even the space and ecology in which we live as socializing agents.

Neville (chapter 3) has studied the various subgroups of Christianity in the South as a participant-observer. Her thesis is that Christian denominational groups in America represent a continuation of various European cultural traditions. There is a particular behavior and lifestyle associated with the world view and membership in each denomination; every member of a religious group is "ethnic" in the sense of having an in-group identity. Each of these "ethnic enclaves" has shared social networks, ceremonies, and rituals, and also a way of finding suitable marriage partners for its young people and enculturating their offspring.

A ceremonial gathering for a birth, wedding, funeral, family reunion, or homecoming is the only place where a significant cultural group assemblage appears within our mobile society. The functions of such a gathering are: 1) the reenactment of shared values and the rehabituation of participants into culturally-defined behaviors; 2) the perpetuation of in-group marriages; and 3) the protection of individuals during their important life-cycle transitions.

In chapter 5, Neville discusses the significance of *ritual*, a culturally patterned behavior that functions like a language in that it is mutually intelligible to the speakers but not to the nonspeakers. Ritual behavior is any behavior that is stereotyped, repetitive, and nonobligatory; this does not make it empty or meaningless, however. Within sacred rituals a form of "telescoping" of the meaning and values that are most dear to that culture takes place. Individuals are provided rituals by their culture to help them through periods of transition. These "rites of passage" involve a *separation* from a person's former group of associates, a phase of actual *transition* (having an in-between status), and then an incorporation into the community with a new social standing.

Feeling that the process of values clarification is incomplete by itself, Westerhoff (chapter 7) explores how values are *learned* by individuals, concluding that the structure by which values are transmitted communicates the content. He shows how social structures, particularly the family, have had to be modified in response to certain historical situations. This has resulted in a change in values to meet changing needs. To respond to the current situation of the small nuclear family living in a single-family dwelling apart from kin, Westerhoff suggests that the church become a model for an extended family, providing a structure and process for intentional socialization based on the Christian faith: *koinonia*.

In chapter 8, Neville lifts up a critical concern in her discussion of sex and socialization. Schools and churches have given much lip service to sexual equality, yet the structure of our society continues to prevent women from attaining equal status with men. In the learning process, women are socialized not only by what teachers and parents and churches *say* but by what they, in fact, *do*. Presently there are few flexible role models for women in our culture (and churches), particularly for married women. Neville is not optimistic about the possibility of liberation within the present cultural ethos, but she does envision the possible emergence of new cultural groups (by the "maypole dancers") which will invent new kin relationships, rituals, and community forms.

One of the most up-to-date pictures of the American teenager is presented in *We Never Had Any Trouble Before* (1975), by Roger W. Paine III. Paine discusses the major areas of conflict that are presently occurring between parents and adolescents. He offers advice to the parents as to how they might comfort and confront their teenage sons and daughters in a rational and loving way. Two important propositions undergird the thesis of this book: 1) keeping communication open and honest is a must in relating effectively to young people; 2) youth will make mistakes (despite advanced warning), and adults should accept this fact and let young people live their own lives.

There are three areas which are especially pertinent to our study:

1) *What is "normal?"* We are now in a period that combines values from both the 1950s and the 1960s. As was true with the youth studies in the 1950s, the main goals of today's youth center around achieving material security in life, not propounding idealism. The factors that now complicate the lives of adolescents in a unique way are: the birth control pill, the availability and social acceptability of drugs (especially marijuana), the lack of parallel experiences between parents and youth (e.g., the rock music culture), the public use of obscene language by both boys and girls, and the phenomenon of growing up faster than one's age (especially in broken homes).

2) *The ethical dilemma* facing youth is in trying to decide

which moral philosophy to use in making moral choices. No longer do code ethics hold the absolute validity that they have for thousands of years. Situation ethics have become popular, in which right and wrong are viewed in relative terms. Young people are also confronted by a "do your own thing" form of existentialism that values only the moment. The constant in this confusing ethical matrix is *responsibility*, which adults should encourage in all of the actions and activities of young people.

3) *The Jesus movement* is a cause of concern for many adults wary of cultism. This movement is positive in that it includes youths from any background (nonexclusive), offers good, clean fun, and gives a young person a sense of direction. The negative consequences of this movement can be that it replaces one addiction (e.g. drugs) for another (religion), makes young people view everyone else as a potential convert to their beliefs, tends to stifle intellectual interests and questioning, and overstresses the advent of the eschaton, with a dualistic world view (i.e., there is a pervasive apocalyptic eschatology).

BEHAVIORAL STUDIES OF YOUTH AND THEIR RELIGIOUS EXPERIENCE

Our second section considers books that are concerned with the study of youth from a behavioral (especially developmental) perspective. The first subsection summarizes the important theories contributed to this study by psychology. The second subsection presents books that explore how these developmental theories bear upon the religious experience of youth.

Behavioral Studies of Youth

Three books that pull together the main contributions of developmental theorists in a usable way are Erikson (1968), Muuss (1975), and Manaster (1977).

In *Identity: Youth and Crisis*, Erik Erikson reviews and restates his theories concerning the life cycle and identity formation, particularly as they apply to adolescents. The chapter most relevant and helpful in the book is "The Life Cycle: Epigenesis of Identity." Erikson moves from the biological development of the person to the psychological development of the individual ego. Common to both biological and psychological development is the principle of *epigenesis*. The epigenetic principle is derived from the growth of fetal organs *in utero*. Each organ has its appointed time for emergence. If it does not arise at this time it will never be able to express itself fully because of the ascendancy of another organ. If one organ does not develop properly according to this timetable, the growth and development of the whole organ will be impaired.

Apply this developmental scheme to the process of ego development. Erikson outlines an epigenetic schedule of eight major stages of intrapsychic conflict that are dealt with sequentially in identity formation:

1) basic trust vs. mistrust (birth to 1+);
2) autonomy vs. shame and doubt (2 to 3 years);
3) initiative vs. guilt (4 to 6 years);
4) industry vs. inferiority (school age);
5) identity vs. role confusion (adolescence);
6) intimacy vs. isolation (young adulthood);
7) generativity vs. stagnation (middle adulthood), and
8) integrity vs. despair (older adulthood)

For Erikson the main challenge of the stage of adolescence is the conflict of identity formation vs. role confusion. The adolescent begins to question how to connect the roles and skills cultivated earlier with the ideal prototypes of the day. The question is whether there is continuity between "who I have been" and "who I will become." This tension becomes an abiding conflict. Youth needs a psychosocial moratorium to facilitate the integration process of ego development. This interlude is a period during which former conflicts are "replayed" to establish that they have been adequately resolved. The identity gains involving the first four stages are now reinterpreted for the adolescent in a new way. (These stages correspond to Freud's stages of psychosexual development: oral, anal, genital, latency.)

1) Basic trust = "I am what I am given." The adolescent searches for people in whom, and ideas in which, to have faith.

2) Autonomy = "I am what I will." The adolescent wishes for opportunities to decide *freely* in what duty or service to become involved.

3) Initiative = "I am what I can imagine myself to be." The adolescent seeks out peers and influential adults who can give imaginative scope to his/her aspirations.

4) Industry = "I am what I can learn to make work." The adolescent searches for a vocation which will be personally rewarding.

If these identity factors are not satisfactorily achieved the resultant role confusion may leave the adolescent isolated and also vulnerable to persuasive ideologies.

The goal of development is wholeness, which finds its culmination in generativity, the "driving power in human organization." One's *ego identity* is a sense of confidence that the ego is *unconsciously* integrating itself toward wholeness by maintaining an inner continuity and sameness. Erikson thus maintains that psychosocial well-being is the solution to the identity crisis. (This becomes problematic, for Erikson also stresses the necessity of the *conscious self* in identity formation. The conscious self will reveal to an individual the brokenness and finitude of human existence, thereby disrupting any psychosocial well-being that was present.)

As suggested in its title, *Theories of Adolescence*, Rolf Muuss does not attempt to derive *a* new theory of adolescence. Rather: "The main purpose is to give a systematic and comprehensive picture of different theoretical positions and to show whenever appropriate the relationship among them" (p. 4). Muuss covers a wide range of theories, summarizing the contemporary issues and drawing out the educational implications of each theory.

James Marcia's expansion of Erikson's developmental stage "identity vs. role confusion" is an attempt to subdivide Erikson's stage to make it less general for youth. Marcia bases the attainment of a mature identity on two essential variables: crisis and commitment. Four identity statuses involving these variables provide a typology of adolescence:

1) The *identity confused subject* has neither experienced an identity crisis nor made any commitments to a vocation or set of beliefs.

2) The *foreclosure subject* has not yet experienced an identity crisis, but has adopted as commitments the ready-made values of his/her parents or other adults.

3) The *moratorium subject* is in a state of crisis, exploring alternatives and making only tentative commitments.

4) The *identity achieved subject* has experienced and resolved crises that have led to personal commitments concerning vocation, religion, and sexuality.

Muuss claims that secondary education keeps youth in the foreclosure stage instead of providing meaningful frustration that would encourage young people to struggle with and form their identities.

In summarizing Kohlberg, Muuss concurs that schools cannot pretend to be "value neutral," and that a pluralistic society must not accept all sets of values as equally valid.[1] As is suggested by Piaget's developmental theory, Kohlberg maintains that the advance from one moral stage to a higher one may be brought about by creating cognitive conflict (disequilibrium) in the individual, for resolution of this conflict leads to a reorganization of structure. Such creative disequilibrium in adolescents may be brought about by challenges, interactions, role-taking opportunities, and debate with their peers.

Muuss points to some of the important contributions from the relatively new field of social learning theory. The basic assumption of Bandura et al., is that adolescents learn most complex skills more effectively by *imitating* the behavior of their parents, teachers, and peers rather than through other methods of instruction. There are three types of effects that the observation of a model's behavior has on the learner:

1) A *modeling effect*—the person imitates the behavior of a significant other;

2) A *inhibitory or disinhibitory effect*—the person observes the consequences of the model's behavior to determine if the model is rewarded or punished for it, and on this basis the person either does or does not emulate that behavior;

3) An *eliciting effect*—the model's behavior provides specific cues, or serves as an eliciting stimulus that facilitates the release of a similar response (which was already present) in the observer.

Peer groups have greater influence as models for adolescent behavior than do parents or teachers because the peers share common characteristics and have control over the rewards that matter to adolescents.

Adolescent Development and the Life Tasks (1977), by Guy Manaster, is one of the most comprehensive and usable books available in this field. Manaster has combined the developmental tasks of Havighurst with the holistic approach of Adler to produce five life-task headings that encompass our problems and efforts from early adolescence until death: love and sex, work and school, friends and community, self, and the meaning of life.

In Adlerian terms, the adolescent is viewed as "a total, complete individual (holistic), whose own feelings and perspectives (phenomenological) influence his or her own personal goals (teleological) within his or her own environment (field-theoretical) as he lives as a member of society, as he must (socially oriented approach)" (pp. 12–13).

In a discussion of physiological changes which occur during adolescence, Manaster claims that early maturers have a number of advantages over late maturers, including greater social and physical prestige. Both adults and peers expect more from an early maturing adolescent, and the adolescent must cope with this increased responsibility. One factor to consider is the earlier mean age of menarche for girls in recent decades: there is now a 1.4 year age difference between the average age of menarche of a mother and her daughter. This compares with an average .8-year difference between the onset of maturity for a father and his son. The greater gap is the *three year* difference between the average age of maturity for a father and his daughter; this could explain some of the tensions and misunderstandings that arise between a father and his "little girl."

Although adolescents are supposed to be in the stage of formal operations (Piaget), Manaster believes that not all adolescents will develop this cognitive ability, and of those who do it will be developed in various patterns or chronological sequences. Psychological research has been conducted primarily on in-school youth (from good schools) and on college youth, and the results are thus not a conclusive description of the "normal adolescent." Manaster posits that a higher I.Q. and an earlier attainment of formal operations are related to early maturation, bigger size, high socio-economic status, better education, and particular cultural backgrounds (pp. 35–50).

There is a relation between formal-operational thought and affect in the adolescent, as the young person begins to experience life in terms of *possibilities*. Elkind (1969) presents two constructions of adolescent egocentrism that stem from a preoccupation with the potential for one's appearance and behavior: the "imaginary audience" and the "personal fable." Young people feel self-conscious about always being on stage before an "imaginary audience" that judges their successes and failures. Such youth invent a "person fable," a story, that each young person tells himself or herself to accentuate his uniqueness, greatness, and worth, and to evaluate the reactions of others to his victories and defeats. The fable reinforces the adolescent's feeling that his thoughts and behavior have universal significance.

In analyzing Kohlberg's theory of moral judgment, Manaster perceives a difficulty in that Kohlberg is interested in the structure of thought, and not in the content of a moral decision. Manaster further believes that the moral judgments of high school youth, which appear to be principled (Level III), are probably a sophisticated form of conventional (Level II), authority-maintaining moral judgment. Thus, few adolescents have attained principled moral judgment upon graduating from high school (pp. 53–67).

Cross-sectional research on personality reveals that there is apparent personality inconsistency among adolescents. Much of this "inconsistency," Manaster claims, comes from a young person experimenting with new potentialities of formal-operational development or trying out various modes of behavior (roles) in the novel situations he/she confronts. Longitudinal studies are more revealing, and indicate that the most significant change in the age group occurs over time. This suggests that instability is produced in a large group (not just in an individual) because of particular historical events and environmental situations. By and large, youth will retain a similar ranking relative to other youth in important personality dimensions; the major personality adjustments will have occurred prior to adolescence.

Manaster offers an interesting critique of Erikson, refuting the theory that youth go through a *normative* stage of identity vs. role confusion during their high school years. In proportion, the *fewest* number of adolescents have problems that are strictly neurotic-personal (corresponding to acute role confusion); a *greater* number of adolescents have identity problems in late adolescence, as they reinterpret a world previously formulated in concrete terms in light of their capability for more abstract formal-operational thought; the *greatest* number of adolescents have difficulties and problems that are the result of limited knowledge and experience as they confront new situations (learning to cope is not identity crisis). The "psychosocial moratorium" is a luxury of time which is not afforded to many young people, particularly those who do not attend college (pp. 114–124).

There is a quest for autonomy as the adolescent moves from family to become a member of the community. Goodman (1969) developed three stages in the growth of autonomy: "they-me" of infancy and childhood, "I-me" of adolescence, and "I-them" of maturity. (The structure of interpersonal dynamics is depicted in each stage by nominative and objective case pronouns in relation to the individual.) Youth is caught in the middle stage, having one foot in the door of childhood (controlled by others) and one foot in the door of adulthood (controlling others). To express a degree of autonomy and power, the adolescent calls upon a sub-group of the total reference group when interacting with another subgroup. Thus, adolescents conform more to parental values in their peer role and more to their peer values in their adult role. An end to this dual value standard is signaled by a part of the parental image being internalized in a mature way.

Manaster points out that adolescence is a time for forming friendships with those with whom one can share thoughts and feelings from the most mundane to the most important. "Friends are people who will like you anyway" (p. 254). In early adolescence, friendships are more superficial, and are based on doing concrete things together. Middle adolescence is a period of trying out various roles, testing the limits of friendship, and revealing one's innermost thoughts. In late adolescence one builds friendships on the basis of personality and talents; there is less need for the continued support from a friend for all of one's feelings and behavior. These three stages are well characterized by the friend-ship of the three boys in the movie *Summer of '42*. Benjie repre-sents the early stage of adolescent friendship, based on doing things together, whether spying with field glasses or eating ice cream. Oscky is in the role of a middle adolescent, sharing his thoughts about the opposite sex. Hermie moves from middle to late adolescence; he "grows up" as a result of his romantic encounter with an older woman and no longer needs his friends as a support group for self-affirmation.

Manaster concludes by examining the existential life task: religion. Often the first religious doubt is brought on when a young person near puberty experiences the death of a loved one or of a close friend. There is little profound agnosticism or atheism among high-school students, for moral law is usually associated with the existence of God at this age. The most consistent conclusion is that females of all ages are more religious than males, more active in the church, and more conservative in doctrine. Many American youth, like their parents, exhibit a "hedging stance": a reluctance to deny the idea of the supernatural, yet an unwillingness or inability to commit themselves to faith with conviction.

Youth are more likely to experience a "definite crisis" conversion if this is a requirement of group membership, and if this meets parental expectations. Commitment to doctrine or to an unquestioning faith is also strongly influenced by the demands of the particular group. During middle adolescence, Lutheran youth showed a tendency of "backsliding" (Strommen, 1972), Presbyterian youth showed no significant change (Woods and Klever, 1971), but evangelical youth showed a steady growth in commitment to conservative doctrine (Zuck and Getz, 1968).

Religious youth movements attract young people for two reasons, one extremely conventional and the other extremely ideal. For those adolescents in the stage of concrete operations, these groups require a simple, basic lifestyle, and mandate a definite, right-or-wrong system of moral values. For youth who are in the formal-operational stage, these groups offer the Utopian answer and provide the possibility for youth to usher in the new world which is imminent. Since most youth are in process stages of cognitive development, such religious groups may provide satisfaction for them in both contexts.

The paradox of youth is that this is the time of the most frequent overt expressions of disbelief in God, yet it is also the time of the most intense religious feeling; often, both of these moments occur within the same young person.

Behavioral Studies of the Religious Experience of Youth

In this subsection, we will examine two books which apply developmental theory to the religious sphere and consider *faith development:* Fowler and Keen (1978) and Wilcox (1979). Additional resources that provide significant data concerning the religious experience of youth are found in these research presentations: Strommen et al. (1972), Strommen (1973), Strommen (1974), Woods and Klever (1971), and *Religion in America* 1979–80.

Life Maps is a stimulating colloquy on the nature of faith development, between Jim Fowler and Sam Keen. Fowler examines the developmental structure of "faith as knowing" and analyzes what happens to faith as our way of knowing changes. He draws on the work of Piaget, Selman, and Kohlberg in the construction of his six-stage schema; stages 2, 3, and 4 encompass the probable range of adolescent development from least to most sophisticated.

Stage 2 is termed "Mythic-Literal," and is grounded in the individual's ability to perform concrete operations and think empirically. Role-taking ability is achieved, and the resultant level of moral judgment is reciprocity ("you scratch my back and I'll scratch yours"). A sense of transcendent meaning is best conveyed by dramatic narrative and myth; the most favored images for God are anthropomorphic. Stage 2 is usually indicative of early adolescence.

Stage 3, the "Synthetic-Conventional," is the most common stage of adolescence. The ability to perform early formal operations makes possible mutual role-taking, and a structuring of the world in interpersonal terms. With the development of third-person perspective, the "group" becomes important in defining one's social and moral standards. Metaphor and double entendres can be understood, and there is no longer a literal correspondence between a symbol and its referent. Images of God at this stage are based on personal qualities of God such as "friend," "companion," "comforter," or "guide."

At Stage 4, the "Individuating-Reflexive," there is a personal awareness that one has a determinate outlook or faith that differs from that of others. This ability to stand apart requires full formal operations and a self-awareness that do not usually emerge until late adolescence. There is a "relative hermeneutic" operating at this stage: The individual tends to demythologize symbols and ritual; their import is conveyed in terms of ideas or propositions which can be handled with emotional detachment. Control over one's self-consciousness minimizes the power of a myth or symbol to transform the understanding. Theological ideas can be rationally discussed at Stage 4 without having a real bearing on the individual's faith.

Sam Keen's presentation critiques Fowler's schema by pointing to the onesidedness of viewing faith development *only* as a cognitive process. Keen emphasizes the psychosomatic unity which must be restored to our view of human nature as we learn how to *trust* God and our environment. Fowler responds that his concept of *valuing* includes both cognitive and affective assent to a philosophy. In spite of differing approaches, in their respective "life maps" both Fowler and Keen suggest that the highest developmental stage involves an individual who is "selfless" (whose "self" is given over to God's will). This is the rare individual who can transcend the paradox and ambiguity of life and experience unity of being and purpose in this existence.

In the introduction to *Developmental Journey*, Mary Wilcox explains that this book is a response to the recent concerns of religious and secular circles alike that values and decision making must be an acknowledged part of the educational process. While

many institutions have chosen a "values clarification" curriculum, based on the presupposition that values are relative,
Wilcox presents another option: the process of valuing and decision making approached from a theory of gradual growth and
development. In describing our developmental journey, Wilcox
suggests an educational model that builds on and enhances the
development of thinking and perceiving, as well as feeling. She
deals with three major areas:

1) Logical reasoning, based on Piaget;
2) Social perspective, based on Fowler, Kohlberg, Kegan,
Rest, and Selman;

and

3) Moral reasoning, based on Kohlberg.

A fourth area, the role of symbols (Fowler) is a minor part of
her presentation.

Chapters 5 and 6 of this book are the most relevant for our
study of adolescent development. The concluding chapters 10,
11, and 12 are the practical applications of Wilcox's developmental theory. She lists six basic elements in teaching the whole
person which are useful guidelines for working with youth:

1) The instructor must provide the learner with information to
be acted upon.
2) The instructor must be aware of how the learner is appro-
priating the information developmentally.
3) Emotions should be used constructively in the learning
process.
4) Both the right (creative) and the left (rational) hemispheres
of the brain need to be engaged.
5) Physical involvement produces the optimal learning experience (enactive learning).
6) Learning should be facilitated by a support community
(family, peer group, church).

A *Study of Generations*, by Strommen et al., is a research portrait that attempts to dispel surface impressions and presents, instead, the variety of religious alternatives which are possible in a denomination (Lutheran). The researchers' self-understanding is that of the artist's, using words, statistical analyses, and charts rather than paint, brushes, and canvasses. They also have a vested interest in the subject of their study. (A caveat to Strommen's research: it is often of American Lutheran youth and would tend to reflect a Northern European background.)

This 1970 study reports the beliefs, values, and religious lifestyles of a representative sample of 4,745 persons between the ages of 15 and 65 from the three major Lutheran bodies in the United States: the American Lutheran Church, the Lutheran Church–Missouri Synod, and the Lutheran Church in America. The information was gathered from a questionnaire of 740 multiple-choice statements and questions, from which 78 dimensions were generated relating to what Lutherans believe, value, and do. The questionnaire, a description of these dimensions, and the statistical data and computation process are explained in thorough detail in the appendices.

A major focus of this study is the future of youth, which Strommen defines as the age span 15 to 29. The study divides youth into three subgenerations by the clustering of similar responses: 15 to 18, 19 to 23, 24 to 29. There is no "generation gap" between youth and adults, although there are seven clearly discernible patterns of tensions which center primarily in differences of belief and value:

1) Youth show frequent distrust of adults.
2) Youth give higher priority to personal piety.
3) Youth show an unwillingness to delay gratification.
4) Youth have more feelings for people as human beings.
5) Youth express more openness to change in congregational life and ministry.
6) Youth experience stronger feelings of alienation.

Twenty percent of youth were found to be almost exclusively peer-oriented. This age group differs from adults in that they are less willing to help others in time of crisis, less desirous of a dependable world, less fundamentalist, and less convinced that hard work pays off. Youth are more likely than adults to favor the church's involvement in social issues and to encourage pastors to participate in social action and preach relevant sermons. A basic problem is that youth feel that congregational life is adult-centered with no real concern for youth and their needs. Only one out of five young persons perceives his/her Christians beliefs as foundational to his/her approach to life.

Strommen has expanded his findings on youth from A *Study of Generations* in his *Bridging the Gap*. This follow-up report focuses on youth ages 15 to 23, providing a more accessible and readable resource for youth ministry. This book presents a profile of Lutheran youth who are "typically American youth" with the exception of three areas: a greater identification with their parents, a more positive attitude toward their congregation, and a greater understanding of what makes their Christian faith distinctive.

Strommen classifies two kinds of high school youth: peer-oriented and broadly-oriented. Peer-oriented youth tend to be more trouble-causing, while broadly-oriented youth are more conforming to social expectations and customs. Within Lutheran congregations, about one-fifth of the young people are peer-oriented. Peer groups can have a positive and value-shaping effect on the individual if key members of a group have had leadership training.

Youth who are uncertain about their relationship to God exhibit two major characteristics. The first is a sense of isolation from others: Youth inhibit their emotions, to become cool, suave, and in control. There is an increasing self-centeredness and an over-valuation of one's importance, and this leads to greater social alienation and less social contacts. The second predominant feeling is a sense that life has no meaning: many youth believe that salvation by works is the theology of the church, and they confess having no personal experience of God's grace in their lives. For these youth, the church has failed to convey a sense of purpose in the Christian message.

Even so, 63 percent of the high school youth estimated that their future giving to the church will increase. They want to be excited and involved in worship, however, and react negatively to the controlled, formal, and unchanging liturgical service. Strommen suggests two imperatives for youth ministry: *mutuality* and *mission*. Youth need and want the warmth, empathy, and genuineness of an accepting group, and also the understanding, hope, and involvement of one-to-one relationships in this group. This is mutuality. There is a need and desire for activities which give youth a sense of purpose, such as the Youth Tutoring Program. Most youth groups have been concentrating on "feeding and keeping" young people; innovative models are needed for "equipping and sending" young people into areas of need and mission.

Following the procedure of research used in *A Study of Generations*, Strommen's *Five Cries of Youth* evaluates the experience of 7,050 high school students with a 420-item Youth Research Survey (1970). Of those surveyed, 6,239 sometimes or often attended church; church and nonchurch-goers, however, were found to be alike in their reactions to common adolescent problems. There are three assumptions underlying the discussion in this book:

1) That young people can be insightful and their reports valid;

2) That adolescent psychodynamics are evidenced by verbally expressed problems which tend to cluster symptomatically around an underlying concern (the "five cries");

3) That a knowledge of youth's concerns is important to an effective youth ministry.

The most commonly voiced and intensely felt of the five cries is the cry of *self-hatred*. The main contributing factors were found to be distress over personal faults, lack of self-confidence, and low self-regard. Acute loneliness has led a number of youth to contemplate suicide at some point.

The cry of *psychological orphans* results from family pressures, distress over relationships with one's parents, disappointment in family unity.

The cry of *social protest* is marked by a sensitivity to others, a desire for change, a concern over national issues, and a criticism of the poor model which adults present (as groups) in caring for the less fortunate.

The cry of the *prejudiced* comes from "consensual religious" youth who conceptualize their faith in specific do's and don'ts, rarely applying their faith thoughtfully in daily activities and behavior. These youth have a law, rather than Gospel, orientation to Christianity; they tend to be loyal to institutions (faithful attenders of youth groups!) and they usually form self-oriented values. One out of seven young persons exhibits prejudice, and there is a positive correlation between the occurrence of this trait in youth and the prejudicial views of their parents.

The cry of *joy* is one of the most dominant ones among youth, whether taking the form of quiet exuberance over the simple pleasures of living, or the shout of celebration and hope in the face of existential despair. One-third of all church youth express joy in their sense of identity and mission that centers in the person of Jesus Christ. The four most typical characteristics of such youth are:

1) They participate actively in congregational and private religous activities.

2) They pray especially for people who need God's help.

3) They seek God's help in deciding right or wrong behavior.

4) They reflect strong interest in help provided by the congregation.

The World of Youth (Woods and Klever) is another important research document, which presents a profile of teenagers in the

United Presbyterian Church. Five interest groups are considered: senior highs (grades 9–12), their peers, parents, volunteer adult leaders, and ordained leaders. This multidimensional study is divided into five areas: cultural, family environment, psychological, religious, and institutional.

1) *Cultural*—the way youth function in groups, particularly around adults. The appropriate image for United Presbyterian youth at the time of the study was white, middle class, suburban. The median response for the number of one's close friends was six to ten. Active church youth had either dated one person steadily (22 percent) or had never dated (26.2 percent). Their self-perception was highest in academics and lowest in artistic ability. The active youth were in general younger and less socially mature than the nonactive and non-Presbyterian youth; they tended to join many youth clubs and organizations yet remained individualistic rather than community-oriented.

2) *Family environment*—the way religious commitment and church participation relate to family dynamics. At the time of the survey, most active youth lived in a stable family situation where two-thirds of their fathers were professionals or administrators. The majority of these families owned their houses and were not mobile but stationary. This report indicates a strong continuity of values, beliefs, and politics between youth and their parents.

3) *Psychological*—involving intellectual interests, response to authority, and emotional adjustment to one's environment. Compared to non-Presbyterian youth, active youth are less given to reflective thought, less flexible in the way they view and organize phenomena, less independent of authority, less trusting and ethical in their concern about the welfare of others, and more convinced that the practical is the best way of life. The main goals of this group are self-development and education, career, and occupation. Low on the scale is the degree of altruism shown by these young people.

4) *Religious*—personal involvement and institutional partici-

pation in religious activities. The theological language that appeals to active United Presbyterian youth is characterized by forgiveness and love. (It is suggested that the use of such language may compensate for their group's deficiency in altruism.) Youth show greater familiarity with biblical material than with the creeds and liturgical formulas. Youth express an ambivalent attitude toward the church, often finding the Sunday worship service an empty experience.

5) *Institutional*—relating to the more formal involvement with programs that the church offers youth. Young people see the mission of the church more in generalized humanitarian terms than in institutional categories. They do not perceive the church as being in touch with their community. Youth who are inactive in the church's youth program report that they attend Sunday worship more than the active sample (although not as regularly), and like it better than the actives do. Only 3.7 percent of the active church youth expressed an interest in becoming a minister or a full-time church worker.

The most up-to-date and broadly-based research data on the opinions of American youth are found in the Princeton Religion Research Center publication, *Religion in America 1979–80*. This study is based on information attained from representative samples of the 25 million teenagers living in America today. Part III, "Focus on Youth and the Family," is the most relevant section for our examination.

The findings on young people's views about religion are interesting, even as they often seem conflicting. While one out of four teens expresses a high degree of confidence in organized religion, and 71 percent of this sample say that they are church members, two out of three youth blame the church for not reaching out to them. Seventy-four percent of the Protestant youth (82 percent of Catholic youth) believe that a person can be a good Christian without attending church. Four out of ten young people claim that religion plays "a very important role" in their lives, and 95 percent say they believe in God; 75 percent say they believe in a "personal God." Only 5 percent of the youth express some interest in the religious life, however, and less than one percent desire to pursue a career as a member of the clergy.

In terms of religious practices and experiences of American youth, 87 percent say that they pray, 39 percent pray frequently, and 52 percent say grace before meals. Sixty-eight percent have had the feeling of being in God's presence. Nearly half of the Protestant teenagers (46 percent) have had a "born again" experience, and as many as 71 percent of this group are engaged in efforts to win converts to their faith. Only 6 percent of these born-again experiences were *sudden* conversions, contrary to popular belief that this is the norm. Twenty-seven percent of the youth are involved in Bible studies, 6 percent in spiritual healing, and 2 percent in the charismatic movement. Important to note is that 46 percent of the boys and 57 percent of the girls like the idea of having "religious retreats."

In response to the question, "What are your main reasons for believing in God or a universal spirit?" the answers cluster in four categories:

1) *Authoritative*—41 percent; including the Bible or religious training at home, church, or school as primary reasons.

2) *Rational*—24 percent; proof of God's existence is derived from the order observed in nature or the moral realm.

3) *Empirical*—13 percent; experiential reasons such as deliverance from an illness or having prayers answered.

4) *Utilitarian*—5 percent; the basic reason is to have something to look forward to after this life.

Seven suggestions are given in response to the need for a more effective youth ministry:

1) Teach parents how to provide better moral and religious training for their teenagers.

2) Programs are to be designed that will bring parents and youth together at times other than the Sunday services.

3) Young Americans are profoundly moved by plays, television shows, and movies that have a religious theme; churches can use this to their advantage.

4) Religious retreats have tremendous appeal to teenage youth and can be made available.

5) Bible-study groups can be a basic rebuilding block for families.

6) The natural affinity between the young and old may be nurtured.

7) Churches may encourage parents to take a firm stand on matters such as alcohol, drug abuse, and sexual promiscuity.

YOUTH AND THE CHURCH

In this section, we will examine ten of the most insightful books available on the task of youth ministry. These books provide a combination of theological perspective, methodology, and sound practical advice to those who undertake the crucial responsibility of relating youth to the church, i. e., the Body of Christ.

The first six books attempt to define youth ministry in its broader context: Little (1968), Warren (1977), Evans (1977), Richards (1972), Sparkman (1977), and Zuck and Benson (1978).

The other four books are concerned with the "nuts and bolts" of creative interaction among young people: Bowman (1963), Fletcher et al. (1974), Holderness (1976), and Kilgore (1976).

Sara Little wants to keep the balance between mission and education in youth ministry, yet the thrust of *Youth, World, and Church* is a renewal approach to mission. Her thesis is this:

Youth who are members of the church are called to be Christian disciples *now*, as people of God placed in the world for ministry; they are a part of the ministering Body of Christ, within which they are supported and equipped for the fulfilling of their common calling (p. 11).

The problem has been the cultivation of a youth church alongside the church, expressed by such heresies as these:

1) Youth are the "church of tomorrow."

2) The success of a program can be measured by the number of youth involved.

3) Programs should be set up by the church to keep boys and girls off the streets.

4) Youth should be involved in a variety of organizations to keep them *busy* (though not necessarily nurtured).

Youth ministry is bound up with the renewal of the church as a whole, and the locus of this reconciliation process is the world. The "world" must be understood both as the created universe subject to the lordship of Christ, and as that to which we are enslaved by our human pride. The church's reason for existence is not for its own self-preservation but for *mission* to this world.

Youth are in an "ecumenical situation" in their high schools; they are in a situation for mission. Youth laity are to be trained and equipped for ministry as an arm of the church. The initial consideration is: What can youth offer to the congregation? The secondary consideration is then: What is needed in addition for the youth? Unfortunately, most youth programs begin with this secondary concern.

Opportunities for mission occur on all fronts and in every area of a young person's life. There are dangers in desiring to minister to others, such as false motivations, the temptation to help only as one wishes (disregarding the real need), and the possibility of exploiting those who receive aid. For this reason, Little suggests these seven guidelines to direct youth in their ministry:

1) Young people are to keep their eyes open for the real needs to be met.

2) A problem should first be throughly investigated.

3) A specific proposal for action should be charted.

4) Others are to be invited to participate in serving.

5) The group is to carry through its plans, revising them as necessary.

6) The work is to be evaluated.

7) One avenue of service is to lead to another.

Equipping youth for ministry involves first the preparations for undertaking a particular task, then its theological evaluation. Churches may help youth prepare for mission by arranging youth-adult conferences that focus, for example, on their situation in high school. Retreats are another good (and popular) vehicle for equipping youth. The process of theologizing occurs as the faith heritage is related to a particular mission effort and it is discovered how God is working in our lives through his Holy Spirit.

The structure and process of doing youth ministry is also to be evaluated, and Little suggests criteria for this evaluation:

1) Does the structure make it possible for you to become involved in areas of ministry close at hand and throughout the world?

2) Does the structure make it possible to minister *to* youth?

3) Is the structure so designed that it unifies the congregation across age-group lines, and at the same time allows for particular contributions of various age groups and individuals?

4) Are the structures clearly related to church government and discipline?

5) Do the structures provide for experiences in the broader Christian fellowship beyond the congregation?

6) Do the structures at the same time provide for maintenance of continuing programs and relationships while allowing innovation?

The teaching-learning process is facilitated by the adult servant-leader who is a *guarantor*, *i.e.*, a reference point of identity, for youth. The guarantor is a significant other who affirms youth and gives them "entrée" into a co-personal world.

Youth Ministry, by Michael Warren, is a book of readings covering three general areas: understanding the task of evangelization of youth, setting up programs for doing youth ministry, and developing leadership for authentic ministry in the church. Warren has compiled this book specifically for those doing youth work in the Roman Catholic Church, yet many of the articles are useful for Protestant churches as well.

In the overview, Warren suggests that youth ministry is "an effort on the part of the beloved community to welcome young people into the midst of a rich and enriching communal existence" (p. 5). Youth ministry involves the four basic ministries of the church: the word, worship, guidance and education, and healing. These ministries must be extended to all young people, whether they are members of the church community or not.

Warren then states five guiding principles for youth ministry:

1) The total situation of young people must be taken into consideration, including their broad range of needs.

2) The ministry of friendship is primary.

3) The gifts and talents of youth are to be affirmed.

4) Youth are called to a community that is united by the awareness of Christ's presence.

5) Youth, themselves, are to be called to minister. Concerning this point, Warren notes that most people decide on the ordained ministry as a vocation not because of seminary training but because of meaningful experiences they had as youth.

In Warren's article, "Evangelization of Youth," he states that the true task of youth ministry is now being exemplified by those youth workers who are going into the community to *evangelize*.

We are slowly coming to the realization that the future of the church depends upon this type of outreach. Much of this task is being done by "para-church" organizations which make no concerted effort to bring a young person into the life of a parish. Warren states that a person's adherence to the gospel cannot remain abstract, but must at some point be concretized by a visible entry into a community of believers.

Indigenization is another key word for youth ministry, implying that the gospel can and must grow out of native soil (as has been learned in foreign mission work). Youth learn how to interpret the gospel for themselves and for other youths. This does not mean a marriage between youth ministry and every aspect of youth culture, but does mean that youth ministry is serious about understanding all aspects of youth culture. Currently, for instance, it is important to try to understand the popularity of "New Wave" music among youth.

Warren wrote "Social Processes in Adolescent Catechesis" because youth ministry so often overlooks the way young people come together. Four important points are considered:

1) Teenagers need both formal and informal groups, for they learn by the process of group interaction.

2) Teenagers need to feel relaxed in groups, for they have anxiety as it is concerning their ambiguous status between childhood and adulthood. The more personal the content to be learned, the more relaxed the learning situation must be.

3) Relaxed groupings of teenagers have the potential to become the church, theologically and socially. They are able to share a common faith with one another, and they discover the joy of serving God without turning their backs on life.

4) A new look at the question of content for teenagers is needed; youth learn best when they are *actively* engaged in the educational process.

"Principles and Procedures in Youth Ministry," by Costello

and Warren, reflects on the attitudes needed by a youth minister, and then suggests planning procedures for youth programs. Youth ministers should be ready: to hand over their faith, not claiming to have all of the answers; to hand over true responsibility to the team; to adapt programs to the gifts of other adult leaders, and not to accept all who apply to work with youth if they are not competent for the task; to continue on their own way as a pilgrimage of faith.

These are suggestions for designing programs for youth:

1) Plan short-range rather than long-range, setting specific goals for each meeting.

2) Plan simple rather than complex, covering only one or two topics at each session.

3) Plan inclusive rather than exclusive, involving youth where possible in the planning process.

4) Plan for the youth's needs, not the leader's needs.

5) Plan for atmosphere and consider logistics.

6) Plan to spend a lot of time with young people.

7) Plan to expect, and then accept, failures.

8) Plan to learn by doing.

The popularity of weekend retreats is examined by Warren in "Understanding the Weekend Format." Theologically, these retreats (which Warren prefers to term "Christian experience programs") rest on the solid presuppositions that Jesus Christ is present in the life of each person and that the Christian message is the answer to our deepest hopes and longings. Culturally, retreats provide youth with a sense of status in the Christian community, a status that they often lack in their parish experiences. Retreats also provide *maintenance* (Berger and Luckmann) for the ongoing process of conversion.

Warren feels that these factors must be kept in mind when planning and conducting a retreat:

1) The retreat must be consciously Christ-centered.

2) Adult leaders should be "preoccupied with freedom," encouraging youth to express divergent views and disagreements.

3) Presentations by adults should witness effectively to their own faith.

4) Evaluation sessions are necessary to determine strengths and weaknesses of the program.

5) The sharing of different retreat models among adult leaders will help to pool talents and prevent rivalry and jealousy from occurring.

6) More attention is to be given to the parents of young people; they may also benefit from retreat experiences.

Written originally in the mid-60s, *Shaping the Church's Ministry with Youth*, by David Evans, was revised in 1977 to address the contemporary situation. Evans begins by stating these underlying premises of youth ministry:

1) The church's ministry with youth is person-centered rather than age-group centered. Youth must be viewed as individuals.

2) Ministry implies the biblical concept of *servanthood* to God and to others and is not restricted to the clergy.

3) Ministry *with* youth means ministry to and by youth and to and by adults who work with youth.

Evans maintains that size and numbers and an "active" youth program are not the crucial determinants of a relevant ministry with youth. Youth are the church of *today*, meaning that the church's nurture must be oriented to the *now*, rather than to the tomorrow. Youth must be accepted as full members of the church today and must be challenged to direct their energies and abilities to ministry in this present context, even when they seem reluctant to assume this responsibility.

There are basically four kinds of youth in relation to the church:

1) Youth for whom the Christian faith has meaning and for whom the gathered church experience is significant.

2) The church dropout for whom the church experience is meaningless.

3) Youth for whom ministry seems to be a kind of "holding pattern." They are not ready or willing to make a commitment.

4) Youth who have no relationship to the church and whom the church does not know.

Having young people at these various levels of involvement suggests that the focal point of the church's ministry with youth must be *persons*, not programs or institutions. The church as people of God, is a base or center of operations (usually in a building) to which many may come and from which they go. At this base there are to be meaningful programs to address various needs. Away from this base there are to be outposts to reach those who cannot or will not come to the base.

For the gathered-church experience with youth, there is to be *flexibility* in groupings, setting, and structure; organization should be kept to a minimum. There is to be an atmosphere of *freedom* in seeking after the truth, in exploring all aspects of God's world, and in the way youth seek meaning. Often a low-key, unplanned but honest discussion gets through better than a spectacular, well-planned program. It takes *time* to learn and to love; one two-hour session is more productive than two one-hour sessions. Evans recommends that the best size for a group is between five and eight persons. There is also to be an effort made to promote times of one-to-one dialogue.

Rather than relying on a nonaffiliated youth minister to evangelize youth, churches are jointly to sponsor or call a youth minister to go out into the community and relate to church dropouts and nonchurch youth. School dropouts are special candidates for an outreach program; they need support and encouragement (which they usually lack altogether) and perhaps tutoring in basic skills.

Ministry with youth cannot be effective unless it involves adults in a fundamental way. It is important for adults to be challenged by the idealism, dissatisfaction, and daring of youth. It is important for youth to be confronted by tradition and by the realism of adults. Toward this end, Evans suggests that:

1) We need someone who has a good understanding of both youth and adults.

2) Training must be provided for adults who work with youth.

3) Adults will have to assume their role as adults, realizing their own values, be sensitive to the dynamics of adult-adolescent relationships, and overcome their insecurity of being around youth by studying theology, psychology, and sociology.

There are two useful articles in the appendix. Sharon Ballenger's "Touch a Teenager" asks us to be aware of the total way we communicate with young people, including body language. In "Adolescents Look at Family Clusters," Margaret Sawin discusses the value of youth meeting together in an intergenerational group of families. The "family cluster" has been one of the reasons why Jewish people have been able to maintain a strong faith identity down through the ages. Home communities have been influential models for youth in the Mennonite tradition, as well.

Knowing and Helping Youth, edited by G. Temp Sparkman, is designed to acquaint a person with the various components of doing youth ministry. Half of the articles are concerned with the application of developmental theories of adolescence (*knowing* youth), and the remaining articles focus on youth in the church setting (*helping* youth).

We have already discussed sociological and behavioral studies of youth, yet this book contributes at least two insightful essays on these topics: "Identity—the Major Task of Adolescence," by Gloria Durka, and "Adolescence in the Family and Subculture," by Robert Poerschke. In "Counseling with Youth," Stanley Watson gives some pointers to youth leaders on how to deal effectively with the problems of young people. This article does not, however, cover the scope of problems addressed by Paine in his book (See Section I).

Sparkman's article, "Youth and Affirmation of Faith," is based on the assumption that a conscious appraisal and declaration of one's faith is an important aspect of one's identity quest. The dimensions of "affirmation" are these:

1) It is a voluntary response.
2) It is a gift of God which we might freely choose.
3) It is shaped in some way by the influence of others.
4) It cannot be the automatic result of an educational process.
5) It is radical but not necessarily cataclysmic.

During adolescence, Sparkman believes, young people are able to examine and internalize their heritage of faith, understand the consequences of sin for their lives, and take personal responsibility for affirming baptismal vows.

"Involving Youth in Worship and Learning," by William Cromer, emphasizes the importance of youth taking an active part in the worship experience as a response to their faith. Worship is more than one-dimensional ecstasy; it is an expression and celebration of the deepest and most powerful experiences of our lives. Following Kierkegaard's model for worship, Cromer reminds us that the proper arrangement is not God as prompter, the choir and preacher as actors, and the congregation as audience; rather, we should view the choir and preacher as prompters, the congregation as actors, and God as the audience. Bearing this in mind, creative worship for and by youth should have these characteristics:

1) Use of contemporary thought forms and language.
2) A recapturing of the spirit of celebration, expressing joy in what the Holy Spirit is doing in the world.
3) An orientation to the needs of persons rather than the needs of the institution.

4) An involvement of the worshiper both bodily and mentally.

5) A focus upon *this* side of life and the social application of faith.

Don Boling, in "Involving Youth in Mission and Witnessing," draws a distinction between "mission" and "witnessing," which he hopes will prevent the usual confusion of these two forms of outreach. Mission means "sending," and describes an event that is an organized group activity directed beyond the fellowship of the church. Witnessing is "proclamation," giving testimony to God's work in the world. This sharing of faith can occur in a group or in a one-to-one encounter, either within the church fellowship or beyond it. Boling gives these terms narrow definitions to distinguish two important aspects of ministry by youth.

Witnessing and mission should be encouraged because they are biblical directives and because youth feel that they should be undertaking these tasks. Faith is kept vibrant when it is shared, and mission puts faith into action. Youth are effective in reaching out to others, especially to other youth, and there are many non-Christian youth who need to hear the gospel. There are also many needs in our society that call for mission. Young people gain confidence and grow in Christian maturity as they share in the Christian life together.

Methods of involving youth in witnessing are: witnessing as groups, holding training sessions, presenting models to them, and evaluating a witnessing experience. These procedures help youth overcome their fears and insecurities about sharing their faith with others. Suggestions for witnessing are: youth rallies, youth-led revivals, religious canvassing, musicals, and performing groups.

Methods for involving youth in mission are: having youth plan and finance a mission project; preparing them for what to expect; keeping them from over-extending themselves; making use of the particular talents in a group, and providing adequate leadership. Examples of mission projects are: ministry to the aged, a church crisis closet (food and clothing), tutoring programs, ministry in institutions, day camps and Bible schools, and work trips.

We now consider two works from a more conservative theological perspective. *Youth Ministry*, by Larry Richards, develops a philosophy of youth ministry in the context of the renewal movement in the church. Although Richards espouses a view of biblical inerrancy, he is not a strict literalist in his use of the Bible as the foundation for youth ministry. This flexibility is apparent in part I, in which Richards claims that the Bible is not a "truth" system, but a "reality" system. He stresses that Christian education must involve the learning of culture rather than the learning of static ideas.

In part II, Richards presents youth as persons growing into interdependence and learning to accept responsibility. This process must be facilitated by competent adult leadership, based on the servant model that Jesus taught and lived. Adults are most effective in establishing relationships with youth when they are *self-revealing*. Part III explores the dynamics of this new community in Christ into which youth are growing.

Part IV discusses the structure of youth ministry, and how youth might be organized for ministry. Richards advocates short-term programs that are planned with a specific purpose in mind, yet are responsive to the needs of youth. Youth are not to be preoccupied with programming and system maintenance, but are to be taught how to love and minister. Richards believes that the structure must arrive out of the objectives that youth ministry wishes to accomplish:

1) *Responsive* instead of representative *leadership* involves establishing a "core group" of those youth who are willing to commit themselves to a serious level of discipleship. This group is open to all, yet the members insist on dedication.

2) The core group enables *person* rather than program *orientation*, as members become vulnerable with one another and share their spiritual concerns.

3) The youth in the core group are the true leaders; they have a *communication* rather than a control *function*, providing adult leaders with necessary information for planning programs.

Richards understands organization as having an adult leader in the central role interacting with the youth core group and the "leader core group" (composed of older adults and college youth). The leader also designs ways for these groups to respond to the wider "contact group," which includes other youth who are associated with the church and attend activities but have not committed themselves to the core group. All of these young people are to be trained to go into the world setting and interact with non-Christian teens. As Richards states in the concluding section (Part V), the goal of youth ministry is growth, together, to *maturity* (Eph. 4:13).

Youth Education in the Church, by Zuck and Benson, is a valuable and comprehensive compendium on youth by evangelical scholars who maintain a view of biblical inerrancy. Several informative essays are: "Adolescents in an Age of Acceleration and Crisis," by Warren Benson; "A Historical Survey of Youth Work," by Donald Pugh and Milford Sholund; "Research on Adolescent Religiosity," by J. Roland Fleck; "Adolescents in Socio-Psychological Perspective," by Donald Joy; and "Middle Adolescence," by Rex Johnson.

E. Dee Freeborn, in "Youth and Music," offers a much-needed critique of the plethora of pseudo-rock-folk-pop music which is labeled "Christian," but which often distorts and misrepresents the gospel. In selecting songs, Freeborn advises that we examine the theological content and literary quality of the lyrics as well as the aesthetic and communicative quality of the music. There is some question raised as to the appropriateness of using rock music as a medium for communicating the gospel, particularly in a setting where this music may connote merely a sensual environment.

"Creative Methods," by Marlene LeFever, emphasizes an approach which might inspire youth to learn more about the Christian life. The chapter focuses on student-centered methods which can be directed by a non-professional adult leader. Role play and mime yield high participation and force youth to internalize and use the biblical concepts which they have learned. Choral reading is an easy and effective dramatic form to use with youth. Self-testing for personal values can be an insightful experience and LeFever suggests a number of ways to engage youth in this process. She also presents useful ideas for conducting discussion sessions and for using pictures to involve youth in discussion. As with the other articles in this book, there is a well-selected bibliography for further reading on the subject.

There is a need for very practical guidelines on the matter of interacting with youth in a teaching-learning situation. *How to Teach Senior Highs*, by Locke Bowman, Jr., is an excellent place to begin. This book is written for the volunteer teacher of senior high youth in the church. Bowman's thesis is that the teacher should stimulate youth to think and inquire rather than giving them "answers" to the questions of faith. "To teach is to share what you know with someone else" (p. 14); this entails the dimension of a teacher's personal conviction and religious experience. The aims of teaching youth are these:

1) Teaching aims toward *confirming* the student in a personal faith that is clearly related to life.
2) Teaching aims toward *community* with others.
3) Teaching aims toward *action*.

Reading scripture and taking time for reflective thought are the best means of preparation, Bowman claims. He suggests a method for reading scripture and lists resources for undertaking theological study. He also shows how to move from scripture to discussion and vice versa. Biblical truths are often presented as *paradoxes*, and youth should come to examine these paradoxes and relate them to their own lives. Bowman advocates a "dialectic approach" to accomplish this:

1) The claims of faith are to be explored from every angle.
2) Youth are to look for inconsistencies and discrepancies.
3) There is to be debate in a genuine sense.
4) Nothing is to be exempted from analysis.

There is a twofold concern for those who are teaching youth. The teacher must help those who are thoughtful youth to find *in the church* a freedom to follow their thoughts wherever they may lead. The teacher must help those who have not reached a "thoughtful" stage in their development to come to an awareness of what it could mean if they were engaged in a personal quest for truth. In terms of knowing where youth are, Bowman suggests these methods for becoming informed:

1) Know what courses they are studying in school.
2) Know what community events they are involved in.
3) Interpret current events for them from a Christian perspective.
4) Find out what jobs youth have, and what ethical considerations may arise in these jobs.
5) Promote sports and recreation in a wholesome and positive way.
6) Know the social clubs and organizations to which youth belong.

Extend: Youth Reaching Youth, by Fletcher et al., outlines a program to help young people to extend themselves in friendship to others. The concepts and materials were developed and tested by Project YOUTH, under the direction of the Youth Research Center. Three hundred and fifty young people were involved in the program, but these were divided into "Home Base" groups of 10 to 12, each with its own leader.

There are ten sessions outlined in this manual, and each session includes a number of useful and flexible ways for involving a group of mature youth in interpersonal relationships. The best method for proceeding is to begin with a long session (a six-hour block of time), perhaps in a retreat setting. The intervening sessions will develop relationships in the Home Base groups, and then another long session is suggested to tie the program together.

The Exuberant Years: A Guide for Junior High Leaders, by Ginny Ward Holderness, is a practical guide and resource book growing out of her experience as a director of Christian education working with youth aged 12, 13, and 14. The thrust is an approach to ministry that will enable the building of relationships. The first section describes how youth leaders should prepare themselves for working with this age group. Junior highs are a special challenge because of their high energy level, short attention span, and peer-pressure conformity. Holderness states her underlying assumption that a leader does not build a youth group, but rather than youth build a youth group.

Section II presents various options and methods for structuring youth programs. In addition to making suggestions for weekly meetings, Holderness describes the organizing of special events such as church-ins, car caravans, and retreats. She presents a chapter of reliable methods ranging from group builders to values-clarification activities.

The final section is a well-assembled set of eleven mini-courses, with each mini-course designed for four sessions on a particular topic. Such topics as value process, identity formation, and death are relevant not only to junior highs but to senior highs as well. The last chapter instructs youth leaders on how to design their own mini-courses.

In *Eight Special Studies for Senior Highs*, Lois Kilgore presents eight concepts that are especially related to the needs of youth: happiness, fear, tradition, obedience, sin, forgiveness, justice, and faith. Each concept is organized into a unit of study that is intended for six sessions. The first and last sessions should be an activity involving the entire group; the intervening sessions are designed for the use of learning centers, in which the youth teach themselves and the adult advisor acts as an enabler/facilitator rather than as an instructor. The organization of each study unit makes this a useful resource for retreats. There is also a section which explains how to recycle the plans into traditional forms of teacher-led learning experiences. A brief look at the Index of Major Concepts is an indication of the wide range of topics covered in this manual.

A SUMMARY OF FINDINGS

What has our excursion through these various resources on youth and youth ministry contributed to our understanding of this task? The purpose of this section is to summarize the major findings to serve as basic guidelines for our ongoing inquiry.

What have we learned about youth sociologically? Youth need both formal and informal institutions, yet it is the informal institutions that satisfy many of the basic socialization needs of youth. Reference groups are the most influential and predictive factors of a youth's current behavior; of various reference groups, a young person's peer group is a greater influence on current behavior than parents or teachers.

Adolescence has been viewed as a rite of passage between childhood and adulthood. Youth is idealized as an age of unlimited possibilities, yet a polarization of the sexes occurs during this period: Traditionally males have been limited socially by their vocational choices and females have been limited vocationally by their social choices. There is need for both male and female role models for youth who successfully integrate their vocation with meaningful social relationships, since youth learn more effectively when they have models with which to identify.

The family remains the locus of basic enculturation; it is also the best paradigm for understanding how pluralism must function at the level of social organization (unity within diversity). There is a growing lack of parallel experiences between parents and their teenagers, but it is up to parents to keep communication open and honest, letting young people live and learn from their mistakes.

What have we learned about youth developmentally? The main challenge to youth seems to be to establish their identity over against role confusion. Males tend first to achieve identity in relation to their vocational choices, and then to be concerned about their intimacy needs. For females, identity formation and the achievement of intimacy seem to be concomitant tasks. (This is culturally conditioned, however, and not to be construed as "human nature.") Our society has made possible a *psychological moratorium* for youth to integrate this process of ego development. A problem with the educational system, however, is that it often does not provide adequate stimulus to bring about creative conflicts in youth. Most high-school graduates are leaving school at the level of conventional, rather than principled, moral judgment.

There is no "generation gap," but rather an "experience gap" between youth and adults. What has been described as an "unstable personality" in young people is actually a young person learning to cope with new situations, trying new patterns of behavior. Adolescents are very self-conscious in this different social setting. They believe that they are always on stage before an "imaginary audience" and they invent "personal fables" to affirm their own uniqueness and self-worth. A young person's closest friendships may be formed during this time, for youths need constant support and feedback from a friend concerning their feelings and behavior.

What have we learned about the religious experience of youth? Three characteristics have influenced the existential consciousness of today's youth: 1) a lost appreciation of history and tradition, with only the "now" being important, 2) a lack of enduring commitment to any value or philosophy, 3) a search for immortality which is no longer grounded in the Christian symbols of hope (heaven, the kingdom of God). In terms of traditional structures, a high percentage of youth believe in God and pray, but the majority do not feel that a person must attend church to be a good Christian. Religious movements have offered something to meet the needs of youth. For youth in the stage of concrete operations, there is a simple, basic system of right-or-wrong moral values. For youth who are in the stage of formal operations, there is the Utopian solution to the world's problems and a chance to participate in the solution. Formal operations enable youth to structure the world in interpersonal terms and to view situations from the other's perspective. This capability also prompts youth to demythologize rituals and symbols, and to deal with religion as a set of intellectual propositions rather than as a transforming reality.

What have we learned about the task of youth ministry? Youth are to be viewed as members of the church *now*, not just as future members. Youth ministry therefore strives to involve youth in mission and outreach programs, and not limit ministry to those who show up at the meetings. Youth ministry is presently exemplified by those who go into the community to evangelize, interpreting the gospel on "native soil." These ministers are reaching youth who have dropped out of the church.

Facilitating friendships and relationships is a primary goal of youth ministry, for relaxed groupings of youth tend to become the church both theologically and socially. Retreats are effective in helping youth to relax with one another and in equipping youth for their ministry. The role of the adult leader as a guarantor of youth is important. Authentic adults use their own gifts and talents and do not try to impress young people with gimmicks. In teaching youth, adults stimulate questions rather than trying to give all the right "answers." Not all adults are competent to lead youth, and should not be placed in a leadership position simply because they have volunteered. The most meaningful characteristic of adult leaders is that they are able to be self-revealing about their own faith journeys.

QUESTIONS FOR FURTHER INVESTIGATION

1. How is youth a construct of culture? How is youth defined differently from one culture to another?
2. Given the influence of the family, in what ways may youth and their parents be involved in meaningful intergenerational experiences?
3. How may the peer relationship be used in a *positive* way for youth?
4. Because young people are constantly told to remain open and undecided (psychosocial moratorium), what type of *commitment* to Christ are they able to make?
5. How may "faith development" be measured in adolescents?
6. How do the findings presented here relate to the experiences and life patterns of minority youth, or urban youth, and of those not going to college where they have the experience of a psychosocial moratorium?
7. What steps may be taken to reawaken in youth a concern for mission?
8. What experiences may be incorporated into congregational worship with youth in mind?
9. What are the criteria for an effective youth ministry and how are these to be communicated to congregations?
10. With the prevailing criticism that youth are isolated from the rest of the church, how is it justifiable to have "youth ministers" who are viewed as somehow different from "adult ministers"?
11. How do we develop models for youth ministry that are relevant for young people in all socio-economic sectors

and geographical regions of this country, and in individually varying degrees of readiness for change or growth?

12. How does the lack of female role models in the church affect young people?

13. What procedures are presently being used to select and train lay persons for leading youth?

14. How have churches overcome their doctrinal differences in jointly engaging a youth minister to serve in the community at large?

REFERENCES

Bowman, Locke, Jr., *How to Teach Senior Highs*. Philadelphia: Westminster Press, 1963.

Erikson, Erik, *Identity: Youth and Crisis*. New York: W. W. Norton, 1968.

Evans, David M., *Shaping the Church's Ministry With Youth*. Valley Forge, Pennsylvania: Judson Press, 1977.

Fletcher, Kenneth R., Ardyth Norem-Hebelson, David W. Johnson, and Ralph C. Underwager. *Extend: Youth Reaching Youth*. Minneapolis: Augsburg Publishing House, 1974.

Fowler, Jim, and Sam Keen (edited by Jerome Berryman), *Life Maps: Conversations on the Journey of Faith*. Waco, Texas: Word Books, 1978.

Havighurst, Robert J., and Phillip H. Dreyer (editors), *Youth*. Chicago: University of Chicago Press, 1975.

Holderness, Ginny Ward, *The Exuberant Years: A Guide for Junior High Leaders*. Atlanta, Georgia: John Knox Press, 1976.

Kilgore, Lois, *Eight Special Studies for Senior Highs*. Scottsdale, Arizona: National Teacher Education Project, 1976.

Little, Sara, *Youth, World, and Church*. Richmond, Virginia: John Knox Press, 1968.

Manaster, Guy J., *Adolescent Development and the Life Tasks*. Boston: Allyn & Bacon, 1977.

Manning, Peter K., and Marcello Truzzi, *Youth and Sociology*. Englewood Cliffs, New Jersey: Prentice-Hall, Inc., 1972.

Muuss, Rolf E., *Theories of Adolescence*. New York: Random House, 1962; Revised 1975.

Paine, Roger, III, *We Never Had Any Trouble Before*. New York: Stein & Day, 1975.

Religion in America 1979–1980. Princeton, New Jersey: Princeton Religion Research Center, 1980.

Richards, Lawrence O., *Youth Ministry: Its Renewal in the Local Church*. Grand Rapids, Michigan: Zondervan Publishing House, 1972.

Sherif, Muzafer and Carolyn W., *Reference Groups, Exploration into Conformity and Deviation of Adolescents*. New York: Harper & Row, 1964.

Smith, Ernest A., *American Youth Culture, Group Life in Teenage Society*. New York: Free Press of Glencoe, 1962.

Sparkman, G. Temp (editor), *Knowing and Helping Youth*. Nashville, Tennesee: Broadman Press, 1977.

Strommen, Merton P., *Bridging the Gap*. Minneapolis: Augsburg Publishing House, 1973.

————. *Five Cries of Youth*. New York: Harper & Row, 1974.

Strommen, Merton P., Milo L. Brekke, Ralph C. Underwater, Arthur L. Johnson, *A Study of Generations*. Minneapolis: Augsburg Publishing House, 1972.

Warren, Michael (editor), *Youth Ministry, A Book of Readings*. New York: Paulist Press, 1977.

Westerhoff, John H., III, and Gwen Kennedy Neville, *Generation to Generation*. Philadelphia: Pilgrim Press, 1979.

Wilcox, Mary M., *Developmental Journey*. Nashville: Abingdon Press, 1979.

Woods, Ray T., and Gerald L. Klever, *World of Church Youth*. Philadelphia: Board of Christian Education, United Presbyterian Church in the U.S.A., 1971.

Zuck, Roy B., and Warren S. Benson (editors), *Youth Education in the Church*. Chicago: Moody Press, 1978.

Zuck, Roy B., and Gene A. Getz, *Christian Youth—An In-Depth Study*. Chicago: Moody Press, 1968.

NOTES

1. It must be recognized that what is termed a "neutral" or "uncommitted" outlook is in fact a commitment to a secular world view and claims just as much authority as does a religious commitment. Because commitment is inevitable, it is better for the commitment of the teacher to be recognized as a significant datum in the learning process. A teacher should acknowledge his/her commitment as a basic presupposition and then operate within the limitations of this commitment. See Edward Hulmes, *Commitment and Neutrality in Religious Education* (London: Geoffrey Chapman, 1979).

Chapter 2

Questions the Church Needs to Answer About Youth

FREDA A. GARDNER

Freda Gardner teaches Christian education at Princeton Theological Seminary. Much of her time is spent helping seminarians learn about youth and how to minister effectively with them. Confronted by the constant barrage of materials, models, and gimmicks for working with young people, she calmly claims that "ministry is life-giving, but running a program is death." An essential aspect of ministry involves understanding the environment and life situations of those to whom we minister. The thought-provoking questions raised in this presentation are evidence of such ministry: Gardner gives her impressions of "what's happening" among today's youth and reflects on them theologically.

INTRODUCTION

With what butterfly net does anyone rush into the American youth scene? No matter where the age boundary lines are drawn, youth, for the present anyway, are still center stage and the focus of research for a broad array of public and private institutions of this country. The data from the research is endless. Education, media, marketing, law, penal reform, physical-mental-emotional health services, nutrition, employment, recreation, publishing, fashion, entertainment, family life, housing—the list goes on and on and the statistics are consistently alarming in either their magnitude or their implications.

To observe the mad scramble on the part of middle-aged and older adults to identify with the youth segment of the population is to be convinced that youth is still synonymous with life no matter what the Gray Panthers or the advertising world try to tell us. It is rare when a youth fad remains such for very long. Clothes, styles, music, dance, play, films, the gimmicks of a consumptive, affluent society are quickly usurped by those who can no longer be considered youth by anyone's definition.

Volumes have been written about each aspect of the youth scene. Only a few have been able to transcend subcultures and/or the individual differences which make even adolescent siblings difficult to describe collectively. Without touching on more than a few perspectives and a small selection of observable data within those perspectives, a wide range of questions emerges from the culture. The extent to which the church must or should consider these questions is, perhaps, one of the first which the church should ask. It would seem that the church must attend to the world, to observe it, to interact with it, to read its data, to discern between its realities and its idealized and generalized promotionally oriented "facts." The church, intended for the world, must watch and listen, must evaluate the sources of its truth, must examine its own constituency for affirmation or contradiction of any claim to describe "the way it is."

DEFINITION OF TERMS

For the purposes of this essay I will define youth as a period in human development, generally beginning with the onset of puberty and terminating when the person becomes independent of his or her family of origin or surrogate family.

In referring to the church, I speak of a people who acknowledge themselves to be God's people through the redemption of the Incarnate Christ of God and, by the power of God's Spirit, to be that faithful body of Christ in the world. In particular, church refers to the mainline Protestant churches in America today.

PERSPECTIVES ON YOUTH IN THE WORLD

With or without a butterfly net, we move into the world of youth with baggage which may either impede our progress or assist our choice of routes.

Some mental arithmetic will perhaps help our baggage identification. If you subtract twelve from your present age, you will have the approximate number of years since you entered the age of our concern; approximate because puberty is not a chronologically assigned phenomenon and even its general age categorization changes with the decade and with subcultures.

That answer you got in the simple subtraction, multiplied by the 365 days of each of those years, will make the length of time elapsed since you were twelve seem unnecessarily long even before you begin to think more specifically about what's happened since you were twelve.

Remember, for instance, what you have done: the first day in junior high or high school, the first time for wearing a bikini or driving a car or kissing someone not in your family, or the first A or F, or the first time you spoke in church or went to an X-rated film or smoked pot or stayed up all night or knew someone who died. On the other hand, think about what and who you have been: personality and character descriptions, physical-emotional-intellectual changes; and changes in the world around you: ideologies, technological changes, theological and ecclesiastical shifts.

All that may be too much, too far back, too difficult to take hold of and if that's the situation, some minutes in remembering the changes in your life in the last six months or two weeks may remind you that ideas, relationships, values, fears, hopes are dynamic, not static. The exercise may also point up the remembrance and the knowledge that change in adolescence is often more rapid and more dramatic than during any other period in life.

To turn away from ourselves is to bring into focus other integral concerns and questions which may be a part of that about which the church must inquire.

What does it mean that in most churches, schools, communities, and families, youth leadership was probably moving in and through adolescence between the late 40s and early 60s?

What world view, lifestyles, major questions, values, hopes and goals marked the lives of these adults as they struggled with identity, sex, occupation, friendship, ideologies? What language, humor, music, recreation, idols, literature shaped their dreams and despair and dictated their choices? These women and men—the parents, teachers, pastors, club and group leaders, policy makers—were born in the late 30s and early 40s to World War I and Great Depression-oriented parents. Those parents, and leaders, were, in this country, intent upon survival and then upon proving themselves able to do better by their children and their country, earning their own way and always on the alert for the next "crash."

"Damn it, folks, things are different from when you were kids." Can't you hear that echoing and re-echoing from each age of humankind?

Or let us focus on youth in the family or surrogate family situation. Where is the adolescent? What is the adolescent in the family? How does her or his past, present, and future figure in the family drama? What is expected of him or her, and equally important, what is not expected?

And in school, the institution for everyone in our society: Where and what is the adolescent in school? Is he or she a participant? A puppet? A pawn of local, state, or national political maneuvering? Is the adolescent alienated from or integrated into this supposedly significant part of his or her life? Is school a social experience? A stepping stone? A place to work out the tensions built at home or a place to make public the values of the home? A time-filler? A time-killer? A context for dignity or abasement? What is the adolescent's intellectual capacity, learning style, motivation, self-concept, socializing instinct and skill, ability in other school valued activities like sports, music, drama, governance?

Each adolescent also lives in a broader community. How is she or he perceived by the community and what sense of identity with which part of the community does each one hold? What is defined as the "good life" in the community? Who are the role models? What earns the community's affirmation, recognition, respect, censure? Are these values affirmed or ridiculed by the media of the culture and what does the adolescent do with the messages received . . . with dishonesty, uncertainty, crises, evil, fads? Or with the message of teenage consumer power? In the past two decades youth has spent ever more billions of dollars on other than education (recent figures indicate a figure in excess of 40 billion dollars). What if you are one of the spenders and what if you are not? What does anyone do with being told continually that youth is where the action is, that life is now at its most beautiful, vigorous, healthful best, that life is affirmed for its lack of responsibility, its use of energies for the pursuit of pleasure? The message appears to be confirmed by a poor employment picture or a totally jobless market for many of the young, confirmed by a rising divorce rate (somehow the statistics on remarriage do not get the same media coverage), confirmed by the pursuit of youthfulness by a large majority of visible adults until there is little to move toward or away from. A significant percentage of reading, TV, and films invites a regression to a state of dreaming illusion or to rage handled mainly through apathy or spasmodic passion, frequently by violence which is often sexual.

How does the adult world respond to the zeal, commitment, willingness to sacrifice, repudiation of materialism, movements toward justice, yearning to love, honesty, and insights of some adolescents? What do we do with the apparent successes and failures of youth (and of adulthood)? With causes and movements? With wars and threats of wars? With technological blessings and their seemingly unavoidable correlative curses? With shifting male and female roles? With the pride and the put-downs of racial struggles? With awareness and ignorance of injustice?

Can our world live with a business-as-usual "Kids are no different today" attitude? A retreat to the arena of physical development seems to bring hope to some. Puberty still arrives with physiological and psychological changes—but earlier. But what about vitamins and antibiotics and teeth braces and corrective or cosmetic surgery and prenatal care and an overabundance of food and the tremendously wide gap between those who take all of that for granted and the others who begin and live their whole lives without them, except as they see them on TV, film, or on the street? What effect does covering up all kinds of blemishes and weaknesses have on a rapidly developing body and body concept? What is the effect of open discussion of masturbation, orgasm, homosexuality, or the effect of open discussion on everything else but those? Pills take care of all problems—acceptably—so there's no need to sweat anything, and if you do, its simply because you haven't been led to the right tube or bottle for your kind of sweat. What is body anyway? And its long-range usefulness may not be a real concern when the draft or a ringing red phone will prove that there's no place to hide even if you do want to survive.

PERSPECTIVES ON YOUTH IN THE CHURCH

Some adolescents in the church can be said to be children of the church. These young people, through infant baptism and/or participation from early childhood, know the church as part of their lives. Their parents and families have been more or less involved and have defined and valued the church in a variety of ways, to be sure, but for these youth, church is, or at least has been, of some significance in their development. They have been through the program of the parish for children and that has become a part of who they are now.

Absent from the group just described are the youth who began with them and have already dropped out. Mobility; loss of parental commitment, interest, participation, influence, or of the parents themselves; personal indifference; shame, despair, or anger; peer pressure; lack of appropriate social or intellectual skills or financial resources; the reasons are many and not all are known or can be known by either the adolescent or those adults who care to wonder.

Both of the groups previously described may have known the church and been known by it to some extent in the rituals of the church's life (seasonal liturgical services, weddings, baptisms, funerals), during times of crisis in the family (illness, death, divorce, loss of job), or through ecumenical or extra-parochial activities (coffee houses, Young Life, child evangelism).

There are the newly arrived adolescents—those who were not raised in the church who come now to study or play or work or just to be with others who do. Some arrive with a parent, out of a crisis emerging or survived, from a search for a new community, from a re-evaluation of life and its meaning. Some drop in—testing themselves or anyone who will stay still long enough to hear a challenge or a confession, looking for an oasis or an eye in a storm. These come with little or no knowledge of what the church is or does except for what has been absorbed from hear-say, headlines, or participation in the civil religion of the culture.

And, of course, there are those who have never been the con-cern of the church as individuals but only as a group who are a focus of the mission of the church. "The youth in our area" or in our community who, most often, are last on any list of priorities of a church's mission to youth. These are the unknown, some-times visible, more often sensed for their presence in the com-munity or their identification as a group by other community organizations.

As general as the preceding identifications are, they may suf-fice to remind us that the church has, in the past, chosen to include or exclude each of the groups as it has developed its ministry to youth. A question of primary significance is: Should and will the church choose to minister to all groups or to which groups in the present and in the future?

THE CHURCH'S OBJECTIVE IN MINISTRY TO YOUTH AND QUESTIONS RAISED BY IT

The question of which young people to attend to may not be a first question for some. A first question may be why attend to any at all?

For years The Objective of Christian Education for Senior High Young People as formulated in 1958 by a committee of the National Council of Churches has been viewed as an appropriate and useful articulation:

The objective of Christian education is to help persons to be aware of God's self-disclosure and seeking love in Jesus Christ and to re-spond in faith and love—to the end that they may know who they are and what their human situation means, grow as sons [sic] of God rooted in the Christian community, live in the Spirit of God in every relationship, fulfill their common discipleship in the world, and abide in the Christian hope.

This statement has stood the test of several decades and, when analyzed and discussed, seems to encompass the cultural influences on youth today as well as the prevailing understandings of the nature and mission of the church. A shorter contemporary definition might be: to enable young people to participate in ever more complete ways in the Shalom of God. Elements of identity, the generally accepted major task and force of the life of adolescents, are inherent in both the statement and in the shorter definition. Who am I? must include the historical, relational, volitional, affective, cognitive, and idiosyncratic aspects of the individual. The church, in each of its denominational expressions, affirms life as intentional, purposeful, meaningful, communal, responsible, and as continuing beyond its earth and time-bound existence. Any statement regarding ministry to youth must, if it is to be the church's statement, attest to those truths about life. A question for the church to answer is: Must/should the church's ministry to youth include all dimensions of its understanding and convictions about life, or do the peculiar circumstances of individual adolescents or groups imply a more narrow witness? An illustration: Can a hurting, isolated young person hear or know anything beyond "We're here and we care and you're worth it"?

Narrow witness, as used in the preceding paragraph, might be translated theologically into incarnational or presence ministry in some situations. The question then becomes: Is it possible and appropriate that the church minister to youth by simply being available in the person(s) of a member of the church staff or of the church itself? Being there may mean in the church building, on the street or in the community contexts for youth. Being there may incorporate particular skills (conversation, listening, counseling, referral, etc.) or may be presence alone.

A developmental perspective at this point might put the question in such terms as: Should the church order its witness to the gospel to match the developmental stage of the adolescent? Is knowledge (yàda) of one's redemption a prerequisite to self-affirmation that leads to commitment that is both lasting and communal? Or, to illustrate in another way, does identification with the people of God precede any capacity to know oneself as valued and redeemed by God and thereby to be freed for a life of discipleship?

In many of the "successful" extra-church movements which attract youth and hold them, the gospel is indeed tailored to their most evident needs for affirmation and acceptance, for the sense of group identity, for truths to live by. Such programs come replete with expectations and ritualized ways of responding to those expectations. The latter speaks to the underside of identity—to know who I am not. Rituals of language and behavior serve as quick indicators of who is in and who's out and leave no wondering adolescent with the uncertainty of where she/he stands. Mainline denominations are critical of the tailoring, of what is left unproclaimed or proclaimed by default, even as those same established churches envy the numerical success and the ethusiasm which such groups and movements enjoy and engender.

The questions posed so far, from a variety of perspectives have a political dimension also. Not infrequently it gets put this way: If the church gives youth what they want in terms of their felt and generally expressed needs, won't many of them remain in the church in their young adult years when they can share in the work and witness? That kind of reasoning has been employed by the church in regard to more traditional forms of missionary endeavor. Feed them so they'll stay around to hear the word. It implies first of all that physical need, in this illustration, and the gospel are two unrelated realities. Such reasoning also implies that adults minister and youth are only ministered to, an implication that is questionable when identifying either the gospel or the church.

Westerhoff's description of the four stages of faith development clearly asserts the relational and communal dimensions of an individual's growth in faith. His stages can be and have been interpreted as "ministry to" in the first three stages and "ministry with" reserved for the fourth stage, "owned faith." This need not be so, nor do I think that is what Westerhoff intended. A question then becomes: Can the good news of God's redemptive action in Jesus Christ and the will and power to participate in God's Shalom come, apart from engagement or ministry *by* youth?

To return to the theological perspective, surely the church must address the question of the new life in Christ. What does it mean to be redeemed, transformed, empowered to live as Christ's disciple? In particular, what does such transformation mean for youth and to youth? Participation in God's Shalom is predicated on taking to oneself the redemptive liberation wrought by Christ's death and resurrection. Only the one who knows himself or herself to have been claimed by God can discern what is the glory and the cost of Shalom.

ADOLESCENCE AND THE MEANING OF BEING HUMAN

Questions that emerge under this heading may be generalized to ask: What human experiences are of particular significance and urgency during adolescence?

Sin is one of the two names the tradition has used to describe the human condition. Sin is not a common word in the vocabularies of a majority of today's youth. The same might be said of a majority of their parents and leaders. Even when defined as "alienation from God" we cannot assume that everyone can now understand it. For many people today, alienation is not an experience that is consciously known. To be cut off from family,

place of origin, or customary institutions is a familiar phenomenon to many, but to experience the sense of loss of self and
self-with-others may not be felt, dealt with, or acknowledged in
any way. Loneliness, depression, despair, anger, confusion,
apathy, weariness—all may be experienced without ever knowing
them as separation from self or that they may be a part of one's
separation from God.

To feel less than whole, fragmented, unsettled is no longer an
adolescent experience or the experience of the maladjusted or
neurotic adult. It is a more general human experience and as
such, adolescents receive little help from those older people simi-
larly afflicted or little hope that it, like teenage acne, if endured,
will one day go away.

It may be said that the adolescents of today know the world in
ways that their parents never did. From birth the images and
symbols of this and other cultures have been the backdrops of
their lives. A street in Honolulu or in Tehran may be more
familiar to many than another part of their own community.
Coca Cola's red sign and McDonald's golden arches are recognized in news reports and documentaries from places around the
world, giving rise to the sense of familarity which precludes
knowing anyone there or knowing oneself in another context.
More significantly it removes any felt need to learn how to know
oneself or another. To watch a teenager walk a street crowded
with people, with his or her senses centered on the sound coming
from the ever larger radio held to the ear is to wonder about the
meaning of life. To watch the parent generation, in increasing
numbers, take mini-TVs to sports events so they can duplicate in
those settings the only way they know how to be a spectator is to
ask about loss in capacity to relate directly to any new experiences
or at least to a variety of experiences. If in the past schools could
be condemned for too little attention to the development of the
whole person, the schooling of television may also be questioned
along similar lines.

The previous sketch is of one form of alienation. The question is: Can alienation from God be recognized and thereby make real the need for redemption if alienation from self and others is an unquestioned reality in the lives of youth and increasing in the lives of their parents and leaders?

The other name the tradition has given to the human condition is *imago dei*. In what ways do the adolescents of today know or see themselves and others as made in God's image? Or, perhaps, a prior question: To what extent does the church today see itself as those who bear the *imago dei* in their individual and collective lives? Coming away from nearly two decades of the human potential movement with its emphasis on individuality and the right to develop oneself in one's own image, the church, which embraced many of the various expressions of the movement, is today a people who are both its victims and its loyal subjects. It is not unusual to find clergy in their forties who privately ascribe salvation to their experiences in encounter groups, growth labs, or TA workshops. Equally visible are those, both clergy and lay, who have been increasingly aware that what seemed salvific in the late 60s has left them alone, disconnected from people and commitments and values which, in retrospect, take on an importance that makes "doing your own thing" a childish indulgence.

The implications of *imago dei*—the purposefulness of life, the communal nature of being, the uniqueness of being a human being—suggest disciplines and behavior that are not a part of much of the church today: commitment, renunciation, sacrifice, fidelity. These are words that most of us accept as a part of the identity and intimacy struggles which mark the adolescent and young adult years. Is the church able to help them with those struggles? Are the adults in the church willing to be helped by youth, recognizing that this is for the most part today, an authentic intergenerational task?

According to this description of the human condition—*imago dei*—made in God's image, made with the capacity for relating, living, creating—humankind dreams, imagines, yearns, communes, and reaches toward others. What of *imago dei* in youth?

Status blue jeans may be decried by sociologists as evidence of classism but labeled blue jeans are still less ostentatious than the refinements of the upper classes two decades ago. At the watering holes of the authentic young, when what they are there to see or hear is the first order of the day, materialism infrequently marks off classes. Adult liberal Protestantism, in remorse over some of its heritage of paternalistic, imperialistic missionary endeavors, shrinks from service that might be labeled "do-good" and suggest classism. In so doing, many young people have been left without models and encouragement to try on cooperative, just, peacemaking, advocating ministries. They have been robbed of the tradition's symbols of servanthood and of the vocabulary for describing sacrifice, fidelity, and commitment. Drugs and incense have filled the emptiness which is both a yearning for the mystery and an ache to be at one with others, a hope that there is more to see than meets the eye—a void that God has filled through the body of Christ in rich and varied ways through the years.

THE QUESTIONS RESTATED

Must the church expend efforts in identifying the shaping forces of adolescent identity? To what extent should the church inquire into the world of youth? Should the church minister to the particulars of the lives of youth as they are a part of families, school, community, culture?

Is the church to be concerned for all young people in more than a general way? Can a congregation or denomination expect to minister to all or is "being in place" in community and culture the only realistic way to witness to the good news for those who have ears to hear and eyes to see?

What is the church's intent for youth? What can be identified and lived with as first steps which may become the beginning of a young person's pilgrimage with God? Can the church live with integrity before God and the world in doing what can be done and leaving the rest to unfold when it will? How far can the church go with ministry to youth without involving youth in ministry? In what do redemption and transformation consist? Does sin or *imago dei* describe the human condition? If not, what does, and to what human condition does the church witness and the gospel speak?

To what extent is the whole church appropriately described in the same terms that we use to describe youth and in what aspects are they different? In what sense does church leadership of youth need to see itself as wounded healer, and how does that awareness get nurtured, and how does it become ministry to/with youth?

OTHER IMPLIED QUESTIONS

Dwayne Huebner and others speak of particular ministries in the church in terms of living faithfully together. To live faithfully with youth the church, congregation and denomination, must first face the questions of reason for being and source of authenticity and authority, must inquire into the ways in which people come to know, believe, and live as children of God and disciples of Christ. Only then can the question of living faithfully, relative to that common freedom and calling, begin to be described by acts and programs of ministry.

Ministry words like justice, empowerment, knowledge, advocacy, sacrifice, fidelity, forgiveness, love, commitment appear in response to the questions asked in the preceding sections when living faithfully together is more than a cliché. Ministry words symbolize the church's best and only legitimate response to the human condition and incorporate youth as both recipients and doers of the word.

For such to happen, doesn't the church have to open up to deciding, acting, risking dimensions of its life to young people that they may see not only the realities of life but also the miracles of God's redeeming and transforming power in our midst?

Doesn't the church have to continue to study and reflect on Scripture, creeds, and tradition in order to know itself in relation to God with enough confidence so that exploration and experimentation with Christian lifestyle expressions (in worship, interpersonal relationships and communal patterns, uses of time and resources, etc.) are welcomed as a part of youth's quest for identity and meaning? The welcome referred to here sees the new, or the old done in new faithful ways, as gift to the whole church, not merely as youth's letting off steam or passing through a phase. Renewal of the church, when trust is in a trustworthy God and in an understanding of God's ways with the church, does not have to be the prerogative of the old but can be the ministry of the whole people, addressed by those whose life force is directed to discovering, for their first time, the meaning of living faithfully together.

What leadership is suggested by all that has come before? In Ross Snyder's terms and implied in the phrase "living faithfully together," the answer may be thought of in terms of authenticity. Style, academic knowledge, age, status become secondary when an authentic human being is encountered. If such is called by the church to a particular role: teacher, advocate, tutor, listener, co-worker—that role will dictate particular requirements, but to be related to youth as part of the church's ministry may be said to require a woman or man engaged with faith and life in open, continually growing ways. The church must address the question of leadership in terms of its answers to all the preceding questions. Stereotypes of effective youth leaders may, in fact, minister to/with stereotyped youth and nurture them to a narrow and also stereotyped response to a living God. The traditional form of one or two youth "advisors" in a congregation must be questioned by the intent of the church for its ministry to/with youth. Charis-

matic leaders of youth frequently deny the theological understanding of the gifts of God to the people of God—charisms
which differ in kind and expression, which in turn call forth a
wider variety of gifts than the traditional lone charismatic leader
may be able to evoke.

The questions are not new. The answers are not easily dis-
cerned. The questions, and others like them or quite different
ones which you would see as more or equally important, must be
lived with. The church's ministry to youth and to the life which is
youth's cannot be settled by a program or a series of programs. It
is a ministry which implies a continuing dialogue with our
Creator, Redeemer, Advocate who calls us and all people into a
life of power and glory, sacrifice and service; it is a commitment
to share that life with younger women and men who are also
God's children and whose lives are marked by both searching and
witnessing.

REFLECTIONS: Andrew P. Grannell

Freda Gardner has succeeded in enunciating and raising up
the questions that in fact the church should ask (and so self-
evidently has not asked) concerning its ministry to, for, with, and
by youth. She has examined the questions of ministry with youth
from three quite distinct angles: secular culture, the mainline
church, and theology. In my view, she succeeds best when she
addresses the questions from such perspectives as sin and *imago
dei*. In fact, I found her questioning increasingly well-targeted as
she worked her way through the "cloud of unknowing" in the
secular realm, until she found what she was so evidently looking
for, *i.e.*, the 1958 National Council of Churches statement of
objective for ministry with youth. From that juncture, she finds
her way with greater assurance and the questions are both more
pointed and well-targeted. This opening exploration was a dif-

ficult assignment, but it proved most important for the ensuing discussions. Freda has succeeded, in short, in raising up a great welter of questions and many of the critical ones.

In the following, I have three goals. First, I would like to sharpen up some of the questions and perhaps lift up some that are only loosely present in the text. Second, I will attempt to add some reflections of my own on the subject of intergenerational connections. Third, I would like to outline the key questions that I believe we will need to deal with and in fact continue to struggle with beyond the parameters of these deliberations.

First, we need to sharpen and lift up some of the questions from each of the sections of the paper. Here then are the questions that the secular culture addresses to the church's educators. Finding many of these questions excessively broad and general, I would suggest these rephrasings:

a. In relation to the stress that the contemporary forms of family are enduring, where does the adolescent fit in? How do present-day youth view the future of the traditional nuclear family which still largely claims the adult's loyalty in word, but too often not in deed?

b. What role is schooling playing in the socialization of contemporary youth? What is the present consciousness of the radical critique of the school of only a few short years ago?

c. What role models do youth look to in the 1980s when we are so clearly bereft of heroes and heroines that command a wide following?

d. What is the future for unemployed youth in urban neighborhoods, e.g., the 50 percent of black youth in Detroit who will not find a job this summer?

e. What is the impact on behavior and attitudes of adolescents of the new outlook of honesty or at least openness?

f. What conscious—or unconscious—impact is the arms race to oblivion having upon the hopes, dreams, and willingness to delay gratification?

These then are the key questions that I discover as I reflect upon the welter of questions raised in this first section. The answers that we have at present appear to be partial at best.

Second, before we come to the crucial questions raised by this paper, I would like to add my own reflections. In thinking about the linking of adult youth leadership with present day youth, Freda Gardner has asked us to reflect upon some facts such as the span of time that adolescence has been a part of our consciousness—or, alternatively, to reflect upon the meaning of adolescence for those of us who went through this experience in the 1940s, 1950s, and 1960s. Erik Erikson's concept of the "cog-wheeling of life cycles" helps, I believe, to illuminate this territory.[1] In this view, each generation comes to maturity under the influence of the preceding two generations—if we understand a generation as roughly 15–20 years. Hence, those born in the 1920–58 time period (a 38-year period) are presumably the most formative in the shaping (and the being reshaped by) this cohort of people presently coming of age. The life cycles (adult passages) of those presently between the ages of 22 and 60 are either meshing or failing to mesh with this formative slow turning of the transescent (ages 11–14), adolescent (ages 13–20), and postadolescent (21–24). I would, then, in line with this reasoning, restate the question in the following manner:

How does the intergenerational "cogwheeling" of adult youth leadership with this ever-new contemporary generation mesh or fail to mesh?

or

Should we be looking to the rapidly growing—numerically and influentially—two-generation elderly, *i.e.*, 65–80 and 80-plus to become directly involved with youth?

or

Doesn't the church make a critical mistake by turning to those young adults among both laity and ministers for the great bulk of its leadership with youth?

Obviously, there are many intriguing questions concerning our cultural propensity to look to young adults to bridge the gap between the generations. What we are saying thereby is that in fact there can be no effective meshing of the life cycles, *i.e.*, those critical life concerns, values, interests, of the succeeding generations. The idolization of youth must surely be tempered in the time ahead with the sheer weight of the population shift toward middle-aged and older persons.

Third, in my view the core value of this paper arises with the questions of sin and *imago dei*. The questions that plague us transcend the cultural, historical, and intergenerational. These questions arise from a stock-taking of our spiritual condition. If alienation from ourselves and especially from God appears to be a widespread phenomenon, then it would appear that several issues arise. The cries of youth that Merton Strommen continues to document as a North American phenomenon that persisted year-by-year through this last decade are: loneliness, depression, despair, anger, confusion, apathy, and weariness.[2] Freda Gardner asks, "Can this alienation from self and God be recognized as sin? That is, since we have come to accept alienation as a fact of life is it then possible to claim redemption as possible?" Haven't we been seduced into accepting alienation as a natural phenomenon not only of youth, but also of much of adulthood? What is the meaning of youth ministry when redemption from our isolated selves is no longer thought of as necessary or worse, possible? This I would view as one of three critical questions.

The *imago dei*, that is, our need to view our lives as being created in God's image, is also quite rich for our purposes here. With too few adults in our churches does the meaning of sacrifice, renunciation, advocacy, cooperation, fidelity take on dynamic or visible meaning in their lives. Without modeling that is strong, pervasive, and meaning-filled by the present adult generations, how can the generation coming of age come to understand the fullness of what it means to grow up in God's image? Are adults in our churches willing to learn from youth, on the other hand, what it means to be created in God's image? In what sense does church leadership of youth need to see itself as "wounded healer," and how does the awareness get nurtured? These then are the second grouping of crucial questions raised by this paper.

Finally, perhaps one of the most exciting moments in my reading of this paper came near the end.

> Ministry words like justice, empowerment, knowledge, advocacy, sacrifice, fidelity, forgiveness, love, commitment appear in response to the questions asked in the preceding sections when living faithfully together is more than a cliché. Ministry words symbolize the church's best and only legitimate response to the human condition and incorporate youth as both recipients and doers of the Word. For such to happen, doesn't the church have to open up the deciding, acting, risking dimensions of its life to young people that they may see not only the realities of life but also the miracles of God's redeeming and transforming power in our midst?

There is the task as I know it and would again like to witness to it. There is the meshing of the generations beyond the gaps, patterns of alienation, and shifting cultural patterns. Ministry is intimately linked with the opening up of the acting, risking, deciding dimensions of our lives together. Only in this manner does the ministry to-and-for youth become the ministry by-and-with youth.

NOTES

1. Erik H. Erikson, *Insight and Responsibility* (New York: W.W. Norton, 1964), p. 162.

2. Merton P. Strommen, *Five Cries of Youth* (New York: Harper & Row, 1974), p. 112 especially.

Chapter 3

Culture, Youth, and Socialization in American Protestantism

GWEN KENNEDY NEVILLE

Gwen Kennedy Neville is currently the Elizabeth Root Paden Professor of Sociology at Southwestern University, Georgetown, Texas. By examining ethnic enclaves and cultural patterns in our own country from her perspective as a cultural anthropologist, she has contributed valuable insights toward our self understanding as Americans. Her collaboration with John Westerhoff has also led to a fruitful dialogue between sociology and theology, a dialogue which is much-needed in the field of Christian Education. In the following article, she challenges the church to adopt an ethnological perspective for understanding and educating its youth—and adults.

In the literature of education and religious education the term *youth* has come to refer to a particular stage of life and to be widely used in the labeling of church educational programs and printed materials. The term is elusive, however. Does it refer to people between the ages 13 and 21, 15 and 24, to the same phenomena that goes by the label *teenage?* Is it the same as *adolescence* as defined by the psychologists, or does it come somewhere after adolescence? Is it a physical condition or is it a social affliction? In the educational program of churches, youth refers roughly to all those people who are between elementary school and "young adult"; it comes after the confirmation class, during it, or before-during-and-after it until one reaches the "young couples' class" or the "young adult singles class." In the evening it becomes "youth group," "youth fellowship," "young people" or is marked by some particular denominational marker such as "M.Y.F.," "Luther League," or for older youth "Westminster Fellowship" or "Wesley Foundation." In the summer the term is found in connection with youth conference, youth camp, and youth triennium. One young person told me that youth "begins at the beginning of junior high and ends when the person has been out of school a few years or gets married—if they don't get married too young." Legally, when a young couple marries they are plummeted into adulthood under the law, no matter what their ages, and in some states a youngster can apply to a judge to have his or her youth removed by gaining "emancipation" and being declared an adult.

One of our purposes, as I understand it, is to take a new look at this confusing category of humanity known in America as *youth* and to begin to find some grounding in educational and social theory to assist us in shaping our practical task as church educators. In this essay I will outline a possible theoretical framework. I will first deal with the existing theoretical position in our treatment of life stages in the theory of religious education. I will then explore the utility of the concept of *culture* as an aid in understanding the concept of youth. Finally, I will comment on the process of socialization within American mainline Protestantism.

LIFE STAGE THEORIES AND CHURCH EDUCATION

Theories of education and, especially, of religious education in America have been drawn primarily from the field of psychology and have pertained almost exclusively to individual human growth and development. We have relied for the groundwork of the entire public school establishment on an understanding of human stages of learning and of individual potential. The graded classes represent this idea within the school system, replicated by the Sunday School graded series for children and youth. Two philosophical concepts are embedded in this approach to learning and to the consequent structuring of educational environments—one is that of progress and development, a venerable nineteenth-century idea for all aspects of human endeavor, and the other is the centrality of the individual as the focus of study and inquiry in the American educational climate. Both progress and the individual as underlying meanings have roots as well in the basic tenets of Protestantism and have influenced the development of Protestant theology and ethics at the same time as influencing the development of Protestant religious educational theory.

The idea of progress, with its accompanying emphasis on the benefits of growth, change, increased efficiency, technological sophistication, and human potential, is well known to each of us from having lived our lives in the late twentieth century of the Western world. We are also familiar with the antithesis of this idea—the Limits to Growth, Small Is Beautiful, and other ecological and humanistic movements to curb the runaway results of a nation caught up by the concept of growth. When applied to educational theory, the idea of progress resulted in the creation of the public schools in America—the individual American must be "improved" as a citizen through the introduction of reading, writing, and arithmetic, and must be exposed through his or her schooling to the ideals and goals of the new American civilization in order for the nation itself to continue to grow and progress. [1]

The expression of this faith in development is deeply rooted in the Protestant ethic and in the treasured belief in the "priesthood

of believers." One of the first activities of the infant Congregational and Reformed churches in New England and the Presbyterians in Pennsylvania and the South was to instigate classes in the
home of the minister to teach children to read the Bible. As soon
as possible these same hearty progressive Christians built colleges
and seminaries to continue this educational task for the benefit of
producing a literate and polished clergy to go out and continue to
spread the Word. The churches growing out of this tradition
continue to emphasize the education of persons for their citizenship in the kingdom and the leading along of Christians in the
pathway known as "growing in grace." Whereas some Protestant
groups lean a little more heavily on the Spirit to assist in this task,
and whereas others allow periodic leaving of the path and re-
entering, all of the groups we refer to as mainline Portestant are
in some way products of and generators of this educational philosophy of progress. [2]

The second aspect of the philosophy that has patterned our
religious education is that of the individual as the center of emphasis, the locus of control in change, the target for the ministe-
rial task of the church. In the literature of the field in recent
years, one finds a domination by theories of cognitive process,
identity formation, moral development, faith development, and
so forth, all of which focus on the life tasks of the individual person in an unfolding series of stages moving toward some goal of
achievement—self-actualization, human potential, authentic
personhood, or mature faith. [3] The individual is taken as an identifiable traveler on an ongoing pilgrim journey from birth to
death during which he or she passes through trials and tempta-
tions as the original Pilgrim did, but which are now couched in
terms of "tasks" to be performed at each life stage in order that
one be allowed entrance through the very narrow gate or over the
stile that leads to the next stage.

The fascination with *self* and with *identity* as the centerpieces
of our religious educational theory in mainline Protestantism is

not surprising when we look at the philosophical underpinnings of rugged individualism from which our traditions emerged. The freedom of the person, of the will, of the individual have been especially significant concepts in Protestant theology and ethics; therefore, church educators have not surprisingly found a comfortable intellectual home within the psychology of human growth and development and of learning theory psychology. Even when sociology or anthropology have been called on to inform the theory of education in the church, those aspects of the two fields most closely related to the study of the individual have been the ones most often used. Among these are cognitive anthropology, culture and personality as viewed by the neo-Freudian anthropologists of the past thirty years, and sociolinguistics. In sociology the most often cited works are those in social psychology, small group studies, and symbolic interactionism. In the search for explanatory frameworks and analytical devices, the rich areas of cultural analysis, symbolic and interpretive anthropology, and the cultural study of community have been little used or overlooked entirely. The twin fears of cultural relativism and of cultural determinism have been partially responsible for this omission; but in large part the omission is due simply to overlooking that which is foreign to the theological world view of individualism that is so deeply engrained in the Protestant intellectual tradition.[4]

As a result of the emphasis on the individual and his or her learning stages the idea of *socialization* has come to mean a process of turning the individual into a socially acceptable adult through educational and other means, and *religious socialization* (a term which I accept some responsibility for making current) is the version of this process that happens in context of the family and the church. While these definitions of socialization are in part correct, they are too narrow to encompass the very important understanding of the concept of culture, which must always inform our study of education and of the stages of human life.

We cannot ask only "How do human life stages unfold?" or "What is the 'normal' development of moral and cognitive stages?" but we must ask a far more basic question: "Are life stages present in all cultures as they are in our own, and if so, how do they find expression in each of these cultures?" Even after we have established that in fact youth does happen as a category of action in American culture and have seen it in action, we must be wary of studying this phenomenon through limited investigation of cognitive process and moral development of collections of individual youths. Our question becomes one of how youth as a life stage is expressed differently by the different cultural segments of our American population, even the segments within American Protestantism. In other words, we ask not "What is youth?" but "What kinds of youth are there?" "In what kinds of various cultural contexts does youth-as-a-lifestage happen in America?" It is only after we examine these culturally constructed versions of "youth" that we can make any generalizations and come up with patterns of similarities.

In a recent address to the national meeting of the Council on Anthropology and Education, of which he was then the retiring president, noted anthropologist and educator Dell Hymes called for this approach to the study of schools, a cultural examination of schools in context in the same way anthropologists once examined the native peoples of the Americas in their disappearing tribal societies, an endeavor Hymes calls the ethnology of education.[5] In his plea for cultural study of schools, he emphasizes that educational theory and even educational ethnography have dwelt on the school as a socializing agent as if all schools are the same because they are set up in structural regularities with grades, rooms, hallways, teachers, students, and administrators. Ethnographies of schools have tended to emphasize the sameness of "the school" as an institution throughout the continent, sometimes noting that "the culture of the school as an institution" does have to impact diverse cultural backgrounds of boys and girls whose world view and whose cognitive maps do not fit that of the American school culture and the civil religion that is being brought to them by the vehicle of public education. Hymes calls for a rearrangement of categories, for a redefinition of the school, not as a social institution organized to contain the intellectual and cognitive reprogramming of individuals from diverse cultural backgrounds, but as itself a cultural phenomenon. The question now changes from "How does the school impact on the culture in this situation?" to one of "What kinds of schools are there?" and "How is the phenomenon of the school constructed into sets of meaningful action by each culture of which it is a part?"

This same approach is appropriate to churches and to church education. Perhaps we have asked too long "How can the church (as we ask in this way we are making the church into an institution which is similar in structure and content across the nation) have an impact on youth?" Perhaps it is time to ask, "What kinds of churches are there?" and "In what ways do these various kinds of churches include the notion of youth within their boundaries?" In other words, we would begin to explore the question of how the cultural manifestations of *the church* intersect with the cultural manifestations of *youth* in various settings and various specific cultural communities.

YOUTH AS A CULTURAL CONSTRUCT

In a conference on youth in 1974, psychologists and educators affiliated with the National Society for the Study of Education presented papers examining the concept of youth from different social psychological perspectives.[6] It was agreed by these researchers that youth should be defined as including the ages 16–21, the period coming after that of adolescence from the point of view of the developmental psychologist. In an article published with the conference proceedings, though written previously,

Kenneth Keniston defines youth as the ages 15–24, which would include the late adolescence of the psychologists. Other writers in other volumes throughout the literature have lumped together the stages of adolescence and youth so that one long stage emerges between the entry into junior high school and the emergence from college. The literature agrees that the stage or stages of adolescence and youth are transitional stages, a sort of elongated tunnel leading from childhood to adulthood, with entry markers and exit markers, as well as internal stops and narrowings along the way. In an article first published in 1960, before the label "youth culture" had become a household word, Keniston writes of the development of this phenomenon:

> The growth and dominance of youth culture in America means that most young Americans spend their formative years in a special culture only peripherally related to the adult world. We expect teenagers to be different, and they come to expect it of themselves as well. . . . The values and behavior of the youth culture are rarely explicitly anti-adult but they are explicitly non-adult; and the dominant virtues of the adolescent society are not those of the adult world. This means that the average young American must undergo two transitions en route to adulthood; first he must move from childhood to the youth culture, learning its ways and adapting to its requirements, and later when he "drops out" of the youth culture or is expelled by commencement, he must make a second transition into the "real" world of grownups.[7]

Keniston's use of the word *culture* here is different from my own in the previous section. He is using the word culture to refer to a subsociety of adolescent young people who share values, beliefs, and norms for appropriate behavior rather than to refer to an ongoing transgenerational system of meanings and symbols expressed in social form as community and society. His usage, however, did become widespread, and the understanding of a "youth culture" and then of a "counterculture" became quite popular in both academic analysis of youth and in the media coverage of the happenings of the sixties in which young people figured prominently. In order even to have a youth culture and/or a counterculture, one must first have the construct of youth as a life space in which young people are not expected to be full adults even though they have passed up their childhood through the actual onset of puberty and the physiology of sexual maturity. This period between adulthood and childhood is one that has only been clearly observed in industrial societies.

Sociologists of education have discovered that in our own society, in the nineteenth century and in earlier times when most families sent out their children into the world of work at an early age, the break between childhood and adulthood was clearly marked and was not elongated by a period of transition. The same has been observed in nonindustrial societies, where children who come to their pubescence are passed quickly into adulthood through a very short tunnel, a ritual of transition or a rite of passage. Individuals in these cultures are either a child, an adult, or for a very short time they are in the middle of a ritual celebration of their first menstruation or of their arrival at the age of circumcision with the other youngsters of the same age grade. In our own society today within the subcultures that value the simple life and do not emphasize modernization, for instance the Amish or Hutterites, even now there is little recognition of a lengthy stage of adolescence or youth. A child is prepared for the adult tasks and when that child reaches sixteen or the eighth grade, he or she is relieved from the formal study of the school curriculum and exposed to intense contact with the world of the farm, the house, and the community, without recognition of any separate time of the life that should be spent free from responsibility.[8] Adolescence and youth, then, could be thought of as cultural artifacts—creations of a twentieth-century culture whose value on extended education and on growth and improvement of individuals has constructed a space of the life cycle for the express purpose of development, transition, change, struggle, improvement of self in the journey toward adulthood, a tunnel-like period that is neither one thing nor the other. It is a betwixt and between period that does not fit into the adult social world and is therefore often seen to be "anti-adult" or antagonistic to the society.

The first appearance of the concept of adolescence in the literature of social psychology was, in fact, not until 1904 when G. Stanley Hall published his classic *Adolescence: Its Psychology and Its Relation to Physiology, Anthropology, Sociology, Sex, Crime, Religion, and Education.* [9] In that year Coleman tells us that only 11 percent of all high-school age children were *in* school. By 1931 the figure had jumped to 51 percent. [10] It cannot be disputed that the economic preconditions of industrialism and economic well-being were essential in the creation of the American high school as an institution. It must also be stated, however, that the creation of the high school is in itself a cultural expression to be expected of a nation of stalwart Protestants whose improvement schemes for the world and for their children were certain to include this extension of the educational process into the secondary phase and, by mid-century, into the universal availability of postsecondary education in public colleges and universities. If there are two distinct stages within this lifestage, as the social psychologists define it, then the secondary school created the period we know as *adolescence* and it became elongated when the public college and university created the extension known as *youth.* Because the distinction of these two phases is not useful for our purposes here, I will refer to both together under the label *youth.*

Now that our culture has created youth, what do we do with it? How can we best understand this transitional phase that apparently has within it its own rules and symbols, and its own separate norms for behavior? Keniston suggests that there are a number of regularities one can observe in youth in America even though the exact ways of expressing these will vary from group to group and

from social class to social class. Youth, says Keniston, is characterized in America by a tension between the individual's concept
of self and his/her concept of the society. It is a time of pervasive
ambivalence, of wary probing, exploration, testing of ideas, al-
ternations between isolation and what Keniston calls feelings of
"omnipotentiality." There is a refusal of socialization, a redefinition of earlier ideas, a development of identities taken from the
symbols and roles of youth, emphasis on change, movement,
transformation, process, on individual growth and development,
and a suspicion of adulthood. While embroiled in the tasks of
social awareness development and the continuing tasks of sexual,
moral, cognitive, and interpersonal development, the young person is in the process of defining himself/herself over and against
the world of childhood from which he/she has emerged and the
world of the adult which appears to be in constant need of repair.[11]

Because we have removed youth from the competitive arena of
adult work, we have allowed the freedom to be idealistic and to
hope for a better world. After this stage ends, we expect an individual to have become "realistic," and "serious." We contrast the
"irresponsible youth" with the "responsible adult." Behaviors and
values appropriate to the one stage are not appropriate to the
other. At the same time we have labeled aspects of youth nonre-
sponsible, we have for this very reason often romanticized the
stage as a carefree succession of summer afternoons before one
has worries and responsibilities. Poets, novelists, and songwriters
have constructed a vision of their "lost youth" and of a happy
time of romance and gaiety epitomized in the folk saying "Youth
is so wonderful: what a shame to waste it on the young!"

The emergence of youth as a separate period of life in America
has at times raised anxieties among those concerned over
tradition-maintenance and transgenerational continuity, points
out Keniston. He characterizes the rift between generations in the
sixties, carrying over into the early seventies, as between "those

who have not had a youth and those who have."[12] Those youth of the sixties are now solid citizens living in neat rows of suburban houses or condominiums, each with a spouse and their 2.1 children. The generation gap has seemingly closed. Even the social psychologists have turned their attention away from the "problem areas" of youth such as drugs and dissent to the study of other areas of the life stage: socialization for work, sex-role typing and gender identification, peer-group identification and socialization, and so on. In fact, a great deal more attention is being paid to all phases of the life cycle, including a renewed interest in the sociology of aging. Perhaps we are now at a place in the history of the study of youth where we can turn fruitfully to a systematic investigation of youth in culture.

CULTURE AND THE SOCIALIZATION OF AMERICAN YOUTH

I suggested earlier in this paper that one possible way to get some analytical leverage on the concept of youth would be to ask "What kinds of youth are there?" and "In what kinds of cultural contexts does youth happen in America?" The components of the cultural milieu in which we might conduct such an investigation include the meanings, the human groupings, the outward symbols—what the archaeologist would call "material culture"—that express this particular culture's version of the life-stage of youth. I am suggesting the study of youth by the careful and painstaking methods of the ethnographer, who would search out and then delineate as carefully as possible these meanings and symbols, these evidences of culture expressed in human group-ings, in words, in types of gatherings and dispersals, in the ar-rangement of space and the symbolic use of time, and the organi-zation of the social units on the human landscape—the structures of hierarchy and equality that form the labyrinth of social relations in a human community. This method of approaching a culture approximates the method of the historian and the archaeologist, but it also has elements of the methods used by interpreters of literature and by critics of music and art. Culture is seen not as a thing to be disassembled in order to grasp the mechanics of its pieces and parts but as a unified entity to be experienced and appreciated; in the words of Geertz, it is a *text* to be read and very carefully interpreted. [13]

Let me clarify again that within overall American culture there are a multitude of cultures and that within each one youth will have different meanings. At one level we can talk about an "American culture" that is shared by all Americans in the same way that we can talk of shared language among all Americans and British people. While all speakers of English share certain meanings and some general agreements on words to express those meanings, we know that the person on the street in London or Cambridge can often not understand the American visitor from South Carolina or Texas, whose words and meanings are quite different from the Englanders' English and whose sounds and intonations further confuse the listener, making his conversations or inquiries sometimes unintelligible. The cultures of the U.S.A. can be seen as many separate universes within an overarching universe of meanings that unite them sufficiently for them to co-exist as a society. The cultural expression of youth will vary from region to region, from social class to social class, from one ethnic heritage to another, while at the same time including some common elements drawn from the overall American culture. Whereas the culture at large will be defining youth within its framework of education, growth, progress, and individual initiative, in separate cultural groups where education is not a valued part of the life pattern, youth will be briefer and have more restrictions; where the meaning of womanhood is defined by motherhood, youth may be shortened or denied altogether to young women; and in cultural groups where individual initiative is not a major ingredient in the meaning system, one of the tasks of youth may be not to become an independent person but to explore one's place in the collective unit of the community in order to fit into one's adult role as a cooperating member.

YOUTH AND LIMINALITY

If we are to study the process of religious socialization in cultural context, one way to go about this might be to separate for study the distinct groups one wishes to investigate and then identify the internal processes where intense learning experiences occur. One of these processes of socialization that has been observed cross-culturally as an important mode of cultural transmission is the process of ritual *liminality*, or *communitas*, which takes place within the central phase of ritual. This concept can usefully be applied to the study of American Protestant youth because of the nature of the process of separation from adulthood in the suspended period of youth. It can also be used effectively in analysis of the intense learning experience of youth in the ritual and ceremonial cycles of church life.

The concept of ritual liminality was developed by Victor Turner, following the work of VanGennep on rites of passage.[14] Turner identifies the middle stage of a ritual as the period of transition, following the early stage of *separation* and coming before the final stage of *incorporation*. These three phases were first identified by VanGennep for rites of passage in the primitive world and have been widely used by anthropologists to analyse various rituals of transition, of initiation, and of incorporation. Turner is especially interested in the middle phase of liminality because it is within this phase that he finds a process of suspension, of "betwixt-and-between." Rules are temporarily changed for the initiates who are inside the ritual passageway leading from one life stage to another; the regular day-to-day structures of social relations give way to a set of nonhierarchical relationships he calls communitas.[15] Within liminal experiences coparticipants develop a strong communal feeling, a sense of having shared a powerful experience. Lifelong friendships are forged from liminality. The senses are keenly awakened in this ritually suspended condition, and learning is enhanced. When the ritual ends and the initiates are allowed to emerge from their enforced seclusion, they are in a new status in the community and can assume full adult roles. In our society, where the long tunnel of youth leads from the world of the child to that of the adult, the process of liminality can be seen to be at work.

Within the youth stage in our society, as young people pass through the high school with its elaborate content of cultural symbolism, with the accompanying clubs, competitions, sports, dances, and dates that comprise the extra-school social world, they are in many ways secluded into a life period where liminality is a reality. During this period young people form fast friendships that often are lifelong, they fall in love, they experience conversion, they become communing members of the church, they experience the sense of being at one with nature as they sit on hillsides at church camps in the summer, they become targets for competing religious faiths, as in the Sun Myung Moon Church and the Hare Krishna, and they commit their lives to good causes. Through various means—through styles of clothing and ornament, through use of alcohol and drugs, through listening and sharing music—youth in liminality alternate between periods of rejecting the society's values and periods of acceptance and cooperation.

The liminal phase of ritual manifested as communitas is a phenomenon which, Turner points out, is seen in all those places in society where transitional phases occur, where groups or communities are found at the lower positions in the social stratification system, and on the margins of the system itself.

Liminality exists apart from the day-to-day routines of the business-as-usual industrial society. For these reasons the church itself as a community of believing people contains aspects of communitas, and the church worship services, punctuating the weekly routine with cyclical regularity, give shape and form to the communitas experience. In other recurrent, less formal rituals the same processes are at work in the church community—the family night supper, the work party on Saturday, the youth group that meets on Sunday evening, and the extension of these into more intense ritual experiences in the summertime are all examples of the various social locations within which liminality and communitas take shape in human activity.

I have written elsewhere of the liminality found in the religious summer community of Montreat, North Carolina, and in the periodic gatherings of Protestants in family reunions, church homecomings, campmeetings, cemetery association days, and other ceremonies focusing on kinship and religious ties.[16] In each of these gatherings, and especially in summer church camps, youth transition is intersected by cultural expression of the most intense variety. The enhanced learning situation of the young person going through the tunnel toward adulthood is overlayed in these removed ritual assemblies with the liminality of the ritual occasion itself.

The formal and informal rituals of the Protestant churches have a "hidden curriculum." In the usage of education writers, the concept of the "hidden curriculum" has gained wide acceptance in referring to the often invisible ways that we teach children the values of the culture through the uses of time and space, arrangement of furniture, lines in the hallways, and requirements of holding up one's hand to speak in class. The idea of the hidden curriculum applies, in fact, to other aspects of culture and society. The church employs a hidden curriculum in its coded messages within the structure of the church school, the liturgy, the informal programs it sponsors, and the ritual occasions mentioned above.

In order to understand more fully the process of socialization within context of culture, I am suggesting careful examination of numerous gatherings, churches, schools, and communities in an attempt to grasp the concept of culture as "meaning-in-action."[17] This must be done through the careful uncovering of symbols, forms of groupings, rhythms of assembly and dispersal, ritual celebration, organization of social hierarchies and of their periodic suspension, and the cultural materials that form the symbolic paraphernalia of youth and of youth's cultural context. Carrying in mind this concept of culture and of cultural analysis, I now turn to the final task of this paper, that of commenting on the process of socialization as an aspect of the human life cycle, encoded by the shape and form of the local congregation.

CULTURE, LIFE CYCLES, AND PROTESTANT CONGREGATIONAL LIFE

One of the strengths we have gained from relying on the stage theorists in psychology and cognitive studies in our theory of religious education is that we have begun to see each stage of the human life as related to the other stages, growing from each other and folding into each other in a succession of patterns and processes. In order to fully appreciate the nature of culture and of the interplay of culture and socialization, we must also take into account that each stage of life for the individual is played out according to a well-defined set of rules, never in isolation but within a pattern of interconnected lives. Human communities have been seen by anthropologists as sets of interlocking life cycles in which there are always some individuals going through each stage in the unfolding pattern, where the life of the human group is a web of relationships expressing in social action the set of meanings and symbols that comprise the culture.[18]

The life path for the American Protestant individual is a set of unfolding configurations of roles and social relationships, of

norms and of symbolic representations, appropriate to the segment of the cycle, to the geographic location, and to the position
in society of the person going through it. The child must grow
and develop and play and respond to his/her family, gradually
developing concepts of possible roles and available positions in
the adult society. This process involves the young adulthood and
middle life of nurturing parents, grandparents, teachers, and
childcare people, whose performance of their roles and adherence to certain norms must be appropriate for these culturally
prescribed child-centered life tasks. Youth is a stage involved with
middle-aged   and   older   adults   who   are   the   parents   and
grandparents, teachers, principals, coaches, ministers, and youth
leaders. In addition to these adults, youth are in close touch with
their immediate elders, the 18–25 age group, who forge role
models as college student, fraternity or sorority member, pre-law
or pre-med student, or as members of the world of work—the
young adult store manager at the A & P, the young factory worker
who plays church softball, the couples who have recently married
just out of high school and are having their first baby. All the
stages in the life cycle are interrelated and are interlocking. No
one can go through the cycle alone—the interdependence is a
crucial aspect of being human. The process of socialization is a
constant process of learning, unlearning, and relearning meanings and behaviors of successive positions within the life pattern
for the areas of work, family, and personal development.

One complicated aspect of socialization in childhood and
youth is that learning to be an adult is always learning to be a
male or female adult, learning what it means to be a woman or a
man of one's people. One must learn socially approved ways to
walk, speak, dress, to relate to others. In addition to this basic
information, one must assimilate information on how to be a
man or woman at each successive stage in life—how to be a young
father or mother of small children, how to be a parent of teenagers, how to be an older man or woman when all the children
have gone, how to be a single adult who chooses not to marry

or a member of a couple who chooses not to have children. The meanings of adulthood are meanings about sexuality and about the nature of the ties between generations.

In a society as mobile as our own and as geared to individual productivity and accomplishment, where it is often necessary to move in order to improve one's life chances, we find few places where all the stages in the human life cycle are represented in the form of a human community sharing a culture. One of the few places where this interlocking transgenerationality can find expression in culturally coded social action is in the local congregation. If the culture is a set of meanings and symbols, then the congregation is a visible expression of that culture in social action. The congregation is a part of an institution, the church; it is a part of a bureaucracy, the denomination, but it is also a part of a human community sharing a particular way of life. Theologically speaking, it is a part of "the people of God."

The process of socialization of youth in our mainline Protestant churches is a process of ongoing human interaction of children, youth, adults, and the elderly within the context of a believing and caring community. This participation includes elements of formal teaching and learning, of meeting for youth groups and for summer camps and conferences, of having work projects to enrich poverty areas, of driving for and serving meals-on-wheels to the elderly poor. It also includes the experience of worship on a regular basis, of family night suppers and church barbecues, of annual homecomings at the country church or an occasional campmeeting. It also may include some periods of rejection of the church because it is, after all, a part of the adult society; it may include long periods of ambivalent searching and discarding, then taking up again, of doctrine and dogma or of the Bible itself.

In the Protestant church, in the Christian community, in the local congregation, part of the task of education is understanding the fabric of human group life. To understand what it is that we have on our hands socially and culturally under the heading *youth* may enable us better to accept the more difficult aspects of this life stage and to take some pleasure in the parts with which we feel more comfortable. The fuller understanding may also be of value in the generating of designs for our educational program.

In conclusion, let me review what I have suggested in this paper. 1) I have suggested that our educational theory in religious education has been dominated by an approach that is individualistic and developmental, coming primarily from psychology and the individualistic parts of social psychology; 2) I have proposed that we might fruitfully turn to the field of cultural study, the area of *ethnology* for some alternative models and methods; 3) I have suggested an ethnographic approach in looking at American Protestant youth in various school, church, and family settings; and 4) I have called for an understanding of youth as a part of the larger picture of the pattern of interlocking life cycles we know as the human community.

To study youth in mainline Protestantism is to study children, young adults, families, communities, and congregational life; for the nature of humanness is that life is interconnected and cannot be understood out of context. To be human is to live in culture, in community, and in webs of relationships with one's fellow creatures. The pattern for these webs, these communities, are drawn from a kaleidoscope of meanings and expressed in an intriguing array of symbolic representations. It is the kaleidoscope that draws us to it for study; it is through seeing whole patterns that we may hope to gain an understanding of the elusive bit of the pattern which we call *youth*.

REFLECTIONS: Andrew P. Grannell

This is an exploratory study of the utility of a wholistic, contextual, cultural study of both church and church youth in American mainline Protestantism. This is a beginning look at the necessary theoretical foundations for a cultural study of the varieties of American youth as they interact with the varieties of American Protestant churches. In Gwen Neville's words, this is to be an "outline of a possible theoretical framework" which may help us to "take a look at this confusing category of humanity known in America as youth and to begin to find some grounding in educational and social theory to assist us in shaping our practical task as church educators." In short, this is a call for a revisioning of the theoretical base of much of the present ministry with youth from a psychological or at best a social psychological theory to a cultural or more precisely an ethnographic theory. I would suggest then that this paper might be retitled to read more simply, "Toward a Cultural Theory of the Church's Ministry with Youth."

I would see this call to a new vision of the cultural context for youth ministry as radical, *i.e.*, a strong call for a completely new repatterning of our perspective on the task. For many, if not all of us, this call is radical since it is a call to reimage, repattern, and rethink the whole matter. But it is radical in still a deeper sense, this is a call to not simply broaden psychological categories in order to include an interesting new cultural perspective, but rather, if I am to understand this correctly, it is a call to entirely throw off the old psychological world view and its attendant social psychological views and put on the cultural or more specifically ethnographic world view.

Gwen Neville calls us to move from our present analytical world view which attempts to view the matter of youth ministry through the lens of an individuative world. She contrasts at the outset the psychological stage theories with their propensity to look at the "deep structures" of a relative few in order to generalize about the whole. This psychological or individuative world view attempts to view youth and the church as a product of certain essential individual structures that can be identified, raised to view, and generalized. Gwen Neville, on the other hand, calls us to reimage this patterning, *i.e.*, to stay with the gestalt, with the whole image in which youth and church interact in at least at first, confusing welter, but then eventually emerge as an organic new pattern with inherent symbols, rituals, communities, and their meanings. Whereas the stage theorist continues to identify certain "deep structures" within the psyche of the individual and then seeks to confirm this structure as uniform, unilinear, irreversible, and indeed universal patterning, the ethnographer calls to us to avoid plunging in and to stay at the cultural surface where the complex web will insist upon the relative, diverse, multilinear, and reversible. In this view, our task is to view youth and youth ministry as part of the whole cloth of American society—more specifically, as part of the whole cloth of American Protestantism, not as the cumulative depiction of the American individual, progressing through the inevitable stages of adolescence.

I have chosen to emphasize the radical nature of this call in order to lift up what I perceive to be a crucial issue here. This is not an interesting supplement to the psychoanalytic, cognitive, and social psychological theories that stand behind much of our present understanding of American youth and that inform the practice of youth ministry itself. Rather, this is a call to a whole new theoretical base from the perspective of the social sciences. If we are to answer this call then we must be convinced first that the older theoretical base is deficient in certain essential regards, and, on the other hand, that the promise of a new theoretical base is compelling. I would like to address both of these dimensions briefly.

First, in the section of the paper dealing with life stage theories, Gwen Neville challenges the claim of universality on the part of the cognitive developmentalists Piaget and Kohlberg. She states, "We cannot ask only 'How do human life stages unfold?' or 'What is the "normal" development of moral and cognitive stages?' but we must ask a far more basic question: 'Are life stages present in all cultures as they are in our own, and if so, how they find expression in each of these cultures?'" In fact, however it is widely accepted that Piaget's stages of cognitive development and Kohlberg's stages of cognitive moral development are not confined to our cultural context. There has been extensive cross cultural investigation.[19] If we are to accept the weight of these investigations, then we must ask in what sense the question of diverse cultural contexts is "far more basic." The Piaget/Kohlberg claim to certain universal stages is a radical one. The fact is that the claim stands increasingly challenged, but unrefuted, until the present time.[20] By no means, then, does the variety of cultural expression confound the claim to certain universal stages of cognitive and/or cognitive-moral thinking.

Hence, I perceive here a certain wariness of universal stages that laps over into outright rejection in the final line of this passage, "It is only after we examine these culturally-constructed versions of 'youth' that we can make any generalizations and come up with patterns of similarities." I would like to make the point here that the line of logic through this paragraph is crucial and pivots on the question of universality. This reader fails to find the point well established.

Second, I would go on to state that there is much merit to the argument for taking this cultural perspective seriously as a parallel if not complementary world view. In fact, the cognitive theory of Piaget, Kohlberg, and Fowler or the psychoanalytic social/cultural view of Erik Erikson rarely deal with the cultural expressions of youth. Fowler has been concerned to look at the role played by symbols, social role taking, and ritual as part of his understanding of religious socialization (albeit in response to the lack of same in his mentors).[21] In my view then, I would reject this call to replace entirely the stage theories of the present order with this promising outline of an ethnological theory.

However, I do find much of merit in such concepts as ritual liminality or communitas, culture as "meaning-in-action." I believe that careful examination of the symbols, forms of grouping, rhythms of assembly and dispersal, ritual celebrations, organization of social hierarchies, and the cultural materials that form the symbolic paraphernalia of youth will net a rich harvest for the future of ministry with youth in mainline Protestantism.

In summary, I would argue and hope for the eventual complementarity of this embryonic cultural perspective on youth and youth ministry with the stage theories now extant. Perhaps in the end we shall see more clearly than now, that the structuralist paradigm and contextualist paradigm work in two quite remarkably distinctive manners to inform an increasingly wholistic understanding of the phenomenon we call American youth. To the end that it will inform a more faithful and coherent ministry with youth may it be so.

NOTES

1. For a treatment of this development from a social point of view, see Solon T. Kimball and James T. McClellan, Jr., *Education and the New America* (New York: Random House, 1962).

2. The classic discussion of Protestant ideology as tied to social and economic systems is that of Max Weber, *The Protestant Ethic and the Spirit of Capitalism*, trans. Talcott Parsons (New York: Chas. Scribner's, 1958).

3. Examples include Erik Erikson, *Childhood and Society* (New York: Norton, 1950), and *Identity: Youth and Crisis* (New York: Norton, 1968); Jean Piaget, *The Moral Judgment of the Child* (Glencoe, Illinois: Free Press, 1948, orig. pub. 1932); Lawrence Kohlberg, "Development of Moral Character and Ideology," in *Review of Child Development Research* ed. M. L. Hoffman, Vol. I (New York: Russell Sage Foundation, 1964).

4. The possible exception to this individual and cognitive orientation in religious education writings comes from those who have emphasized the importance of the community. The community as seen by most of the Protestant writers, however, is a collection of *individuals* in interaction networks functioning for the support of persons and the mediating of life crises.

We have not used widely the understanding of community as social form, as structure, as a cultural construct, as a text which can be read and understood, and as a creative agent in interaction with the individual who is its product.

5. Dell Hymes, "Educational Ethnology," *Anthropology and Education Quarterly* XI, Number 1 (Spring 1980), pp. 3–8.

6. Kenneth Keniston, "Youth as a Stage of Life," in *Youth*, eds. L. Robert

Havighurst and Phillip Dreyer (NSSE, 1975, distributed by The University of Chicago Press), pp. 3–26.

7. Kenneth Keniston, "Youth Culture as Enforced Alienation" in *The Cult of Youth in Middle Class America*, ed. Richard Rapson (Lexington, Mass: D. C. Heath & Co., 1971) pp. 81–88.

8. See John Hostetler and Gertrude Enders Huntington, *Children in Amish Society* (New York: Holt, Rinehart and Winston, 1971).

9. G. Stanley Hall, *Adolescence: Its Psychology and Its Relation to Physiology, Anthropology, Sociology, Sex, Crime, Religion, and Education* (New York: Appleton-Century-Crofts, 1916).

10. James S. Coleman, *The Adolescent Society* (Glencoe, Illinois: The Free Press, 1961).

11. Keniston, "Youth as a Stage of Life," p. 15.

12. Ibid., p. 22.

13. Clifford Geertz, *The Interpretation of Cultures* (New York: Basic Books, Inc./Harper Colophon Books, 1973).

14. Victor Turner, *The Ritual Process* (Chicago: Aldine, 1969). Also see Arnold VanGennep, *The Rites of Passage*, trans. Monika Vizedom and Gabrielle Caffee (London: Routledge & Kegan Paul, 1960).

15. Victor Turner, *Ritual Process*, p. 94.

16. See John H. Westerhoff III and Gwen Kennedy Neville, *Generation to Generation* (Philadelphia: Pilgrim Press, 1974) and Gwen Kennedy Neville and John H. Westerhoff III, *Learning Through Liturgy* (New York: Seabury, 1978).

17. David Schneider, "Toward a General Theory of Culture" in *Meaning in Anthropology* eds., Keith Basso and Henry Selby (Albuquerque: University of New Mexico Press, 1976).

18. Alexander Moore, *Cultural Anthropology* (New York: Knopf, 1978). Also see Moore's *Life Cycles in Achatlan* (New York: Teachers College Press, 1973).

19. Lawrence Kohlberg, "Stage and Sequence: The Cognitive-Developmental Approach to Socialization," in *Handbook of Socialization Theory and Research*, ed. David A. Goslin (NewYork: Rand McNally and Co., 1969), pp. 357 ff.

20. Sohan and Celia Modgil, *Piagetian Research: Compilation and Commentary*, Vol. 8: *Cross-Cultural Studies* (Atlantic Highlands, New Jersey: Humanities Press, 1976), p. 70.

21. James W. Fowler, "Faith Development Theory and the Aims of Religious Socialization," in *Emerging Issues in Religious Education*, eds. Gloria Durka and Joanmarie Smith (New York: Paulist Press, 1976), p. 194.

Chapter 4

Problems, Predicaments, and Gravity

ROGER W. PAINE III

Roger W. Paine III works as a youth counselor in Boulder, Colorado. He also writes very readable essays and books to help adults learn how to relax around young people. From his training as a Methodist minister, Paine realizes that profound thoughts and ideas are best communicated by the use of parable and story. A combination of personal anecdote, wit, and wisdom, this paper is truly a work of art: it is both enjoyable and instructive.

Back in one of Colorado's mountain towns, an old man decided that his daughter wasn't much of a mother for her children:

she used a lot of drugs

the kids weren't getting much food

and so he and his wife took in their grandchildren and gave them a home.

The house wasn't very big, and

the old man only made $700 a month,

but the kids seemed to be doing fine.

The only problem was that the $700 was having to stretch too far

for too long

and so even though the old man hated the welfare department, he asked them

for help.

So a social worker enters from stage right
                notepad in hand
                and sees that there aren't enough bedrooms
                    and there are dirty dishes in the sink
                    and there aren't any Wheaties in the
                    pantry.
The old man started muttering:
"Seems if you don't run your life like a social worker, you're not
fit!"

And after his way of life had been picked at for a while, he took
his frustrations to a nearby Legal Services office and told
them the story, which ends with him saying to his paralegal
listener:

                "Yuh know, I'd like to kill that social worker!"
                "Oh no—don't do that. If you did, you'd be in
                real trouble."
                "Yeah—I might be in trouble . . . but she'd be
                daid."

These days we've got more people than ever who make their
living by helping people. Some people have made a fortune
telling us how to flatten our stomachs
                        how to be a good parent
                        how to have a good sex life
                    how to have a fair fight with our lover
                    or how to jog in the right way.

It makes you wonder how people used to make it through the day.
And the things that are being done in the name of "helping"
people also make
            you wonder. . . .
The most jarring incident in the last year happened
                    not in California, as you might expect,
                    but here in the East Coast:
                    you probably saw it in *The New York Times*
        *A man helped sponsor his wife's suicide

cooperated with her in planning it
and even videotaped the whole process. . . .

Sometimes I think that we're tossing out the old traditions and
taboos so fast that we've just got to be in for major trouble—that
videotaped suicide is Cassandra trying to get our attention.

The evidence against the helping professions is not just anecdotal:

* Jay Haley established years ago that 50 percent of the
  people on waiting lists to see a therapist get better while
  they're on the waiting list. He calls this "waiting list
  therapy," and points out that you can have a 50 percent
  success rate simply by leaving your clients alone . . .
* Del Elliott is a Colorado researcher who showed two
  years ago that when a teenager is arrested for a first
  offense crime

  he is *three times* more likely to get back into
  trouble
  if you refer him to a counseling agency
  than he is if the arresting officer simply
  lectures him
  and releases him.

Put that together with Gertsell's book, *Cradles of Eminence*,
which shows us that many of the most influential people in the
history of the world had absolutely *terrible* childhoods

the kind of childhoods that the Department of Social
Services

would rescue them from today. . . .

Or Jean McFarland's Berkeley studies which show—along with a
growing number of other studies on the subject—that children
from divorced families turn out to be stronger

more resilient adults

than children from normal, two-parent families.

It's hard to hear that divorce may actually make a kid *stronger*.

*   *   *

It's hard to hear because, based on the values we've always be-
lieved in
                    by all that's fair and logical
                            it doesn't make sense.
But don't worry: this is America
                    and that means that somebody will make it make
                    sense!
We are the inheritors of Aristotelian logic.
Every problem has a solution.
A leads rationally and inexorably to B.
We are extremely uncomfortable with paradox.
Which means, I submit, that we are uncomfortable with human
nature.

To illustrate my case, I offer just four of the paradoxes that we live
with every day. These are not "problems" to be solved—they are
predicaments
                    and predicaments cannot be solved.

Paradox Number One: The better things are, the worse they seem.

Revolutions don't happen when things are at their worst
                    they happen once things start to get better.
I realize this is nothing new—it's the theory of rising expectations—
But what *is* new is our awareness of how far-reaching that theory
is. . . .

    For example: it's the reason why good marriages
                    are more likely to fail
                            than bad marriages.
                    In a good marriage (by 1980 standards), the man
                    and woman continually challenge each other to
                    do better and so the possibility of disappointment
                    is that much greater. They keep reaching for the

brass ring. . . . That stuff never occurs to Archie
and Edith Bunker. They could stay together
forever, never realizing what a terrible marriage
they have—-

unless some counselor pointed it out to them.

*Paradox Number Two: Second marriages are better, but they're
shorter.*

Pepper Schwartz up in Washington State has the latest data on
this one. Couples in second marriages *do* feel lots better about
what they've got

than they did in their first marriages

but the relationship isn't any more durable as a
result.

Pepper satisfies our craving for explanations by telling us that in
second marriages—or second primary relationships—there's a lot
of

my table—your lamp

my chest of drawers—your kid's dental bill

a lot of fixing it so you can get out of the relationship if you need
to

with the least amount of carnage. . . .

And both the woman and the man are clearer than ever about
what they *want*.

Paradox Number Three: Sex education causes sexual dysfunction.

One thing is sure: you can't *try* to have an erection.
The seventies produced a technology of sex

and that technology has made some people start
to worry:

am I doing it right?
am I doing it enough?
am I really a boring sex partner?

Once again the therapist has won out because now that we've

raised everyone's consciousness about sex habits, we've helped cause an epidemic of impotence and thus have generated a lot of new business for ourselves.

Paradox Number Four: Communication often makes matters a lot worse.

At the bottom of every counselor's kit bag you'll find this line:
"Let's talk it over."
So let's see what can happen when you invite a couple in for marriage counseling and ask them to talk it over. Suppose the woman has made up her mind

> that she wants out of the marriage.
> That puts her in the power position.

But suppose the man wants to stay in the relationship
and has been trying to persuade her to work it out.

> You ask them to express their feelings,
> the woman obliges
> and talks about why she wants to end
> the marriage.

> She has thought about the risks
> she is sure about what she wants
> and her strength and her resolve shine
> through.

Hard stuff for the man to hear, right?
When he starts talking, he's feeling more powerless than ever.
And his arguments for saving the relationship

> coming as they do from his newly-weakened ego
> state

> sound too much like pleading
> and cause his wife to detest him that
> much more . . .

It often happens that when you ask a strong person to communicate with

> a weak person

                    the strong person will be stronger
            and the weak person will be weaker in the end.
It does not matter if the rock hits the jug or the jug hits the rock:
the jug

                                            still gets it.
The same dynamic is true in family counseling:
If a teenager is ready to split, then he has the power—
            it's the power that comes from knowing you have noth-
ing to lose;
And no parent can fight that power effectively. What happens is
that both the parents and the kid unload all their crap on each
other and by the end of your session, the family is farther apart
than ever. [Any fight: damage done in

                            the first 60 seconds.]
Communication often makes matters a lot worse.
You can see it happen on a larger scale, too. Richard Farson tells
about an encounter weekend between a group of Navajo Indians
from a reservation and a group of whites from Marin County.
The weekend was a marvelous success:

                    everyone made friends
                there was lots of good confronting
                people handled it well
            and in the end the Navajo went back to the
            reservation
                    and the whites went back to Marin
                    feeling that they really *knew* each other.
            They planned to see one another again—
                    to visit in each other's homes in the fu-
                    ture.

The Navajo soon discovered that they had lost something during
that weekend. . .

                    they had lost their target
                    they had lost their enmity
                        their hatred of the white man.

And that hatred was the driving force that had helped their brothers and sisters

> in the past
> that could have helped many of them
> get off the reservation.

The strong people in the weekend—the whites—were still strong. But the weak people were weaker.
The medical profession actually has a name for all of this: iatrogenic disease. An iatrogenic disease is a disease that is caused

> by the practice of medicine.

Hospitals are full of people with iatrogenic diseases,

> some of which are worse than the
> disease that brought them into
> treatment to begin with.

The next time you get the urge to help somebody, just lie down until it goes away!

*   *   *

I've spent my life in the helping professions—as a minister

> as a counselor
> as an author
> and as an administrator. . . .

It's not easy for me to hear that people in trouble might be better off if I just leave them alone. I also don't deal well with paradox.

> I'm a problem-solver.
> People have told me that I'm good at it.
> I *like* feeling that there is something I'm good at.
> I *believe* in the value of getting people together to talk
>> through their problems.

But I also believe that we have compelling reasons to be extremely careful about the circumstances under which we get involved in someone else's life—

there are too many of us out there doing it now
and it's easy for egos to start bouncing off of each other
                        like pucks in an air hockey game.
Recently I asked several different people to give me their most
spontaneous memory from childhood. Here is a sample of what I
heard:

- I remember my mother and father sitting in the dark together
  on the back porch talking quietly and necking for hours. . . .
- I remember playing chess with my father—we lived in the
  deep south—and I never won because he was a master, and
  he would tell me that he wanted me to grow up and be an
  independent woman. . . .
- I remember running into the woods that stretched out behind
  our back yard and picking wild flowers for my mother, and
  seeing the expression on her face when I held them out for
  her to take. . . .
- I remember trying to learn to water ski one summer, with my
  father up in the boat, and trying so hard but never getting up
  on the skis and wanting so much to please him, and feeling
  warm later on when he held me and told me it was all
  right. . . .
- I remember my father, who had never paid much attention
  to me, coming to my bedroom once when I was very sick and
  sitting on the edge of my bed for a long time watching
  me. . . .
- I remember standing in the side yard of our house playing a
  game of catch with my father, who was often gone for
  months or longer, at sea in the Navy, just the two of us
  tossing a softball back and forth. . . .

Those were some of the memories. All of them were intimate
                        touching
                    and important. . . .

If you wanted to, you could make a psychology out of those memories

you could play with the themes
expand on them
and offer some conclusions.

But you could never make a *technology* out of it.

The hardest lesson for the Western mind to learn
is that people are not "problems" that can be "fixed"
And there is no such thing as a technique for doing counseling.

* * *

In his book *Cat's Cradle,* Kurt Vonnegut describes a bored and lonely God who creates the earth and then decides to make living creatures out of the mud—so the mud can see what he has done. The last of God's creatures is man, and man is the only one who can speak—so God leans close

as man sits up
looks around
and speaks:

"What is the purpose of all this?" man asks politely.
"So everything must have a purpose?" asks God in return.
"Certainly," says man.
"Then I leave it to you to think of one for all this," says God.
And then he goes away.

Well, what *is* the purpose of all this?
Not to mention—what do we *do* about all this?
If communication often makes matters worse,
and since the better things are, the worse they seem,
and since lots of fine people had rotten childhoods and, in fact,
may have been fine people *because* they had rotten childhoods,
does it really matter what we do?

I believe the answer is yes—of course it matters. . . .
And, without intending to trivialize the subject in the least, I want to suggest
                           skiing
                 as a conceptual starting point.
Skiing is a long, controlled fall
                      from the top of the mountain to the bot-
                      tom.
                      What you've done is fall—
                      some of us with more finesse than others
                              but it's a long fall all the same.
Gravity is the controlling force
              just as, for a fish, the ocean is the controlling force.
If you're a good skier, you learn to use gravity like a dolphin uses water.

Being a parent is also a long fall
                      from all-powerful and all-knowing angel
                      to just plain Herb and Alice.
The arch-enemy of the skier is apprehension.
It is the fear of what *might* happen.
It creeps into the bones and stiffens the muscles.
Toes curl to clutch at the snow.
You look at that sea of moguls coming up
        you ski into it with a fixed knee and an unbending position
                              and you wind up in the trees.
Being a parent is like that, too.
The beginning skier is told:
     "Keep your upper body pointed straight down the fall line!
     Don't throw that shoulder!
     Relax!"

Point myself straight down the mountain, you say—if I do, I'll kill myself.
It doesn't make sense.

It doesn't make sense because it's—a paradox.
When you let gravity have its way,
when you combine the force of gravity with the edges on your skis
   you actually *gain* control.

The force which pushes you down is also
the force which holds you up—once you make friends with it.

The paradox is that the struggle is best won simply by *letting go*.
And letting go is not the same thing as giving up.
Letting go means you begin to live in each moment,
   it means you collect the energy that apprehension has been
stealing from you
   it means you let gravity be your ally.

In adolescence, gravity is blooming sexuality
                        it's curiosity
                        it's self-doubt
                        it's the need to question
                        it's the need to test authority
                        it's the power of a first love
                           and the heartache of first love lost.

For parents, it's very, very hard to let go and ski into those moguls
with knees loose
      ready to let the body respond to each bump naturally
         and looking forward to the fun of it all.

I love to listen to Bill Glasser tell stories about his own children.
And my favorite illustration of what it means for a parent to let go
is his story about his daughter's first date. She had not been very
social as a teenager, so she was older than most kids are when
they have their first date—I think she was sixteen. She came to
her father and said:

   "Guess what! I've got a date."
   "Well, good," her father said, "I'm glad you've got a date."
   "When do you want me to be home?" she asked.
   At this, Bill apparently looked a little shocked, and then said:

"I don't know when you should get home."

That did not satisfy daughter's image of what a father was supposed to do.

"Don't you watch television? Fathers on television tell their kids when to be home at night!"

"Well, I just don't know . . .

Suppose I tell you to be home by 11:30.

So you tell your date you've got to be home by 11:30.

But what if you go out and have a lousy time with him— maybe you'll want to come home at 9 o'clock . . . but now you'll feel obligated to stay out until 11:30.

Or, may be it'll be a great date.

What if it's just starting to get *good* at 11:30.

But if I tell you 11:30 you'll resent me for making you come home just when things are getting good. Just come home when the date's over."

*   *   *

It would be an enormous mistake to recommend to parents everywhere

that they all handle the question of curfews the way Bill Glasser did.

His was a particular response

to a particular child

who he believed could handle the responsibility

who, in fact, needed to be challenged to decide for herself

But he was on the right track.

He was using gravity to help them both.

By contrast, consider the case of "Parents Who Care," a parent organization in Palo Alto, California. Joann Lundgren, one of the organizers, says she was shocked when she learned about the pressures on her daughter to drink and smoke dope. The parents got together and agreed on some community norms that they would all try to enforce. They agreed on weekend curfews

They agreed to monitor the kids' parties

They agreed to get to know their children's friends and the friends' parents

They agreed to contact the parents of children hosting parties to find out

if there would be adult supervision.

Now, as you listen to all that, what are you thinking?
Aren't you thinking about how appealing it is? That's what I thought.
Here's a group of parents getting together to solve a problem!
It's so *American!* It's so "Can Do!"
It's so linear and Aristotelian!
I can't imagine a group of *French* parents getting together to do that.

John Gall in his book *Systemantics* tells us about the Egyptian pyramid of Snofru.
Snofru's pyramid is a ruin

a two-hundred foot tower surrounded by rubble.
For years people thought this was the result of an earthquake

or bad weather

or vandalism
even though the other great pyramids were all doing fine just down the block

from Snofru's.

Then a physicist on vacation realized that Snofru's pyramid had simply *fallen down.* The problem was that Snofru had wanted his pyramid to have smoothly-sloping sides and so he had not used the time-honored stepped-tower technique for building pyramids. He didn't realize that the stepped-tower technique was what made pyramids stand up.

Snofru's son was Cheops
            and Cheops was not a dim bulb like his father had
                                                                    been.
He calculated all the stresses and designed a smoothly-sloping
pyramid that
    wouldn't fall down: in fact, it became a model.
                            Several more just like it were built.
                            And none of them ever fell down.
    What *did* fall down was the entire Egyptian state
                            because so much national energy had been
                            diverted
                            into building pyramids.
    I commend the story of Snofru and Cheops to Joanne
Lundgren and the
                    Palo Alto "Parents Who Care."
Parents usually have the idea that they are supposed to mold their
children
                                        as if their children
                                    were unformed piles of clay.
The truth is that none of us are very good sculptors.
The truth is that we are running along and we *fall* into a pile of
clay.
                            It does leave an impression.
                            But it may be different from the one we
                            wanted to leave.
You can make a *psy*chology out of it
but you can't make a *tech*nology out of it. . . .

I knew a psychiatrist several years ago who was a master at family
therapy. And I watched him once work with a family which I had
worked with myself. The family dynamic was to make the oldest
child
                    who was an eighteen-year-old girl
                        be responsible for holding the family to-
                        gether.

She accepted this responsibility, but she paid a price:

> she grew up without ever having any real
> fun.
> Her fifteen-year-old sister was a hell-raiser.
> Her twelve-year-old brother was turning de-
> linquent.
> Her mother was a burnout, and
> Her father was a drunk.

The whole family was gathered in the psychiatrist's office, and they talked for a while about who was the caretaker for the family, and each in his or her own way acknowledged that the eighteen-year-old daughter did most of the work in that regard. The psychiatrist

> who looked a little like Allen Ginsberg
> and was as wide as he was tall
> walked over to the girl
> who was a tall, dark-haired beauty
> and he plopped himself down on top of her
> settling onto her lap
> and half squashing her.

"What are you going to do about me?" he asked her.
She barely managed a shrug.
He settled himself more comfortably and smiled contentedly.
The girl started to squirm under his weight.
He looked at the other family members and asked:
   "What do you think she should do with me?"
The other kids both said:
   "Shove him off!"
She gave a little push which did no good at all.
   "You'll have to push a lot harder than that to move me!" he told her.
And now mother and father joined in with the other kids:
   "Push harder! Get him off you!"

So she pushed
and he resisted
and she pushed harder
and he fought to hold his position
and finally with an enormous effort she shoved him to the floor.

"Good!" he said, as he got up and brushed himself off, smiling
congratulations to her. And looking straight into her eyes he said:
"The next time anyone in your family tries to get you to take care
of their business, you do the same thing you just did to me—
                    and remember
                    it will take a lot of strength to do it
                    because it weighs a lot more than I do. . .
                    but you've got to give it back to the person it
                    belongs to."

                              *   *   *

Now, you can admire that man's skill, as I do
    you can tell that story to other people who work with families,
and
    you can use the idea behind what he did, *but*
    you can never duplicate the technique. You'd look foolish if
you did.
You have to come up with something which is *yours*.

Guy de Maupassant gave this advice to writers who wanted to be
original; he said:
    "In order to describe a fire burning
                    or a tree in a field,
    let us stand in front of that fire
                    or that tree
    until they no longer look to us like any other fire or any other
tree.
    That is how one becomes original."

And for those of us who work with people
    let us be willing to look at each and every one of them

until they no longer look to us like any one else we have ever known.

With teenagers, we need to read their books
see their movies
listen to their music
watch their television shows
and learn about their sex symbols.
We need to be able to see from within.
That is how we will become original.

When I left my first wife in 1971, my daughter was eight years old.
Now she's seventeen.
Back then, once I had moved into my own place,
I saw her for several hours every Sunday afternoon.
I never knew quite what to say to her, and so we often
walked quietly around a lake
or went to a Walt Disney movie, and afterwards
we made supper together.
Last year, during one of her visits to Colorado,
we had a long talk about how she had felt back then.
She remembers feeling concerned about how her mother felt at the time
but something told her that I was all right
and then she told me this:

"Actually, I got to see more of you after you left than
I did when you were living with us."

She went on to explain that once I'd left, she *knew* she was going to see me
for a certain number of hours
on a certain day each week.
The time was guaranteed
and it was all hers
and she knew she could count on it.

Her memory of that time was very different from mine, and it

reminded me that if we're going to work with kids
   we've got to be willing to do our homework
   and that means—just to pick on a single subject—
      that if your own parents never got divorced
      and if you've never been divorced
      then you've got some questions to ask:
         ask kids what it's like.
        They love the chance to be our teachers!

All the outcome studies on types of therapy are pointing to the same conclusion:
   it's not the technique, it's the rapport between counselor and client
      that makes the difference.

Urie Bronfenbrenner was asked in a *Psychology Today* interview what he thought kids needed more than anything else, and he said:
   "They need someone who is crazy about them."

He called it an "irrational attachment,"
      a closeness which means that you will stand by that kid
                   no matter what.
      And he believes that if you have someone like that in your life
         then no matter what happens
         you'll be okay in the end.

So if you are a counselor
and if you are using a technique which you understand and your client doesn't,
   stop using it
  because if you keep on using it
      you will gradually lose your respect for the other person
        and in the end, you will lose your compassion.

When you let a teenager or a parent know the rationale behind what you're doing in therapy, you stop the god-game
   and you empower *them*.

Once you empower them, you allow their uniqueness to shine.

*   *   *

In the last few years of his life, Winston Churchill was invited to give the graduation speech at his old public school.
It was a very small town
    and no one expected Churchill to accept
        but he did accept and it became a major event.
Everyone turned out
            there were banners and bands
            and when it came time for the speech, Churchill stood up
                looked across the crowd from behind the podium
            He said: "Never give up!"
            And then he sat down.
His words bring me to a final paradox—
            Lost causes are the only ones worth fighting for.
            This is the paradox of the cross.

            Selfless love is a lost cause.
            Loving one's enemies is a lost cause.
            Interpersonal harmony is a lost cause.
            The perfection of human beings is a lost cause.

            They are lost only because they are so important.
            And that was the message of that day on Golgotha.
            Lost causes are the only ones worth fighting for.
The church, of all institutions and groups, should understand lost causes. And the church, of all institutions and groups,
            should understand the paradox within which lost causes are won.
What *never give up* really means is: Don't give up when they think you're going to. Hang in there a little longer.

When a kid is used to seeing adults give up on him after a certain
time
        you'll surprise him if you're still there
                        still listening
                        still suggesting ideas and offering sup-
                        port.
I believe that the church, in relating to parents and teenagers,
                needs to play the role of a friend
                        a well-informed friend
                a friend who can be counted on to stick around
a friend who will go so far out on a limb for you that you can
                                hear the wood cracking.
As a friend, we can do what is most important for teenagers:
        we can help them survive their own adolescence.
                How do we do this?
                                        We offer ourselves.
                We give gentle lessons in human nature, for a start.

The first chapter of my book for parents is called "What's Normal?"
I know that it's impossible to describe "normal" teenage behavior,
        but I wanted the chapter there in the beginning
        because I wanted parents to relax about some things
                I wanted them to know that some of the crazy things
                                their kids are doing
                                are *normal*.
                I wanted to help parents make a distinction between
                        normal crazy behavior
                        and dangerous crazy behavior.

For example:

- It's normal for a teenager to have very little to say to his or
  her parents between the ages of thirteen and sixteen. . . . One father I know calls these years "the secretive
  years." It is also normal for a teenager to grow out of the

secretive years and have quite a lot to say in conversations with parents—usually around age sixteen or seventeen.

Not all kids go through this phase, but many do—and what's important is that parents be forewarned
    so they don't freak out
        and over-react
if their child, at age 13 or 14, stops telling them much of anything.

One of the most helpful things any organization can do is get parents of teenagers together and talk about phases like the secretive years.

- It's also normal, according to the latest surveys, for the teenager of 1980 to be a practical, down-to-earth person who is interested in making money—but who is also interested in style, and thus will plunk down $60 for a pair of designer jeans.

- Drinking and smoking dope are common practices in high schools today, but the reactions are more mixed than ever:

  —You have parents who smoke dope themselves
  —You have parents who get high with their kids
  —You have parents who never used drugs when they were teenagers
          but who started smoking dope
            or using cocaine
              as adults;
          they wonder if they should take a stand against their teenager's use of those same drugs.

This means that it's more and more normal for parents to feel confused,
                for the boundaries they set to be hazier
                    and more doubt-plagued than ever before.

- It's hard to find a survey today that doesn't indicate that about half of today's high school students are sexually active.

- It's still normal for the brightest and most sensitive kids
  to go through the scariest experimental stages
      both sexually
      and with drugs.
- And it's still normal for junior high school kids to be the best
  proof of Reinhold Niebuhr's "moral man and immoral society." As individuals, junior high kids can be a delight
                    but as a group—
  Well, have you ever sat near a group of junior high kids
                    at a movie theatre?

The church can help parents understand what's normal—
but the church is obviously up to more than mere sociology:
  we can also make some value judgments.

For example, we can suggest that parents need not know everything about what their kids are doing. Did *your* parents know
everything you did?

                    Did their ignorance harm you in any im-
                    portant way?
                    I suspect not.

    But some parents who *had* to know
        and who sneaked a look at daughter's diary to find out
            wound up damaging their relationship with their
            child
                irreparably.

Katherine Hepburn was asked in a television interview last year
how she was feeling, and with a twinkle in her eye she answered:
    "Oh, I feel *fine*—if you don't ask for details!"

Almost all kids are fine, too—if you don't ask for details.
We need to help parents learn to relax with the basic minimum
of information.
We need to help kids learn some basic values
            and then trust them to do a good job with those values.

Successful parents have told me again and again that when they were bringing up their children, they tried to take a "mostly yes" approach to parenting. There's another Bill Glasser story involving the same daughter which is a good illustration of the "mostly yes" approach:

Bill and his daughter
        who was fifteen at the time
                were driving down the Santa Monica freeway
                        when she asked him a question which seemed to come
                                                right off the wall:
                                "Dad—can I go to Japan?"

After a brief pause, Bill said: "Yes, you can go to Japan."
The question did make some sense because his daughter had been involved in a hot correspondence with a Japanese pen pal. There was a long silence in the car, and then she asked:
                        "How do people get to Japan?"
                        "Well, I think most people probably fly in an airplane."

Another long silence, and then:
                        "Will you buy me a plane ticket to Japan?"
                        "No, I won't."
                        "Then how am I going to get there?"
                        "I guess you'll just have to figure out a way, that's all."

In the end, she did go to Japan.
                        She worked at a number of odd jobs for the next year
                        and earned about half of what she needed
                        and father chipped in with the rest.

We can encourage parents to take a mostly yes approach to parenting, We can encourage kids to learn how to be responsible for themselves, *and* we can show parents how to take a firm hand when it's needed.

It's a popular fad these days to make everyone responsible for creating their own experience:

   it is at the center of est

   it's the theme of dozens of self-help books

and it's what Bill Glasser was doing with his daughter there on the Santa Monica Freeway.

Like most popular fads, it has lots of good, healthy stuff to offer us—

   but we need to go forward with some caution on this

   because some people—both adults and kids—can't handle the responsibility.

   They may accept it

      and try to live up to it

      but they just can't do it.

When people feel both responsible

               and helpless

               they are likely to do something excessive.

The feeling of both responsibility and helplessness is what cause child abuse

                         and suicide

                         and homicide.

When a person is feeling like that and you ask him to take control of his life, he very well may take terminal control:

            "I can't fix my marriage, but I can end it."

            "I can't fix my job, but I can end it."

            "I can't fix my life, but I can end it."

When I worked in the church, I felt that the church nationwide was working just about one year behind the latest national fad.

   If it was social action, the church got into it a year later.

   If it was human potential, the church got into it a year later.

But maybe that's okay—*if*, in that year, we take the time to size up what's being promoted and offer people something more than a warmed-over bill of goods.

I'd also like to see us do this with a sense of style and grace.
One night I ate dinner at one of the Attention Homes in Boulder
just after a new set of houseparents had taken over the home, and
the meal was a nightmare:

everything happened short of a food fight;
the kids were yelling
                swearing
                complaining about the food
                insulting each other
                you name it. . . .

It was clear that the new staff people just thought that this was the
way things were. But even the kids knew that this was not the way
things were—and all they needed was for someone to make the
point:

                that there is such a thing as civility
                and civility is living your life in such a way that it is not
                        a burden to other people.

Richard Farson tells a nice story about a consulting job he did for
the park service. The park maintenance crews were upset.

                They were upset because the park management was dis-
                satisfied
                        with the way they were cleaning up the camp sites after
                        people left.

It seems that management wanted all the trash picked up
                and they wanted the sites raked in between occupants.
                Some members of the maintenance crew felt that picking up
                the trash

                                                         was enough.

Farson asked the group: "You mean they want to be able to see
                                rake marks on the ground once you're
                                through?"
And they said yes, that was it.
And he couldn't help but think:

You know, if I were a camper just arriving at a camp site
            I'd like to see rake marks.
            It would be reassuring,
                a clear sign that someone who really cared had
            been there.
There is such a thing as civility.
There is such a thing as style and grace.
There is such a thing as doing what we do very, very well.

I am an optimist, but even if I were a pessimist I would point out
that when the last life boat was lowered from the decks of the
Titanic, Benjamin Guggenheim went below and changed into
evening clothes.

I would like never to give up
        when they think I'm going to.
And I would like to leave some rake marks behind.

REFLECTIONS: Andrew P. Grannell

This was for me a highly enjoyable piece. Not only because I
found the style and insights refreshing, not only because I agree
with much, if not all, that Roger Paine shares with us, but especially because it represents a perspective that mature persons have
to share with all of us who still engage in adolescent forms of
thought. This, in my view, is a prime example of the hard-won
fruit of working through many of the insufferable dilemmas of
adolescence—*with* youth.

If we can have any confidence in shifts of logic detailed in
moving from conventional to postconventional world view, then
certainly the movement from strict unilinear logic to paradox is
critical. How in fact can we engage youth across the gulf that
separates these dichotomous and paradoxical world views? All of
the dilemmas of war/peace, materialism/spirituality, idealism/

realism bear down upon the adolescent and they admit of no solution. All of the "answers" from the adolescent perspective appear to require an either/or solution. Indeed, the often remarkable sense of clarity and honesty combined with the zealous passions of youth appear to admit no other. Either you are for me or you are against me. The hard sayings of the Sermon on the Mount fascinate, frustrate, and often ultimately alienate thinking youth. So it is with youth who have been sojourning with the highly-principled people called Quakers. Here among an "oddly-out-of-sync folk," youth often find just what they are looking for. Then comes the late adolescent shift toward realism with an increasingly painful awareness of life's duplicities, vagaries, and cruel ambiguities.

Can we communicate when what we have to offer may sound like poetry in our ears, but sounds like gibberish, or worse, double-talk to the adolescent? How can you in fact say that we should both learn to "let go" and on the other hand "never give up?" Which is it? When is it? *Why* is it?

I would like to share some personal communication to illustrate the struggle here. (I have substantially changed the details but the contents remain nearly verbatim.) Beth wrote to me last winter just months prior to graduation from a New England college. She had written earlier and shared with me some of her extensive personal struggle on the decisions facing her upon graduation. We had known each other over nearly an eight-year period. In her early teens she had elected to attend and then to join her local suburban Friends Meeting. She is one of four siblings belonging to a struggling-but-comfortable family that had seen the mother return to the marketplace to help with college costs. Beth is tall, athletic, determined, increasingly poised, and fun-loving. Above all she values honesty and the fruits of hard work. Earlier she had been a candidate for a Rhodes Scholarship.

The letter arrived in mid-February, 1980. I hope that you will look for the unilinear (Aristotelian) logic in her note to me and

critique my attempts to meet her need. Unfortunately or fortunately, it is youth who must decide for themselves how they will
respond to the value systems of our banking empires and military
establishments.

Dear Andy,

Much delay in writing because my life seems in constant flux and I'm
never sure what to say. One thing is certain, however, much thanks
for the Rhodes recommendation! I'm sorry to say that I did not get
one, but formulating my essays and interviewing was a real learning
experience.

School is slowly winding to an end. Should I say slow? I guess not, it
seems like only yesterday that I was in Young Friends. I'm currently
looking for a job which is a *really* interesting process, because it all
seems to work out to how much one is willing to compromise oneself
to get the job (*i.e.*, a Morgan Guaranty Trust interviewer in NYC
asked me my opinions on investing in South Africa, on the candidates in the presidential election and on nuclear power—I was not
asked back for a second interview). It's very difficult to assess how
much individual freedom one will have on the job. Especially, since
I am interested in business and banking which tends to be *very*
conservative. I am not frightened as much by not getting a job as I am
by being placed in one where I am unhappy with my position and my
employer. Oh dear.

All of this talk of registration leaves me very confused. I see registration as the most equitable way that the armed forces can exist (*i.e.*, all
classes must go). However, I am not comfortable with the rising
sentiments of militarism that are accompanying this all. I suspect the
draft will soon follow. I am also bothered that the people who will not
pass the ERA because of coed bathrooms are eager to register women.
I am, however, bothered by the implications of the Soviets move in
Afghanistan, but wonder how clean the story is that we are getting
from the press. In summation—I am befuddled. I am not a straight
pacifist, however. All the athletics and intense competition have
made me recognize a certain violence in my nature. Also, the
Friends Meeting has been picketing the firm where my father works.
What this jumble is leading up to, I guess, is a problem I am having,

politically, with Quakerism. Has all my economic training turned me into a gross conservative? I worry that it has. I don't know where I stand, but it is not as simple and peaceful as my meeting may wish. Oh—I seem to be in constant dilemmas. My faith in God is solid, but how I apply that to my life and attitude remains confused. So much for my continuing dilemmas—I am working on them!

Love,
Beth

A short while later, I responded with the following:

Dear Beth,

It was good to hear from you both in letter and on the phone. I have sent off a letter of recommendation to the Peace Corps and am enclosing the address that you requested.

Dorothy and I talked a bit about your encounter with the recruiter from Morgan Guaranty Trust. You are undoubtedly correct in sizing up the attitude and atmosphere of banking as being very conservative. From our family experience, it is apparent that a certain amount of conservatism goes with the territory. It is a much more difficult thing to size up the amount of latitude that an individual can be allowed to deviate from the conservative norm. . . . I was certainly glad that you took with utmost seriousness the questions regarding divestment and the generation of nuclear power. The first demonstration that I ever tried to attend was a rally in front of the Chase Manhattan on the question of divestment of gold holdings in the Union of South Africa: . . . I couldn't find a parking spot and missed the rally!

The Soviet aggression in Afghanistan is sobering. We cannot help but be affected by the allegations especially of the use of certain chemicals and possibly of poison gases. I, for one, do not believe that we ought or can dismiss or turn aside at this juncture from the grimness of it all. Every possible measure should be taken to both call attention to it and to attempt to force the Soviets to reconsider their actions. I support the President in much that he has attempted to do to date, e.g., Olympics boycott, but I am doubtful that the measures taken will have much real effect. Still, in regard to the Arms Race, I believe that his actions have been precipitous in that he has jeopardized the

SALT II process for an indefinite time and he has helped to unleash the forces in this country which continue to rush blindly onward toward the MX system, chemical/biological warfare, laser beam or particle beam defense systems, and the use of outer space for a "limited nuclear war," et al. While the invasion of Afghanistan is sobering, it does not warrant in my opinion, the worst instinctual measures now being researched and funded. . . . The draft is, in this light, just another part of the new phase of xenophobic reaction to this invasion. We are still, however, not in any mood to start up registration or the draft fortunately (this was soon to be dispelled as an illusion).

I very much like your sensitivity to the question of the draft. We should have a fair and inclusive process—if we are to have one at all. We are all too content to have the ranks filled with the poor and the unfortunate. However, the question of the draft itself raises the question of whether a free society can or should demand that a person involuntarily submit to train for the destruction of other human lives. Thus we pit two quite different principles against each other, i.e., the obligation of all to share the load coequally (or equally as is possible) as against the principle of the individual freedom to choose to participate in a system deemed to be inherently immoral. This type of question also pits the realistic against the idealistic as you so readily point out. This is tough terrain to manage. I believe we must press on to resist the institutions of war at every level. War as the recourse to the resolution of conflict between peoples will surely be the death of the species on this planet. There are no "holy wars;" they are all unholy alliances with the unmitigated furies, i.e., the Dionysian mentalities in our own constitutions and our own propensities to hack out our own destiny—at any cost. "Defense" budgets that continue to escalate and reinstitution of the draft are visible witness to the grimmest human propensities possible, i.e., we will have our own way for this is our time, our land, our freedom, our resources, our children, our destiny, etc. and we will see that this is defended at any cost. All of this negates our responsibilities to use all that has been so graciously given to us to God's glory and not our own. For at root is our utter presumption, our pride, our greed, our uncaring that feeds the flames of war, i.e., that Afghanies or Iranians cannot manage their own affairs. In my view, we must continue to resist the draft not because its democratic or constitutional assumptions are errant, but because it feeds the insatiable propensity to even kill whole peoples to have our own way. There is no logical limit to our technological genius in all this, thus only our will to resist gives us hope. We always forget the most important ingredient in all our calculations of hope and despair. May God save us from ourselves yet, just as we look to the sacrifice of those who, following after Christ, have paid with their lives that it might be so. I hope that this response is not an overreaction of another kind. As you can see, I believe that we need to come to grips with this question at profound levels of our reasoning and begin to address it for what it is. I support you in your willingness to grapple with it. May you never lose your openness or your honesty! Keep looking hard for your answers to these questions for we need your answers, too! We think of you often and hope that the final term goes smoothly enough. Will look forward to hearing which direction your life moves on from here.

Love and peace,
Andy

Chapter 5

Desired Outcomes of Religious Education and Youth Ministry in Six Denominations

DEAN R. HOGE
ESTHER HEFFERNAN
EUGENE F. HEMRICK
HART M. NELSEN
JAMES P. O'CONNOR
PAUL J. PHILIBERT
ANDREW D. THOMPSON

The research reported in this chapter was carried out by the staff of the Boys Town Center for the Study of Youth Development, Catholic University, Washington, D.C. We would like to thank the many persons who helped us gather the data, including Bob Taylor, Kenneth Hayes, Richard Harp, Warren Hartman, Susan Hay, Beth Downs, Mildred Cooper, Guy Baer, William Forbes, Lynn Foley, David Perry, Elizabeth Crawford, and John Westerhoff. We would like to thank our Advisory Committee for guidance, and Scott Wolfe and Ella Smith for research assistance.

Dean Hoge is a research sociologist at Catholic University in Washington, D.C. Working with statistics and doing factor-analysis provides the most com-

prehensive picture of what a large number of people are really thinking about, opining, and wondering. Invited as a participant to our conference, Hoge shared these recent findings of his research team with our group. This data summary moves beyond speculation to reveal the current trends concerning the education of youth which are prominent in mainline Protestantism.

Religious groups differ in their goals for Christian education and youth ministry. This diversity has been analyzed by several theorists, including R. M. Rummery and Harold Burgess.[1] One reason for the diversity is that religious work with youth is inherently pluralistic in its goals. Every denominational statement on youth ministry sets forth several discrete goals, whose relative importance may vary from parish to parish. Also, theological positions vary from denomination to denomination, causing further differences.

In 1978, the Boys Town Center staff began planning empirical research to discern the experiences and settings which enhance growth toward the desired outcomes of religious education and youth ministry during the high school years. We needed more precise information about the outcomes actually desired by educators and parents, so we decided to carry out an empirical study. It was hoped that the results would be helpful to religious educators in long-range planning.

METHOD

We decided to design a questionnaire which would articulate specific goals and also obtain information for explaining variations in desired goals. We collected many outcome statements from various sources—statements which describe the desired characteristics of youth after participating in religious education and youth ministry. They included such qualities as personal religious commitment, understanding of the faith, personal maturity, identification with the denomination, devotional life, and so on. Our initial collection, made in spring 1978, had over 100 items. We pretested them with friends and associates, reviewed the comments, and then pretested a second version. The third version we presented to our Advisory Committee, and in summer 1978 we carried out a major pretest of a 91-statement questionnaire. [2]

After the pretest data were in we tallied all the written-in comments, and on the basis of them we eliminated or rephrased about 20 items. Also, the comments indicated that the final questionnaire should be shorter. Thus we deleted most items not clearly belonging to any factor. The final product was a list of 62 goal statements which showed promise of covering the diversity of goals held by various persons and of producing 10 reliable scales in the final study. The final questionnaire also included 7 items on approaches to religious education, 18 items on theological attitudes, and 12 background questions.

We decided to gather representative samples from six denominations, including the largest ones in the nation—Roman Catholic, Southern Baptist, and United Methodist. Also we included the Episcopal Church and Presbyterian Church in the U.S. (Southern), since we had good contact with them. Finally we enrolled the Church of God (Anderson, Indiana) to ensure enough data from theological conservatives. In all six denominations we asked national staff to help us gather representative samples of about 150–175 educators and 150–175 parents of adolescents. We asked that the educators be parish-based youth ministers and religious educators, either professionals or nonprofessionals who are responsible for programs. We did not want volunteer Sunday School teachers or other helpers who were not thoughtfully engaged in planning parish programs. We asked that not more than one or two educators be from any one parish or congregation. The purpose was to assemble samples maximally representative of each denomination.

All the denominations used the same sampling method—they wrote to their rosters of religious educators and youth ministers, asking each to fill out the questionnaire. A small number were asked to get 5, 10, or 15 of their parents of adolescents to fill it out. This method worked well for the educators but not for the parents, requiring that additional efforts be made in most of the denominations to bring in more questionnaires from parents. The final sample was deemed to be representative by the denominational persons gathering the data; we recognize that this method of data collection produces responses from parents who are relatively more involved in church affairs than the average.

Data collection took a long time, but in the end we completed all the desired samples except in the smallest denomination, the Church of God, where the total was 126 educators and 50 parents.

FINDINGS

The questionnaire began by asking: "What characteristics of youth near the end of the high school years should be the main goals of Christian education? What should the well-educated and well-socialized youth be like? What should religious education and youth ministry be producing?" Then the 62 goal statements were given, followed by numbers from 1 to 7, labeled "1 = highly desirable—highest priority;" "2 = quite desirable;" "3 = somewhat desirable;" "4 = neutral;" "5 = somewhat undesirable;" "6 = quite undesirable;" and "7 = highly undesirable." The respondents were asked to circle one number. We expected that they would circle 1, 2, or 3 most often, and they did.

The list of 62 items is too bulky to list here, but Table 1 depicts the twenty which were rated as highest priority by the entire

TABLE 1: RANKING OF 20 ITEMS GIVEN HIGHEST PRIORITY

	All	Baptist		Ch. God		Presby.		Methodist		Episco.		Catholic	
		Ed.	Par.	Ed.	Par.	Ed.	Par.	Ed.	Par.	Ed.	Par.	Ed.	Par.
31. Has a healthy self-concept about his or her value and worthiness as a person.	1	5	12	4	4.5	1	1	1	1	1	1	1	1
*1. Sets an example of Christian behavior among his or her friends and associates.	2	7	5.5	5	6.5	2	2	2	2	2	4	2.5	2
*25. His or her religion is meaningful in everyday life.	3	6	7	3	2	3	6	3	5	3	10	4	5
43. Takes a responsible view toward moral questions such as drug use and sex behavior.	4	21	13	16	10	8	3	7	3	4	2	11	3
59. Has a personal relationship with Jesus Christ.	5	1	1	2	1	11.5	11	9.5	6	17	29	5	9
54. Understands sexual feelings and has responsible ways of handling them.	6	20	21	17.5	11.5	9	7	6	7	8	5	14	11
*46. Discovers the meaning of the love of God through personal relationships.	7	13	20	9	16	4	10	5	10	12	9	9	14
61. Is acquiring knowledge about human sexuality and has formed a responsible Christian approach in sexual matters.													
*58. Is not embarrassed to identify himself or herself as a Christian	8	19	19	15	18	10	9	9.5	12	9	6	8	12.5

136

No.	Item												
9	and to speak of Christian beliefs.	17	17.5	13	13	16	14	16	11.5	18	10	5.5	8
10	*19. Considers helping others as central to Christian commitment.	7.5	2.5	7.5	5	9	8	15	5	18	25	32	32
11	*7. Is able to act responsibly in various social situations.	16	17.5	3	6	8	4	4	14	26.5	28	29	26
12	62. Distinguishes between the values of the popular culture and the values of the Gospel.	20	16	14	7	20	12	12.5	6	22	17.5	18	15
13	27. Attends church regularly.	4	22	17	21	11	23	22	30	4.5	19.5	8.5	18
14	3. Sees daily prayer and reflection as worthwhile.	21	12	30	20	14	21	18	24	8	19.5	10.5	11
15	*4. Cooperates with parents, school authorities, and church authorities.	12.5	33.5	7.5	30	4	22	5	37	13.5	30	15	24
16	*60. Associates with friends who hold responsible Christian moral values.	19	21	15	27	15	25	8	27	11.5	23	10.5	22
17	*37. Exhibits in daily life and contact with other people a personal faith.	28	19	21.5	25	23	15	23	20	21	12	16.5	10
18	10. Has come under the influence of spiritually authentic Christians.	34	10	28	24	29	18	20	21	6.5	6.5	14	12
19	*9. Is actively involved in the church community.	31	25	27	22	13	13	17	15	20	26	22	14
20	40. Forms relationships with mature and trustworthy adults.	23	26	12	19	21	20	12.5	13	23	24	31	30

*These 10 items did not fall on the main dimensions found by factor analysis, hence are not in the goal scales.

sample. It lists them in order of overall priority and also gives the ranking for each goal within each of the twelve sample groups. In the table, "E" indicates educators, and "P" indicates parents. Ties are ranked halfway between, so that, for example, items tied for 5th and 6th place are both ranked 5.5.

The Southern Baptist Convention and Church of God are somewhat different from the other denominations. They give higher priority to a personal relationship with Jesus Christ and personal conversion, and lower priority to moral development and social justice. The goal which the Baptists and Church of God respondents often ranked in second place—#39 ("Has experienced a personal conversion and commitment to Jesus Christ"), did not make it into the top twenty items overall. Also on certain items the parents in all denominations are higher than the educators, showing that they see the items as more important. The items are #43 on drugs and sex, #27 on church attendance, #4 on cooperation with parents and authorities, and #60 on associating with Christian friends. On one item, educators consistently give a higher priority than parents—#62 on distinguishing the gospel from popular culture.

To form reliable scales we factor-analyzed the 62 items. The procedure discerns underlying dimensions, or patterns of interrelationships, in the responses. The most interpretable solution had 10 factors. Below are listed the items in each scale. The order in which the scales are presented is arbitrary.

1. *Conversion* (intercorrelation = .67)
    #23. Has experienced being "born again" as a Christian.
    #39. Has experienced a personal conversion and commitment to Jesus Christ.

2. *Personal Religious Life* (alpha = .88)
    #3. Sees daily prayer and reflection as worthwhile.
    #12. Sees God's rule of the world as demanding a personal surrender to his will.

#13. Lives each day with a sense of divine forgiveness.

#15. Has a daily private prayer life.

#50. Values the Bible as inspiration for personal spiritual growth.

#59. Has a personal relationship with Jesus Christ.

3. *Moral Maturity* (alpha = .88)

#31. Has a healthy self-concept about his or her value and worthiness as a person.

#43. Takes a responsible view toward moral questions such as drug use and sex behavior.

#54. Understands sexual feelings and has responsible ways of handling them.

#61. Is acquiring knowledge about human sexuality and has formed a responsible Christian approach in sexual matters.

#62. Distinguishes between the values of the popular culture and the values of the gospel.

4. *Importance of Sacraments* (alpha = .81)

#2. Understands the Lord's Supper (Eucharist) as a time of God's presence and activity within the community.

#14. Participates frequently in Holy Communion.

#26. Understands the importance and meaning of the Eucharist (Lord's Supper).

#38. Appreciates the importance of participating in the sacraments (including Baptism and Holy Communion).

5. *Loyalty to Denomination and Parish* (alpha = .84)

#16. Feels loyalty to his or her own denomination.

#27. Attends church regularly.

#33. Has a positive feeling toward the local church and church activities.

#45. Has a positive view of ministers, priests, and other religious workers.

#51. Is happy to be identified as a member of his or her denomination.

6. *Christian Fellowship* (alpha = .70)

#10. Has come under the influence of spiritually authentic Christians.

#21. Develops friendships within the church community.
#24. Desires to live in a church community of Christians who love and trust each other.
#40. Forms relationships with mature and trustworthy adults.

7. *Universalizing Faith* (alpha = .73)
  #18. Believes that other religions of the world make worthwhile contributions to humanity.
  #20. Holds that literal interpretations of the Bible have definite limitations.
  #22. Appreciates religious expressions and experiences—not necessarily those normally within his or her religious tradition.
  #30. Has appreciation for and some understanding of the great religions of the world.
  #32. Brings a searching, questioning way of thinking to his or her religious tradition.

8. *Reflective Understanding of Christian Truth* (alpha = .80)
  #28. Has knowledge of the history of the Christian church.
  #44. Understands Christianity both from within his or her own tradition and also critically, as if from outside.
  #48. Feels that he or she shares faith with those who have been closest to God through all ages.
  #55. Can identify important assumptions and implications of Christian teachings.
  #57. Knows the stories of the gospels, the Acts of the Apostles, and the Old Testament.

9. *Social Justice* (alpha = .85)
  #5. Actively works for justice in the local community.
  #17. Emphasizes that the struggle for justice is a rightful concern of the church.
  #29. Shows concern about liberation of oppressed people.
  #41. Is willing to work publicly to protest social wrongs.
  #52. Appreciates his or her personal responsibility as a Christian for combating social evils.

10. *Charismatic Experience* (alpha = .86)
  #11. Participates in the charismatic movement.

#35. Has experienced the gift of tongues.
#47. Appreciates the charismatic movement.

Each scale score is the mean of the items comprising it. "Alpha" is a measure of the homogeneity of the items as perceived by the respondents; the alphas of our scales are at generally acceptable levels.

Of the 10 scales, one was rated so much lower than the others that it cannot be seen as an important goal held by the sample groups—"Charismatic Experience." Hence it is ignored in our analysis.

Figure 1 depicts scale scores of parents and educators. We should note that the educators in this study varied somewhat from denomination to denomination. The samples are generally representative, but we make no claim that our data exactly describe the total group of educators in any denomination. Of all the educators, 68 percent had taken one or more college or seminary courses in religious education, and 66 percent said they were professional religious educators; 46 percent were female (this varied from 6 percent in the Church of God to 73 percent in the Catholic Church); 39 percent were ordained members of the clergy (this varied from 7 percent in the Catholic Church to 91 percent in the Church of God). The median age of the educators was 38.9 years; of the parents it was 44.0 years.

In Figure 1 three lines are plotted within each denomination on the 9 goal scales (the vertical lines). The lines are for educators with college or seminary courses, for educators without formal training, and for parents of adolescents. Note that for four of the six denominations, moral maturity is clearly the most important outcome of religious education and youth ministry. The moral maturity scale stresses personal responsibility in matters of sex, drug use, and popular culture. For the other two denominations—the Southern Baptists and the Church of God—conversion is an even higher priority.

The six denominations fall into three types. First, the South-

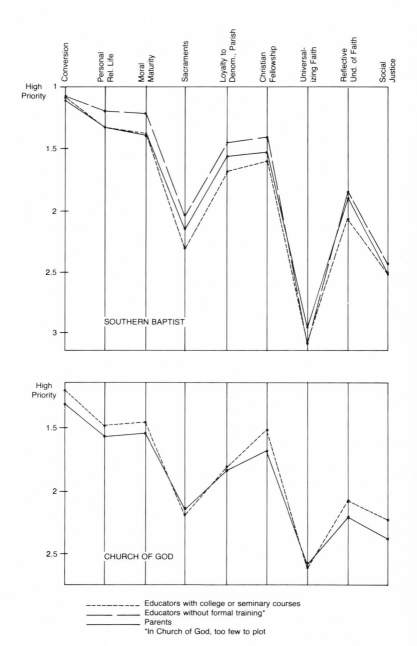

Conversion

Personal Rel. Life

Moral Maturity

Sacraments

Loyalty to Denom., Parish

Christian Fellowship

Universal- izing Faith

Reflective Und. of Faith

Social Justice

High Priority 1

1.5

2

2.5

3

SOUTHERN BAPTIST

High Priority

1.5

2

2.5

CHURCH OF GOD

---------- Educators with college or seminary courses

— — — Educators without formal training*

———— Parents

*In Church of God, too few to plot

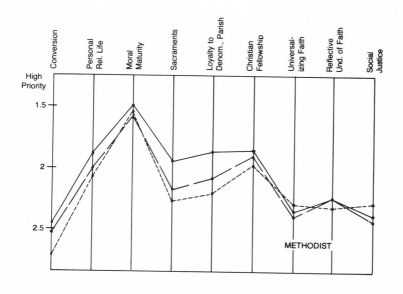

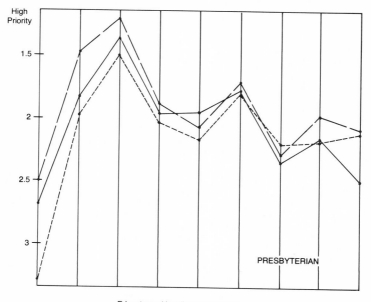

------------ Educators with college or seminary courses
———— ———— Educators without formal training
———————— Parents

143

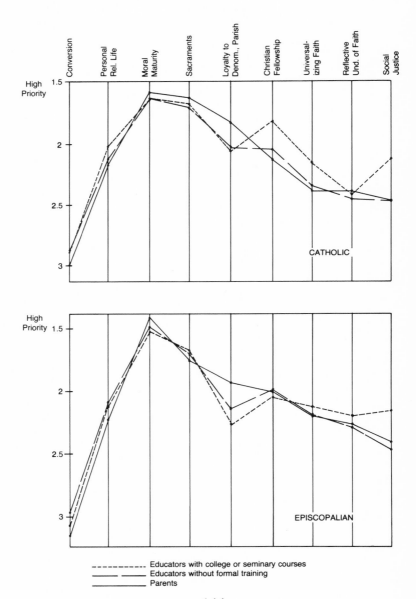

Conversion
Personal Rel. Life
Moral Maturity
Sacraments
Loyalty to Denom., Parish
Christian Fellowship
Universal- izing Faith
Reflective Und. of Faith
Social Justice

High Priority 1.5

CATHOLIC

High Priority 1.5

EPISCOPALIAN

---------- Educators with college or seminary courses
— —— — Educators without formal training
———— Parents

144

ern Baptists and Church of God are distinctive in stressing conversion and personal religious life and in deemphasizing universalizing faith and sacraments. At the other extreme, the Catholics and Episcopalians have almost no interest in conversion but a high priority on sacraments and quite high priority on universalizing faith. Between these, the Methodists and Presbyterians form an intermediate group, with much less emphasis on sacraments and somewhat less on universalizing faith. The three lines in each denomination are quite close, showing little educator-versus-parent difference of opinion. This surprised us, since we expected that parents would prefer more practical, immediate goals. Figure 2 summarizes the goals preferred in each denomination. One line for each denomination summarizes the views of both parents and educators. A few of the lines are drawn broken (not solid) solely for visual clarity.

The questionnaire also gathered attitudes on theological orientations. The theological items formed four scales: (1) A *Relativism Scale*, composed of four items, measured religious relativism versus a belief that one's own church has God's truth and other religious groups are in error. One item stated, "All the different religions are equally good ways of helping a person find ultimate truth." (2) A *Creedal Assent Scale*, composed of four items (borrowed from King and Hunt),[3] was made of creed-like statements, such as "I believe in eternal life." (3) A *Moral Concreteness Scale*, composed of four items, measured whether Christian moral decisions are to be made by direct reference to New Testament moral rules, or whether Christian ethics is contextual, depending on responsible decision making. (4) An *Ongoing Revelation Scale*, composed of two items, stated that God is revealing himself today just as much as earlier.

We divided the sample into high, medium, and low groups on each of these scales, then plotted the scale scores for each subgroup. The plots were so similar that we concluded we had used theological dimensions highly associated with each other. A

Dean R. Hoge et al.

FIGURE 2
GOALS OF PARENTS AND EDUCATORS, BY DENOMINATION

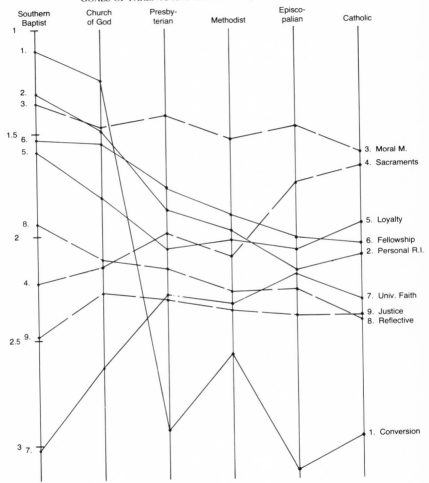

conservative-versus-liberal axis seemed to underlie all four scales. The goals most affected by theological attitudes were #1 (conversion), #2 (personal religious life), and #7 (universalizing faith). Theological conservatives gave quite high priorities to #1 and #2, but very low priority to #7. In all theological subgroups, goal #3 (moral maturity) remained highest priority of all. And one goal, #9 (social justice) was ranked quite low by all the theological subgroups.

The questionnaire asked for information on age, sex, race, amount of education, amount of training in religious education, and city size. Breakdowns on these variables showed less variation than the theological breakdowns, indicating that theological views are stronger determiners of educational goals than such background categories.

DISCUSSION

This is the first empirical research study of its kind, so far as we know, looking at the precise priorities of religious education and youth ministry as held by various denominations. It resembles in some ways a market research survey to see what customers want. Religious educators can see from its results what outcomes are most wanted, and if the educators dissent from the outcomes the people want, they can see where thoroughgoing theological discussion is needed.

Notable is the high priority given to the adolescents' self-concept formation and their preparation for handling the difficult adolescent problems of sex, drugs, and popular culture. These goals are so prominent in the outcomes that one might say that moral education is the most-desired part of religious education. These goals are ahead of the more traditional religious educational goals of appreciating Christian history or identifying with the denomination's tradition.

The most-desired moral education is not the kind leading to postconventional thinking or sensitivity to social injustices. It is less radical than that, more aimed at personal adjustment and fulfillment in the existing social and moral order.

Several recent nationwide surveys done by Gallup and by religious researchers have shown that the vast majority of Americans see religious training of children and youth as very important. Even the majority of unchurched people want religious training for their children. Exactly what do they want? Research such as the present study can help specify more precisely what various groups want for the youth of their families and communities.

NOTES

1. R. M. Rummery, *Catechesis and Religious Education in a Pluralistic Society* (Huntington, Indiana: Our Sunday Visitor Press, 1975). Harold W. Burgess, *An Invitation to Religious Education* (Birmingham, Alabama: Religious Education Press, 1975).

2. The 1978 pretest was done in a series of churches and in summer school courses on religious education. There were 296 respondents in the pretest, of whom 204 were professional educators. We factor-analyzed the 91 items and found eight distinct factors. One factor combined two concerns—social involvement and ecumenism. Hence items were added to create reliable scales for each. Also we decided to add four items on charismatic involvement in the final questionnaire.

3. Morton B. King and Richard A. Hunt, "Measuring the Religious Variable: National Replication," *Journal for the Scientific Study of Religion* 14, No. 1 (March 1975), pp. 13–22.

Chapter 6
Youth and Church Renewal

LAWRENCE O. RICHARDS

Lawrence O. Richards is one of the few educators who has perceived the need for and developed a theology for ministry with youth. The very practical dimension of his work comes from his personal involvement in living out his theological convictions. He is presently doing consulting work for church-renewal movements in East Lansing, Michigan, where he is living in an extended-family situation similar to the one described in this article.

It is my goal in this chapter to (1) state theological and sociological assumptions relevant to youth ministry and church renewal, (2) suggest aspects of renewal which are salient to youth ministry, and (3) illustrate the impact on young people of a developed renewal lifestyle in a local congregation. This essay is meant to be suggestive only: No prescriptions for action are advanced here.

THEOLOGICAL AND SOCIOLOGICAL ASSUMPTIONS

Theological. The basic assumption theologically is that it is appropriate and necessary to extend the family symbol to the broader Christian community, and that the church-as-family is the divinely ordained context for nurture.

The extension of the family symbol is in complete harmony with Scripture, which speaks of God's "whole family" as "deriving its name [identity]" from one who is by nature Father (Eph. 3:14). In a prayer for the strengthening of the people of God, Paul asks that "being rooted and established in love, [they] may have power, together with all the saints, to grasp" Christ's love and "be filled to the measure of all the fullness of God."

Each of the biblical writers who speaks of the church uses family language, talking of brothers and sisters and fathers and mothers, and urging that since "you have purified yourselves by obeying the truth so that you have sincere love for your brothers, love one another deeply, and from the heart" (1 Peter 1:22).

The New Testament documents consistently stress the family nature of interpersonal relationships in the Christian community. "Keep on loving one another as brothers," says the writer to the Hebrews (13:1), and John affirms that "we know we have passed from death to life because we love our brothers" (1 John 3:14). Over and over in his epistles, the Apostle Paul describes in detail a love lifestyle for the family to experience together. Relating to one another in affirming, accepting, and nonjudgmental ways, we are to share faith's life and worship, as well as sharing our burdens and our joys (see particularly Romans 13:8 - 15:5).

The Scriptures thus assume that it is in this context—this community which is an extended family—that children and youth will grow to Christian maturity, and that the converted will come to understand and to live as members of God's kingdom.

Sociological. In a 1975 address on "The Next Generation of Americans,"[1] Urie Bronfrenbrenner, then Chairman of the Department of Human Development and Family Studies at Cornell University, summarized hundreds of investigations over three decades into the "developmental antecedents of behavior disorders and social pathology." The results, Bronfrenbrenner asserted, "point to an almost omnipresent overriding factor: family disorganization."[2] In his address he went on to point out that investigations of cross-cultural child-rearing practices "call attention to a distinctive feature of American child rearing: segregation not by race or social class, but by age."[3]

This same segregation has been noted to extend beyond the nuclear family. Forum 15's report in the White House Conference on Children a decade ago observed,

> In our modern way of life, it is not only parents of whom children are deprived, it is people in general. A host of factors conspire to isolate children from the rest of society. The fragmentation of the extended family, the separation of residential and business areas, the disappearance of neighborhoods, zoning ordinances, occupational mobility, child-labor laws, the abolishment of the apprentice system, consolidated schools, television, separate patterns of social life for different age groups, the working mother, the delegation of child care to specialists—all of these manifestations of progress operate to decrease opportunity and incentive for meaningful contact between children and persons older, or younger, than themselves.[4]

There is no question that, as an institution, the church in the United States has conformed to this cultural pattern, and in its programming has systematically isolated youth from meaningful contact with persons older, or younger, than themselves.

This is particularly significant if we accept the renewal perception of the church-as-extended-family, and the associated implication that Christian faith is communicated in a socialization process. Kellman[5] has suggested three types of social influence understood in terms of three different psychological processes: *compliance*, produced when the influence source has some means of control over the individual; *identification*, when influence is based on desire to establish or maintain a satisfying relationship; and *internalization*, when the content (ideas and attitudes and behavior) of the induced behavior is adopted as intrinsically rewarding. When affectional motivation for identification is high, the likelihood is increased that the influence source will serve as a model and that the content of faith's life (beliefs, attitudes, and behaviors) will be perceived as intrinsically rewarding.

A survey of behavioral science literature[6] indicates general agreement that the following relational factors are significant in enhancing identification, and thus have a major influence on shaping the lives and character of young people.

1. Frequent, long-term contact
2. Warm, loving relationships
3. Exposure of inner states (sharing of feelings, etc.)
4. Consistency and clarity with which behavior models beliefs and values.
5. Explicit instruction (talk about beliefs and values that underlie behavior)
6. Correspondence of behavior with verbalized precepts.

INTERLUDE

It is interesting that this perception of the importance of significant relationships across generations is not reserved to the behavioral scientist.

Some time ago I spent two hours with youth ministers from fifteen Phoenix-area churches. These were in general large, well-organized congregations, with many resources and active youth programs. The youth ministers represented a variety of theological traditions. I led them through a process of defining their own goals for youth ministry,[7] and then asked them to specify what conditions were absolutely necessary for achievement of those goals.

The group suggested and agreed on only two necessary conditions: interaction with Scripture, and interaction with "spiritually sensitive adults" (not suggested in that order). In exploration of what they meant by relationships with spiritually sensitive adults, the group members spoke of the importance of modeling, of stable long-term relationships, of relationships with parents, and of relationships with spiritually sensitive adults who were not parents.

I then asked the group members to write down one-word descriptions of the relationships existing at that time between their own youth and the adults of their congregation. The words suggested, and agreed to, were: surface, transient, nonexistent, sporadic (defined as unsustained), toleration. Not one "positive" descriptive term was suggested by any of the youth ministers!

The highly suggestive responses at this session indicated clearly, in spite of the fact that the youth workers themselves expressed the conviction that their ministry goals could not be achieved apart from significant personal relationships between their youth and spiritually sensitive adults, that no such relationships existed in any of the fifteen churches. Moreover, when questioned, not one youth minister was making an effort to facilitate development of such relationships, nor had any plans to do so.

The assumptions underlying this discussion of youth ministry and church renewal are, then, (1) that the church is by nature an extended family, "family relationships" being the divinely ordained context for growth in faith, and (2) the societal and cultural patterns of segregation by age group have in fact been institutionalized by the church to the extent that "family" relationships between youth and adults in local congregations seldom exist.

SALIENT ASPECTS OF RENEWAL

The term "renewal," like most theological labels, is a rather slippery one. It is difficult to agree on a common meaning. Thus, some background and an explanation of how I use the term are appropriate prior to focusing on the aspects of renewal salient to our discussion.

Background. In the sixties a number of books and articles appeared that were critical of the institutional church. *God's Frozen People* were described as occupying *The Lonely Pew* on Sundays, and going out to live a split-level life during the week. The church was taken to task for superficial relationships, lack of personal commitment, and general irrelevance to the real lives of men and women. At first, more conservative Christians chuckled, for the first criticisms were made by "liberals." But soon it became apparent that the criticisms struck home across the theological spectrum.

A number of solutions were suggested. Relevance might be restored by changing the format of worship services. Perhaps guitars and dialogue sermons would restore God's people to vitality. Probably the most helpful thrust came from people like Robert Raines and Keith Miller and Cecil Osborne, who called for the personal renewal of individuals through recovery of intimacy. For a time, "small groups" were viewed as "the" answer.

While the small group movement did make a significant contribution to the lives of many individuals, the ecclesiological issues had still not been faced. The questions that had been raised were, ultimately, about the very nature of the church itself. Only an attempt to grapple theologically with the nature of the church and the identity of the people of God could adequately address the issues.

Very slowly these issues of theology were to be addressed, and in the seventies the superficial solutions were gradually set aside. There was no great turn to a common "renewal" ecclesiology. But a literature has developed around a distinctive view of the church as a community of faith. This view has found expression in the Catholic tradition (the Cursillo movement) as well as in most Protestant traditions. Its greatest strength is probably to be found among the centrist evangelicals, rather than in either the "fundamentalist/conservative" or "liberal" wings. As an illustration, just in the past year my own work in renewal has led to a consulting ministry with renewal groups in Southern Baptist, Presbyterian, Nazarene, Methodist, Mennonite, and several other fellowships, as well as to relationships with one Roman Catholic community which is strongly charismatic.

Renewal. From similar personal experiences and my own theological convictions, I suggested in a 1975 book[8] that several things tended to characterize renewal churches. These were:

(1) A sense of community
(2) A love lifestyle (stress on close interpersonal relationships)
(3) Servant leadership
(4) Ministering laity (stress on priesthood of believers)
(5) Growth emphasis (focus on nurture as the key ministry of the gathered church)
(6) Scripture/response (involvement in the Word of God, but less concern with doctrine than with personal response and obedience)

Since that publication, I have given much time to developing theological and practical implications of these areas for local church practices.[9] They still appear to be the distinguishing marks of what, to me, is church renewal.

Salient aspects. While it appears that a strong case might be made for the importance of each of these elements in ministry with youth, our present study demands a sharper focus. What specifically are the most significant contributions a renewal orientation makes to our understanding of ministry with youth? Here, in view of the theological imperative of the church as extended-family, and in view of contemporary social patterns of segregation by age group, it seems clear that the most important contribution of renewal is the development of congregational community and the faciliation of a love lifestyle which builds close relationships across the generations. Development of significant, sustained "family" relationships between youth and spiritually sensitive adults is, as the youth ministers in Phoenix affirmed, a necessary condition for achieving the varied goals of ministry with youth.

But a critical question is raised here. Considering the patterns existing in our society, is it possible to build a true community? Is the symbol of the family something which might be extended to the church of the first century, but is no longer relevant in a modern, technological, industrialized society?

While it is important to understand Scripture and to interpret it from a historical/cultural point of view, and while we can affirm the importance of contextualization of the gospel in varying human societies, it is also important to affirm that certain realities portrayed in Scripture must have cross-cultural validity. The critical question here, and a question seldom easy to answer with certainty, is this: Is the concept with which we are concerned *rooted* in theology or in culture?

It seems clear that the extended-family symbol is both rooted in theology (as Paul's statements in Ephesians 3 assumes) and is also a universal human symbol. Thus to call the church an extended-family, and to stress love relationships growing out of the family relationship which now exists between believers, strongly suggests that the family symbol does have cross-cultural validity, and that *to be the church, we must become family.*

We can say that there is a theological imperative which calls us, in this aspect of our lives together, not to be "squeezed into the world's mold" (Romans 12:2, Phillips) but to seek a transformation of our corporate experience. Where this renewal—this recovery of *koinonia* is experienced by youth and adults together, we would expect healthy processes that promote growth toward Christian maturity to be at work in youth/adult relationships.

AN ILLUSTRATION

In order to gather some empirical evidence of a measurable impact of renewal on youth/adult relationships, I went to Evergreen, Colorado, and visited a local congregation that meets the "renewal" criteria suggested earlier.

Evergreen Fellowship began some seven years ago, the outgrowth of a Bible study begun by a woman who now serves as minister to women in a large Presbyterian church in the South. Over the years it has had leadership which is committed to a renewal understanding of the church. As it has grown to its present size of some 250 adherents, meeting in a public school, it has consistently given expression to renewal principles in its practices. The church has no youth minister, althouth two couples serve as youth sponsors; one for the young teens, and one for highschoolers.

I visited a typical morning service, which included worship, a twenty or twenty-five minute time of spontaneous sharing, and a sermon. During the sharing time, several of the teens present spoke, as did a number of adults. Afterward, ten teens who attended the morning service stayed and completed a very simple questionnaire. Five girls and five boys participated. Two were 9th graders, four 10th, three 11th, and one 12th. Others who attended the service were not able to stay for the survey.

Of those who completed questionnaires, four considered themselves members of the congregation for less than six months, and four for five years or more.

The questions I asked, and my rationale, were:

(1) *List the first names of adults in the congregation who are your friends.* The goal was to count the number of adults that the teens would designate as "friends."
(2) *How do you define your church?* The goal of this question was to gain some insight into the teen's perception of "church," and see if any relationship between the perception and extended-family symbol would be indicated.
(3) *Why do you come to church?* The goal was simply to see what motivations the teens would identify.
(4) *List the first names of any adults you would like to be like*

in ten or fifteen years. The goal was to see if adults in the congregation functioned as role models.

(5) *Why would you like to become like the person(s) you just listed?* The goal was to find out what it is that attracted the teens, and if any of the motivation was in fact related to Christian faith.

A summary of the results points up a number of suggestive responses and patterns.

Three of the four teens who had come to the Fellowship within the past six months listed as friends 8, 8, and 6 adults, respectively. Inquiry later showed that in two cases, adults had become known prior to the teens coming to the church. The fourth newcomer listed only 2 names, explaining that she had only been coming a month and "didn't hardly know any." The other six teens each listed approximately 8 first names.

Very significant is the fact that the ten teens named 42 *different* adults on their lists. It is evidently not the case at Evergreen Fellowship that only a few adults, those dedicated to youth ministries, have significant relationships with the youth.

The definitions of the church given by the youth were of great interest. One 11th grade boy defined their church as "where people get together to worship Christ the way they think is right," while a 10th grade girl wrote that the church is "a group of people who care for each other and support each other, and they also learn the Word together." Of the ten teens, only one gave a definition without some strong relational dimension. To the youth of Evergreen the church is:

- A group of people with the same religious beliefs that come together as a family and worship the Lord.
- A gathering of Christian people to share happenings and a learning experience of Christian ideals.
- People who care about you and want to share God with you.

It also strikes me as significant that, along with the emphasis on relationships, five of the ten specified worship in their definitions.

Personal reasons for coming to church varied. They included such typical reasons as "being with friends" and "I really don't know" to such things as "the lift I get for going through the week," "you feel very secure," and "I can have fellowship with God."

Of great interest was the response to the request to list adults which the youth would like to be like in ten or fifteen years. The lists were drawn in most cases from adults identified as friends, but in five cases the list also included other adults from the Fellowship. This list was shorter than the "friends" list in each case, and typically identified 2, 3, or 4 individuals. In all but one case, the role models named were of the same sex. One 10th grade girl named two men and two women as her models.

The final question had to do with the qualities or traits about the persons named on the "be like" list that motivated his or her choice. A variety of reasons were given, some of which were typically adolescent. "Carol is outspoken and easy going, plus being caring and intelligent," and "because they seem to have fun and a lot of friends" summed it up for two of the teens. Yet others did mention specific aspects of Christian faith and/or values that attracted them. They mentioned "their honesty and straightforwardness," and the fact that they "have a (seemingly) good life and are happy and love God a lot," as well as "they seem to care for everyone. They include me in their activities. They are just plain beautiful people." To one girl, her models "shine with an inner something . . . love and sincere happiness. Jesus in them is very enthusiastic and is really neat."

The youth seem to be observing the adults closely. Three teens used the word "seem" in describing their role models. To date the adults at Evergreen have not disappointed their young observers.

I conducted this very simple research project in Colorado for several reasons. First, if a theory describes reality with some degree of accuracy, there should be empirical evidence available. I was convinced both theologically and theoretically that a strong case would be made for the impact of a renewal orientation in the church as a context for youth ministry. If the theological and sociological concepts have validity, it should follow that some evidence of meaningful relationships between youth and spiritually sensitive adults would exist in a congregation with a developed renewal lifestyle. I also felt that some evidence that identification processes were at work should exist. I wanted to do some preliminary testing to see if the assumption of empirical evidence was valid.

Second, I wondered if there might be some simple approach which would be adaptable to help generate later experimental designs. Such designs might be useful later in a variety of ways, from raising the awareness of a given congregation to problems, to suggesting hope of attaining in contemporary Christian communities that "extended-family" lifestyle which is a context for "natural" spiritual growth and nurture.

Third, I wondered if the approach might in some preliminary way suggest avenues for further exploration by the Princeton Seminary youth research project steering committee.

FINAL CONSIDERATIONS

If we accept the notion that renewal (and especially the aspects of renewal which emphasize interpersonal "family" relationships across the generations) speaks to the basic needs of youth in our society, what conclusions can we validly draw?

First, we can *not* imply that there is a single "renewal" structure which should be imposed on every local congregation. Many models of congregational life have potential for encouraging a renewal lifestyle. These range from the house church, so readily adapted to intergenerational experiences, to the "small group" church (like the congregation in Colorado, which stresses sharing at the Sunday gatherings), to congregations with very traditional Sunday gatherings, supported by a variety of weekday ministry settings. Our primary concern is not with renewal *structures*, but with a renewal *lifestyle* for the people of God.

Second, we must recognize the fact that the renewal lifestyle extends through the weekday interactions of the congregation. There are to be a number of activities and settings in which youth come into sustained and significant contact with adults and of the congregation. It is characteristic of the believers at Evergreen Fellowship that teens are frequently in the homes of adults, that social activities often include youth and adults, and that the adults of the church actively attend and support the athletic and dramatic activities of their teens in the public schools. There are some peer group activities just for youth. But there are many activities shared regularly and informally by youth and adults.

Third, our extension of the family symbol to the congregation and our renewal perspective on the nature of the church makes it clear that we cannot deal with "youth ministry" as an issue separate from the life of the congregation as a whole. "Youth work" is not a matter of programs which can be organized and conducted in isolation from the total life of the congregation. If the church-as-extended-family is theologically and sociologically essential as a context for the growth of youth in Christian faith, then any approach to youth ministry which fails to deal with the quality of life for the whole congregation must prove inadequate.

REFLECTIONS: Andrew P. Grannell

The thesis of Larry Richards's paper is succinctly stated as follows:

Where this renewal—this recovery of the community as family—is experienced by youth and adults together, we would expect to have healthy processes that promote growth toward Christian maturity at work in youth/adult relationships.

The key terms here are renewal and family. They are linked by the understanding of a multi-aged integrated community. Urie Bronfenbrenner has aptly depicted the chief form of segregation in our present society as "not by race, or social class [and I would add sex] but by age." In this view, we are under a biblical imperative to seek in the church a recovery of a non-age-segregated caring community. Here in Larry Richards's experience and beginning research lies the chief hope, not only for authentic youth ministry, but for the dynamic and ongoing renewal of the local Body of Christ. Much of our discussion has pivoted around this unique, intergenerational, culturally verifiable, and increasingly economically-necessary opportunity or challenge that is the church's.

This is meant to be a suggestive sketch of two empirical probings, long-term personal theological commitments, and I would guess some gut-level hunches. As such, it is a useful exploration which can help us examine more closely one clear option, strategy, model, or approach to ministry with youth. In this spirit of tentativeness, I would like to attempt to accomplish four goals: first, a critique of Richards's use of the term family; second, to attempt to answer the question of the roots of the family in culture or gospel; third, a critique of the stress being placed upon community as family; and finally, a look at the meaning of family from the perspective of faith development theory.

First, I find here no clear theological or sociocultural definition of family. Instead, there is a continuing confusion in this reader's mind as to whether family is a *metaphor* for the Body of Christ, whether it is a *cultural artifact*, *i.e.*, a symbol for intimate relationships, or whether finally, it is used to define the *quality of intergenerational relationships.* I find all three being used at will and at points interchangeably. Certainly, social scientists will want to press for clarity on this matter of definition which is of increasing importance to us all. I would interpret Richards as using the term to refer to the traditional two parent, two generation, bisexual, nuclear unit, but we must then exclude communal, common law, single parent, childless couples, et al. My answer to Larry Richards' question, "Is the symbol of the family something which might be extended to the church of the first century, but is no longer relevant in a modern, technological, industrial society?" is: The symbol of family is in fact *not* a truly representational and inclusive one. As an aside, it would be important to see how the church's families of the first century church were also represented by this supposedly prototypical contemporary model . . . of the family.

Second, Larry Richards asks, "Is the concept (of family) with which we are concerned rooted in the theology or in culture?" In a recent article, James W. Fowler of the Candler School of Theology speaks to this question.

> Karl Barth was right in refusing to use the term family (familia) in his discussion of the Christian ethical understanding of the relation of parents and children in *Church Dogmatics.* The term family, he points out, is of pre-Christian, classical pagan rootage, and as such defines the boundaries of the retinue of a ruler, lord, or military leader. [10]

The term family then is in fact culture bound and can be legitimately viewed as the loose-knit, self-protective, in-grown, indulgent clan so perfectly represented by the television show *Dallas.* We need to take every care to understand youth as being nurtured by a sponsoring, open, disciplined *koinonia.*

Third, I find little evidence in the preliminary research as presented by Dean Hoge that either parents or educators view this renewal through the recovery of community as family as the key desirable means or ends of youth ministry. [11] Of the eight key factors that were isolated out, factor six "Christian fellowship" appears to target much of Larry Richards's concern here. Such items as "come under the influence of spiritually authentic Christians," "forms relationships with mature and trustworthy adults," and "desires to live in a church community of Christians who love and trust each other" speak to the heart of this concern. Yet this cluster/factor rated only a relatively moderate fourth; well down from the top two factors of personal morality and sacraments, and finding a comfortable clustering with "loyalty to denomination" and "personal religious life." Thus, preliminary evidence, except in the cases of the two more conservative denominations, would tend not to support the stress being placed upon youth ministry through recovery of community-as-family.

Finally, we should be aware of the need for adolescents to prepare for their leaving the nurturing community of faith in order to move toward what James Fowler calls the individuative/reflexive (stage four) or what John Westerhoff has more simply recaptioned "owned faith."[12] Again, we need to be aware that the faith ethos of our communities defines the search for social justice, religious questioning/doubts, and cross-cultural awareness. Indeed, it is precisely the confining nature of this synthetic/conventional world view that forces many to leave. In this sense, renewal becomes possible only through rejection of the nominally defined "community-as-family."

These challenges, I hope, will serve to further this exploration. There can be no doubt that the church's continuing renewal is linked inextricably with the manner in which it seeks to confirm and be confirmed by her youth. Only in authentic Christian community can the individual find his/her true freedom.

NOTES

1. From a paper presented to the Annual Meeting of the American Association of Advertising Agencies, given at the Cerromar Beach Hotel, Dorado, Puerto Rico, March 19–22, 1975.

2. Ibid., p. 26

3. Ibid., p. 27

4. Report of Forum 15. White House Conference on Children, Washington, D.C., 1970, p. 2.

5. Herbert C. Kellman, "Compliance, Identification, and Internalization: Three Processes of Attitude Change," *Journal of Conflict Resolution*, No. 2 (1958), pp. 51–60.

6. Adapted from Lawrence O. Richards, *A Theology of Christian Education* (Grand Rapids, Michigan: Zondervan, 1975).

7. The goals suggested by the youth ministers, in order of suggestion, and without necessarily being affirmed by each person present, were: salvation, discipling defined in subsequent discussion as personal maturity, developing love, practicing Christian truth, service, interpersonal relationships, self esteem, ownership of ministry (of the church, or of personal service to others).

8. Lawrence O. Richards, *Three Churches in Renewal* (Grand Rapids, Michigan, Zondervan, 1975), ch. 1.

9. The books and the areas to which they relate, are: servant leadership: *A Theology of Church Leadership*, May, 1980; ministering laity: *A Theology of Personal Ministries*, early 1981; growth emphasis: *A Theology of Christian Education*, 1975. All the books in this series are published by Zondervan.

10. James W. Fowler, "Perspectives on the Family from the Standpoint of Faith Development Theory," *Perkins Journal* 33 (Fall 1979), p. 18.

11. Dean Hoge, et al. chapter 5, above.

12. John Westerhoff, *Will Our Children Have Faith?* (New York: Seabury Press, 1976), p. 98.

Chapter 7

Kairos and Youth: A Call for Community

JACKIE M. SMITH

*Jackie M. Smith is presently living in Charlottes-
ville, Virginia, seeking a lifestyle which is consonant
with her understanding of the gospel mandate: "Follow
me." Formerly a staff executive with the Presbyterian
Church in the United States, she came to feel that the
"church bureaucracy" was failing to address the pressing
social concerns of our time. Although institutions are a
fact of human existence, for the church was instituted
("set up") from the point of its very origin, the Christ/
culture dichotomy has remained a perplexing problem
for the community of faith. Smith insists that our contemporary response to faith must involve youth in prophetic communities which are sensitive to the "new
thing" God is doing in this world.*

THE CHURCH AND WORLD IN THE LATTER PART OF THE 20TH CENTURY

What Are the Signs of Our Time?

> Even the stork in the sky
> knows the appropriate season;

166

> turtle dove, swallow, and crane,
>   observe their time of migration.
> But my people do not know
>   the ruling of Yahweh (Jeremiah 8:7).

It has always been difficult for people within the immediacy of a particular period of history to "discern the signs of their times." To discover what word God is speaking through contemporary events and historical movements requires a kind of standing outside the present context and looking at it with disinterested eyes. Through such a distancing process, it is easier to read the Scriptures impartially so that one can analyze what God's past action and promises for the future indicate about God's activity in and will for the present.

A basic thesis of this chapter is that discerning God's will today is especially difficult for the dominant white church* in the U.S. because it cannot move into a disinterested posture. Our church has become captive to culture by aligning itself with the major controlling powers of our world. We are trapped within an enculturation process that has run full circle. Our perceptions, consciousness, and world view are shaped by the dominant culture. We have grown accustomed to interpreting and reinterpreting the biblical word to support our way of life, our self-interest, and investment in white, Western social values and ways of organizing social, political, and economic life.

A second thesis of this chapter is that through the interrelated crises of our day, God is speaking a word of radical judgment on our present world order. If we could remove our cultural earphones and relinquish our investment in them, we would hear Yahweh's voice affirming that it is end time: the termination of

---

*For convenience throughout this chapter, the word, "church," unless otherwise noted, refers to the dominant white church in the U.S.A. It is this church which is being addressed throughout this essay.

an era, the breaking up of the old order, the shaking of the foundations of the earth itself.

As we listen to the evening news, which one of us does not experience forebodings of doom? We feel uncertain, fearful and anxious. We wish we could shut out such news and simply live our lives through in peace. Yes, we are all too aware that we live in the midst of innumerable and complex crises. But it is extremely difficult for us to acknowledge that these crises point to a basic flaw in our way of life which challenges us to radical change. Who wants to believe that God is speaking to us through Jeremiah affirming that we have forsaken "the fountain of living water and hewed out cisterns . . . that hold no water (2:13)"? Although we see the torrents of water crashing through cracks in our global cisterns, we find it hard to recognize their prophecy of death to our way of life. We are afraid to hope for living water; we still pray for a technological fix or a political/economic miracle.

Let us listen again to some contemporary prophets who believe that the crises we are witnessing indicate God's sharp judgment on the old order.

All the crises of history are converging: racism, sexism, colonialism, the technological depletion of the earth. . . .[1]

Our societies are structured for the unjust privilege of a tiny minority of ruling-class, white males over the majority of people. . . . Our economic system has become global, even if our political systems remain geared to the nation-state. Increasingly, multinational corporations disregard not only the social welfare of the Third World nations from which they exploit raw materials and cheap labor, but even disregard the welfare of the home nation from which they originate. . . . The escalation of the arms race creates a world bristling with missiles and counter-missiles. . . . The very earth, sky, and waters grow poisonous around us as the rich seek profits. . . . For the first time in human history, humanity is faced with the specter of a technological Armageddon. The alternative to the development of a just world is the failure of humanity itself to survive.[2]

Referring to the threats of overpopulation, war, ecological limits, and economic upheaval, Robert Heilbroner, Victor Ferkiss, and Matthew Fox have been warning us:

> The outlook is for... "convulsive change" forced upon us by external events rather than by conscious choice, by catastrophe rather than calculation.... The death sentence.... will permit the continuance of human society but only on a basis very different from that of the present, and probably only after much suffering during a period of transition.[3]
>
> The present convergent crises... have combined to convince all but the most complacent and self-deluded that we are entering upon a new period in world history.[4]
>
> Some scientists feel it is already too late to change both our ways and the deadly direction the... (world) is headed in. Others like Buckminster Fuller, give us seven years to change ourselves and direction.... In many places the lights have already gone out. For example, in areas like Harlem and Mexico City where employment and the pride work brings is limited to only 60 percent of the adult population... and drugs, crime, alcoholism and other symptoms of despair are all that remain to light up people's lives.... The earth hovers on the brink of blowing up.[5]

We must wonder if "the lights have already gone out" for the young prophets quoted below. When asked what they foresee for the year 2001, they answered:

> The concrete begins at the brown, oily water's edge of each continent and stretches right to the other side. The earth is one city.... The earth would explode into fragments.... We all silently close our eyes to wait for the end of our pain.
>
> The human race has stagnated itself by turning life over to science ... there was a worldwide revolution.
>
> By the year 2001 the traditional morals and values will be rare... sex and violence will increase, demoralizing each and every one of us.
>
> I don't believe there will be any religion in 2001. Being caught up

in a modern world will stifle the people so that their religious values will be left behind. They won't even realize that they need God in their lives.

When a baby is born it is separated from its mother and father. Every person would have a place in society already cut out for them. If the person did not meet this role, they may be killed or sent to a prison for further conditioning and fit into the society better.

Family life will be mechanical.

I would like to be a robot. I would enjoy running back and forth . . . when you break down, the family you are living with will send you to the repair shop. [6]

Can the statements above really be the visions of our youth? Traditionally youth are characterized by their hopeful idealism. Such statements cause us to ponder what happens to idealism in a time when reliable sources indicate something like 400 million persons are barely surviving. Fifty million die yearly of starvation. Greater millions struggle for life under repressive governments controlled by powerful elites of the privileged few. Human rights, political and economic, continue to be systemically denied to the majority of humankind through "societal secrets" (Max Weber's term) which hide or seek to justify oppression. Lines of refugees grow, hostages are seized and "terrorism" and violence escalate as frustrated persons seek to extricate themselves from systemic violence. And the familiar cry, "Let my people go!" is echoed from justice movements around the globe.

Yes, to young and old alike it is abundantly clear that time is running out for the old order. With the passage of each hour, the possibility for new life springing from the old order diminishes and the probability of the apocalypse of all order increases. We hear the words of the prophet and know they diagnose our time:

See how Yahweh lays the earth waste,
makes it a desert, buckles its surface,
scatters its inhabitants,
priest and people alike, master and slave,

lender and borrower, creditor and debtor.
Ravaged, ravaged the earth,
despoiled, despoiled,
as Yahweh has said.
The earth is mourning, withering,
the world is pining, withering,
the heavens are pining away with the earth.
The earth is defiled,
under its inhabitants feet,
for they have transgressed the law,
violated the precept,
broken the everlasting covenant.
So a curse consumes the earth.
And its inhabitants suffer the penalty.

(Isaiah 24:1–6)

HOW SHALL WE RESPOND TO OUR TIMES?

Announce Kairos

In a time when converging global crises point to God's judgment on a dying order, the church's most critical task is to announce that judgment with its inherent call to repentance and its challenge for movement into newness of life. A time of judgment offers a *kairos*, a time when conditions are ripe for new decisive actions, a time for new beginnings. Through God's judgment, we are called to announce *kairos* in our acts and words—proclaiming our historical opportunity to acknowledge guilt, to repent and to convert. If we fail to recognize the time as *kairos*, we can expect the convulsive and catastrophic changes Heilbroner feared—some of which we presently experience.

In order for our repentance to lead to a radical newness of life, we must first expose the bankruptcy of our culture, disentangle the Christian gospel from cultural molds, and recover our tradition of faith, permitting "that tradition to be the primal way out of enculturation."[7] This is a prophetic function, described by Walter Brueggemann in this way: "The task of prophetic ministry is to nurture, nourish, and evoke a consciousness and perception alternative to the consciousness and perception of the dominant culture around us."[8] The new alternative consciousness must undergird all justice action and public witness. Otherwise both will serve only to place bandages on a global malignancy, thereby prolonging an illness diagnosed as terminal. Without a new consciousness rooted in an undomesticated identity as the Body of Christ, all our projects, actions, resources, and ministries become empty and powerless tokens—medicinal drops in an ocean of misery.

We can no longer be content with programs that do not call for radical change in our personal and social life; our actions must extend beyond giving relief to the victims and patching up a dying order. Such fragmented efforts produce the illusion of doing something while leaving root evils intact. Through them we are yet clinging to hope that the old order can be saved and save us. It is time to confront the truth that the interrelatedness of all crisis areas points to a deep structural malaise rooted in the values and derivative ways of organizing life in our land. Unless we acknowledge these values and structures as evil and counter to the gospel, we cannot expect newness of life. Until we recognize their illusory, fraudulent nature, the fact that they are death-dealing rather than life-giving, we will be unable to leave them behind. Only through such a repentance can we come to a conversion, grasp the opportunity of our *kairos*, and risk following a God who is radically free from the present regime and who can liberate us from it.

Live Toward a Vision

Our *kairos* calls us to decisive actions anticipating a new kind of life. For Christians this newness of life is not simply extrapolated from the present, because the good news of the gospel is that the world does not have to be organized the way it is.[9] Nor is newness sought in an illusory, unrealistic, idealistic dream. Rather God has given us the shalom vision as a firm foundation from which movement toward new life can be anchored.

Describing shalom, Brueggemann says, "The central vision of world history in the Bible is that all creation is one—every creature in community with every other, living in harmony and security toward the joy and well-being of every other creature."[10] Certainly, for many of us such a vision sounds idealistic or even undesirable since we have been reared in a society that values individualism and competition as key motivating factors for producing personal and social health. Indeed we have so spiritualized, individualized, and rationalized the Bible that we hardly expect our faith to radically transform the very fabric of life in community. Instead we still tend to view social problems as personal problems. We look for "cures" for individual victims of our society through counseling, religion, rehabilitation programs, etc. We fail to recognize the power of social structures and conditions to shape and deform persons and communities. We rarely use the power of our faith to shape corporate life and with it our personal lives—our work, our play, our schooling, our economic and social relationships. The time is ripe for us to desecularize politics and economics. The time is ripe for us to reject society's judgment about what makes the world go round and risk trusting God's promise for creation. Can we recapture God's word, affirming that the creation is intended for shalom *now*— not in some distant, other-worldly future? Can we allow that word to guide us in the common creation of new ways of relating directed toward harmony, unity, interdependence, and mutual security?

If we want to reclaim the power of shalom, we must allow God's promise of *what will be* to produce a creative tension with *what now is*. This tension can inform us about God's present will for shalom, freeing us to turn loose from the way things are and motivating us to join in God's life-giving action. The life of Jesus Christ which enfleshed God's will for shalom illumines our creation of more health-giving ways of relating to one another and the earth. We know we are moving toward shalom when we join Christ's mission announced as the fulfillment of prophetic vision (Luke 4:18–19 [Isaiah 61:1–2]).[11] This vision and mission enlighten our movement toward creative newness of life for all creation.

Later on we will explore concrete steps that can be taken now in movement toward shalom.

Witness to the Brokenness of Shalom

We have looked at the positive function of shalom as it opens up totally new possibilities for the present and the future. The other function of the vision is that it becomes "a measuring rod for testing the present system sternly revealing its hypocrisies and injustice."[12] In this section, using shalom as a rod of measurement, we will examine two basic contemporary expressions of corporate evil.

To expose corporate evil is very difficult, since all of us have been reared to value the belief systems and social structures which result in social sin. As Ron Sider declares, "One can be ensnarled (in structural evil) and hardly even recognize it."[13] Gregory Baum compares the resulting social sin to an illness into which we are born. Through social conditioning, our inherited social blinders prevent us from seeing injustice built into our systems, institutions, and structures. The complex interconnectedness of contemporary crises becomes another blinder preventing us from seeing how our lifestyles contribute to systemic exploitation of our neighbor—near and distant, human and nonhuman, present and future. Indeed, "this false consciousness persuades us that the evil we do is in fact a good thing in keeping with the aim and purpose of our collective well-being. Examples . . . (are) the achievement orientation of the dominant culture, its individualistic and competitive spirit, and our arrogant collective self-understanding with its implicit racism."[14]

Today there are two crucial and interlocking sources of brokenness which deny the shalom vision of wholeness without bounds. They are how our culture (1) views human security and (2) participates in hierarchical thinking and structuring. Although we will be dealing with youth experience later in this chapter, it will be helpful as you read to reflect on how a young person born in the sixties experiences a world with these basic distortions of shalom.

Seeking Security. As has been true in most ages and generations, citizens in the U.S. are led to believe that life is basically about securing their physical existence, that the good life consists in an abundance of bigger barns. Today as in other times we cannot really "live toward the joy and well-being of every other creature" for the values which organize our lives and direct our actions contradict shalom. Are we, more than persons in other eras, expected to be responsive to the gospel? Can we take seriously radical words such as: "Be not anxious about your life . . ." and "You cannot serve God and mammon"? (Matthew 6:25 and 24) Can we be expected to move counter to a culture which assures us that security is in mammon?

Every day through the pervasiveness of media, we and our youth are urged to:

—put ourselves in the hands of Prudential
—improve our relationships with Close-Up
—enhance ourselves with techniques and products
—support transnational corporations who are "protecting" our environment
—worship free enterprise because it allows a parttime newspaper carrier in the U.S. to earn more in a month than the yearly wage of Third World persons
—support what Matthew Fox terms our "lemming-like race to arm ourselves" through seeking a balance of terror.

In our daily experience, economic growth and power is promoted as a primary social good and we are led to believe that control of, power over, and possession and use of material goods (and indeed persons and nations) can secure our existence.

In a pressured, fear-filled world, we dare not give up its kind of activity—its kind of securing—to risk more life-giving values and ways of relating. We are too ensnarled, too confused by complexity, too filled with anxiety and tension, too busy getting, too busy in analysis, too busy writing papers, too busy securing this or that or the other thing.

And yet it is abundantly clear that a basic source of fear, anxiety, and pressured lifestyles is our way of relating to the earth and distributing its gifts. The root issue of our time is an economic issue—how we manage our household, the global community. We have founded and continue to revere an economic system premised on greed and the exploitation of people and the earth. By institutionalizing greed, we permit the economic system to be greedy on our behalf and "we know not what we do." By operating within that economic system, we legitimate and sustain demonic powers and principalities: mammon, as Jesus labeled it. We have deified maximization of profit and control. We have given homage to a system which now controls us by dictating how we shall meet our basic existence needs. It creates false needs and gives us a major identity as consumers. Indeed the system envelops us in a way of life which is life-destroying to us and others.

In allowing the amassing of power and wealth in gigantic transnational corporations, we have turned the management of the entire globe over to a powerful economic elite whose power exceeds most nations and who dictates to all nations. The irony of our captivity is seen in the fact that these global managers are now managed by the system we have legitimated. "And the churches are implicated in the system right up to their steeples, both as legitimators of the satanic values which makes exploitation so easily tolerable to Christians, and as dependents on the financial overflow of its wealthier contributors."[15]

A major reason that we have allowed this amassing of demonic power is that we have cherished a very narrow, exclusive version of shalom—health and wholeness for us, our kind, our nation, our generation. We have ignored how radically the Bible understood the relation of God, persons, and nature in shalom. "The geography of shalom extends to the whole globe. We are to seek shalom not only in our own community, but across political and social boundaries. . . . Shalom is not simply human property, but it is that relationship of wholeness between ourselves and nature as well. The duration of shalom is to all generations."[16]

Participating in Hierarchy. A second source of brokenness of shalom is hierarchy. It is perhaps the most demonic social structure since it infects all other social structures, personal relationships, our relationships with God and nature, our thought processes and means of valuing. Although the biblical vision of shalom leaves no room for such an insidious ladder concept, hierarchy has been regarded as the divinely ordained order of creation.

We are all perhaps aware of how hierarchical thinking has "become the foundation for superstructures of sexism, racism, and anti-Semitism,"[17] but I doubt that we are yet fully aware of the extent to which it has infected our thought, valuing, and everyday experience.

Hierarchy linked with patriarchy has produced a one-sided spirituality, anthropology, psychology, sociology, and theory of economics. It has distorted the way we perceive and use our freedom and power for "dominion and control." Hierarchy has distorted our understanding of human nature, our theories about growth and development; thereby molding our educational institutions and influencing our understanding of meaningful work and play.

When we reflect on human behavior valued by the dominant

culture, we see the influence of hierarchy, arm in arm with patriarchy. A list may be illuminating:

Individualism, competition, aggression
Survival of the strongest, win/lose mentality
The psychology of more, progress/questing mentality
Success and achievement orientation
Exaggerated competence/efficiency drives
Control/domination
Classism, elitism, militarism, nationalism

As Fox points out, "Phallicism, the worship of upness, remains America's dominant religion."[18]

Linked with our economic system in a symbiotic fashion, hierarchy/patriarchy has become a powerful tool for separating, evaluating, and oppressing. It fosters divisiveness and control within a global community created for pluralism, unity, and interdependence. Again we can do nothing more than to list a few of these divisions preventing shalom:

God-human, male-female, old-young, white-black, heterosexual-homosexual, Jew-Gentile, professional-laborer, parent-child, rich-poor, employer-employee, teacher-student, strong-weak, powerful-powerless, we-they, clergy-laity, humanity-nature, mind-matter, reason-emotions, spiritual-sensual, soul-body, first world-third world, nation-state, nation-nation.

Structuring life with these divisions and for nurturance of these kinds of values, needs, activities, and concepts has often persuaded us that indeed they are essential components of human nature and necessary for collective health. In reality they originate with destructive ways of patterning human life and violate our humanness. The brand of human "fulfillment" encouraged by hierarchical thinking can never be "achieved" in shalom but rather must be sought struggling up a never-ending ladder, ultimately destroying one another.

Invite Corporate Conversion

In the preceding section, we looked at two root sources of brokenness deeply ingrained in contemporary social systems. Both hierarchy and our economic arrangements perpetuate evil among us without any one of us consciously choosing behavior which would bring harm to another part of creation. Instead we unintentionally collude with evil forces in our world.[19] Such evil cannot be healed by individual efforts any more than could any one of us take total responsibility for our continued involvement in racism or sexism. Personal conversion and transformation will not change the system, even if individual transformation were possible. The person who wants to change finds herself powerless to do so alone. This reality points to our need for a social transformation which can only come about by corporate conversion. We, like the Hebrews in Egypt, face a *kairos* indicating it is liberation time—we are called to leave the old order behind. And as was true with the Hebrews, our liberation will be communal or not at all.

Gregory Baum emphasizes the corporate nature of our task, saying:

> To promote the illusion that personal piety and personal conversion can interject Christian values into society blinds people to the inherent power of society over consciousness, to the extent that Christians preach personal conversion and hold out the hope for the extension of private values to the public order, they pull the wool over people's eyes and . . . actually help perpetuate the system that generates egotism. The recommendation of virtue can be, under certain circumstances, the legitimation of an unjust social order . . . . For while people may nourish their ideals from a great religious tradition, but participate in economic life, they acquire a new self-understanding, and even without recognizing it, they are transformed in accordance with the public ideals of profit and competition. We become concerned with promoting our own careers; we think of our advantage . . . . We dream of a government that keeps society tidy,

protects property and investments, and leaves us alone to live out our private life without disruption, apart from the work we do to make money and promote our careers, we want to live a private existence, have a good time, enjoy our hobbies, escape suffering, and remain free of obligations. A lively weekend at the summer house on the lake—this makes it all worthwhile. That's the life.[20]

To know that there is something more to life than that, we must recapture the validity and allure of the values inherent in shalom, knowing that the call of shalom is to a people. Communally we can repent of our present attachments to mammon and of our participation in hierarchy. Together we can return to a God who has liberated communities in the past from false consciousness, expecting that God will help us answer two major questions raised by our past allegiance to false gods:

How can we find security in a finite world?

How can life be structured for shalom for the *total* creation?

In the asking of these questions we will be more open to God's present activity expressed through the crises of our day. We will be more responsive to new life-giving options that God is opening by breaking up contemporary powers and principalities.

Yes, it is God who calls us through this *kairos*. We are called to renew our covenant with God and with our sisters and brothers. In that company, we can move into a new enabling consciousness, the starting point for the creation of new social structures that embody shalom and insure the full participation of the total creation in shalom. This is a corporate endeavor.

In the ensuing pages of this chapter we will explore concrete ways this corporate endeavor might be initiated, focusing sharply upon ministry with youth.

PROPHETIC COMMUNITIES AND YOUTH

The Need for Prophetic Communities

The basic conclusion I must draw from my understanding of God's activity in our world today is that God's judgment on our world order is expressed through contemporary converging crises. If we are to accept God's judgment and the *kairos* contained in it, our basic task becomes that of relinquishing support of and involvement in activities and structures that currently result in suffering, distortion, and destruction. This can only be done by engaging in new styles of living grounded firmly in values inherent in *shalom*. Through this common venture, we can generate free spaces where small beginnings of a new world order emerge and a new consciousness is nurtured.

This means that *a central focus for ministry with youth should be that of identifying or generating small prophetic communities of persons who are radically involved with other Christians of all ages, endeavoring to enflesh the gospel in both individual and corporate life.*

Critical times call for radical decisions. If we recognize our times as a *kairos*, then we know radical repentance and conversion must occur. No more business as usual! I do not believe that we can hope for the corporate conversion of the whole church. There is little hope for valid youth ministry in a church enslaved by culture. The church as it is has little identity of its own through which youth can be nurtured in their search for identity and faith. Entangled in a death struggle with false gods, the church cannot reveal the living God who calls for radical and life-giving commitment.

At such a time we are called to let go of the old struggles, deny old loyalties and securities and venture out into a new unknown with Sarah and Abraham.

There are within every congregation persons who are ready for such a venture. They are the persons who perceive the signs of our times. Many are all too aware of their complicity in the evil-being-judged and feel desperate in their powerlessness to bring change. Such persons can be empowered by the biblical vision to risk relinquishment of the old and to give loyalty to the forgiving, liberating God who does new things. Many of these persons know "we die when we settle for the limited possibilities

of a dying order . . . . We come alive and become agents of transformation when we begin to live now the as-yet unrealized possibilities around us, whose time has come."[21]

Let me emphasize that I am not suggesting that such adults be
asked to be in ministry with a group labeled "youth." The setting,
environment and style of life within the traditional church would
contradict and jeopardize what they might do and become. Nor
am I suggesting that such adults be involved with youth in a
"social concerns" group within the life of the church. Vis-à-vis
the crises of our day, our basic task is *not* simply to address
individual public issues, as critical as each may be. Each issue is
only a symptom pointing to the demise of the old order. Our
challenge is not to rally youth to one social action cause or
another or to "find one that interests" them (even the draft).

Rather, I am pointing to the crucial undertaking of building
community among those youth and adults, families and individuals who are in touch both with their own powerlessness
against the pressures of today's society and the promise of real life
from a powerfully free, liberating God.

Such communities can begin "living toward the vision" of the
utter unity of the entire creation anticipated in Ephesians 1:3–
10.[22] They can create life together "as if" there were no dividing
walls of hierarchy separating person from person and persons
from earth.[23] By living an "as if" life together, gradually a new
way of seeing life evolves, influencing all of life within and outside the community, and energizing further movement toward
liberation from the dominant culture in the church and the
world.

I do not envision these Christian communities as being es-
capist, sectarian-style communities, self-righteously segregating
themselves and intent on securing for themselves a "cheap
shalom." Rather, I am talking about persons who are willing to
risk Luther's admonition to "sin boldly, but believe in Christ, and
rejoice more boldly still." Such people are willing to experiment

with and learn from the new, in anticipation of God's shalom. They have what David Riseman calls "the nerve of failure—that is, the ability to face the possibility of defeat without feeling morally crushed."[24] Knowledge of God's gracious forgiveness and will for shalom frees such persons to risk trial and error, knowing there will be both failure and sin in any human endeavor.

It is within communities of this kind of folks that youth can and should be invited—no, challenged—to enter, not just to be taught nor to have their needs met according to our culturally determined developmental stages, not to be served or segregated, but rather to become full partners in the community's ministry.

Theological Reasons for Prophetic Communities

From a theological perspective against the background of our times, the need for attention to community-building is threefold:

1. *Jesus Christ revealed embodied truth:* truth that must be incarnated in flesh and blood—truth that is revealed only as it is lived—truth that is learned only as it is done and witnessed. It is no mere coincidence that after saying, "I *am* the way, and the truth, and the life," Jesus moves on to say that the person "who believes in me will also *do* the works I do; and greater works than these," because the Counselor, the Holy Spirit, the Spirit of Truth will dwell in believers, *doing* Christ's work. (John 14:6, 12–14)

2. *The Spirit does not dwell solely in individuals.* Rather the fullness of the work of the Spirit is expressed through the corporate body, the body of believers who enflesh God's truth. It is this corporate body growing into oneness with Christ and God that expresses in fullness the living truth through works of justice, peace, compassion, and reconciliation. The body of Christ is the incarnated Word moving toward God's "plan for the fullness of time, to unite all things" in heaven and earth in God. Again, it is not mere happenstance that the first acts of Jesus' ministry were to

draw together a community of disciples and that Pentecost occurred in a group gathered.

3. *Then and now individuals working alone are relatively powerless within society.* They are formed and deformed, pushed and pulled by the historical context. If the corporate principalities and powers of our day are to be denied their demonic control of individual and communal life, the Word and truth must be incarnated in the corporate body of Christ, revealing in word and act God's shalom. By God's choice, truth is not belief or doctrine entombed in words, rational thought or printed page. Instead God's truth is *experienced* in acts of justice and love embodied by communities of believers. It is this kind of revelation of incarnated truth for which the whole creation waits in eager longing (Romans 8:18ff).

Youth's Acute Need for Faith-filled Community

If Christian truth is most fully revealed within faith-filled communities, then it seems clear that a church shaped by its culture cannot nurture its youth into full Christian commitment. Youth, reared during the latter part of the sixties and the seventies, witnessed what Ronald Enroth labels a "spiritual counterfeit . . . a Christianity which has been squeezed so far into the world's mold that all distinguishing authenticity has been squeezed out of it."[25]

Let's recall the kind of nurturance that kind of church/world provided for the present generation of youth. The historical period from a North American perspective might be characterized as one of extreme disillusionment. As Morris Dickstein describes it, it was a time of "pinched possibilities, failed Utopian visions, exhausted psychological resources."[26] During the seventies not only did we witness the bursting of our economic bubble which promised growing security and abundance for all but we also discovered that although wants and technological ingenuity may be infinite, natural resources are not. "The belief in 'progress' that sustained over a century of technological growth has literally and figuratively run out of steam. The faith that unlimited economic growth could do away with poverty and inequity without challenging the basic distribution of wealth and power in the country (and world) has proven to be an illusion."[27]

In addition, we have given this generation of youth a generative period of national and international political turmoil with oppressive social systems being countered by rebellions and revolutions, violence and wars, nuclear threat and protest, assassinations, racism, political corruption, and the list could go on and on.

When we reflect on this span of history which has shaped our young people today, it seems obvious that radical measures are called for and that the co-opted church cannot help young persons hear or respond to the radical call of the gospel. With no clear, sure word from the church, individual youth or even groups of youth must feel powerless when confronted with the immediate past and the magnitude and complexity of crises in the immediate present. Even if they could hear the gospel with clarity, how can they respond to the revolutionary call: "Follow me"?

Is not this the fast that I choose:
to loose the bonds of wickedness,
to undo the thongs of the yoke,
to let the oppressed go free,
and to break every yoke.

Is it not to share your bread with the hungry,
and to bring the homeless poor into your home,
when you see the naked, to cover them,
and not to hide yourself from your own flesh?

(Isaiah 58:6–7)

When confronted with this call for commitment in our kind of world, youth response is likely to be like those of their elders whose words are echoed in Beckett's *Waiting for Godot:*

VALDIMIR: "Well, what do we do?"

ESTRAGON: "Don't let's do anything; it's safer."

In a world like ours, a passive despairing may seem an appropriate response, especially if you have been effectively segregated in a world of schooling which indicates you have no real responsibility except to focus intensely on your own development as prescribed by society in preparation for a future which may not arrive. I am reminded of, "Even youth shall faint and be weary" (Isaiah 50:30). It is any surprise that 400,000 high school students attempted suicide in 1978 and another million ran away from home?[28] It seems appropriate that we are witnessing among youth a decline in social consciousness and a rise in a personalistic, pietistic spirituality and/or hope in nightmarish visions of new technological Utopias. It is no wonder that many young people turn to escape through buying into traditional means of securing their futures (buying into the system) and/or seeking immediate refuge in drugs, pietistic and authoritarian religious movements, the psychology of more . . . and more, and instant intimacy. When an old order is crumbling, everything seems to be in flux and "up for grabs."

Youth and the Shape of Radical Christian Community

As Michael Warren suggested in 1978, youth need to enter a community of the faith-filled and to be a part of the total ministry of that community entering a lifelong effort toward growth in community.[29] Such complete involvement in the ministry of a faith-filled community would meet one of the basic needs of youth pointed to by James Coleman and others. They state that youth both need and want broader social involvement than is presently possible in societal structures which compartmentalize and segregate youth. These structures deny youth fulfilling activity, responsibility, and impact on the real world, including the church. A church community can provide one setting in which stratification by age is not given homage and this dividing wall is broken down. Young people could then experience the self-validation that occurs when persons are invited and challenged to responsible action. Through radical involvement within an organic community of mission, youth would have the opportunity for interdependent life with others living toward a commonly held vision validated by God. They would experience collaborative efforts in which the outcome depends on the gifts and faith of all. Supported by others in common and individual endeavors, they could overcome the sense of powerlessness so prevalent in our times—especially among youth who still experience areas of dependency in family, school, and communal life.

Within prophetic communities:

1. Young persons would have a broader, more creative social network for constructing their sense of personal identity through close communion with adults who are not traditional authority figures—an experience not readily available to many youth. Indeed, the community itself would be in search of identity, seeking to move outside hierarchical ways of structuring and thinking about life and beyond life-defining roles of sex, race, class, etc. Such a community would contain new models, youth and adult, who demonstrate the value of commitment and an emerging understanding of what it means to be human. In this expanded human network, youth could more fully explore their uniqueness and experience the effects of their person and actions on others, consequently learning about the responsible use of freedom in community. Perhaps the exaggerated drive for autonomy expressed in our society would be altered by experiences of creative conflict-resolution and the joyful experience of reciprocity and building together. Within an organic community, the abilities of all can be valued and utilized, giving each the experience of being "leader" as well as "follower," receiver as well as giver.

2. The community would contribute needed psychic support

to the adolescent, perhaps easing pressure on the nuclear family and thereby enhancing such support within families. Strengthened by creative interaction across age, racial, economic, and sexual barriers, peer pressure should diminish. Empowered by the community, these youth could become vital influences for shaping norms within outside peer groups. The need for group identity would be partially met within a community that did not establish its sense of identity as over against others. Participation in a community that perceived its major vocation as that of being radically "for and with" others would clearly influence all other social involvements.

3. Interdependent, collaborative activity would counter the self-centeredness and competitiveness built into the worlds of young people which contribute to the extreme individualism that eats away at our society.

4. Moving outside special roles and places presently assigned to them, youth could experiment with new expressions of their whole person, using gifts and abilities which now lie dormant—especially in the arena of significant activity that contributes to the health of the larger community.

5. Experiencing a truth which is lived would broaden youths' understanding of faith, truth, and knowledge, all of which have been narrowly defined in our rationalistic, technological society. This fact alone would have life-changing implications, affecting the way persons perceive the nature and purpose of human existence.

6. Being part of a community which is wrestling with God in the midst of a complex and confusing historical period, youth would be included in a communal process of discovering and enfleshing that which is worthy of human commitment. "If any one is in Christ," a community covenanted to God, that person is a new creation. (2 Corinthians 5:17) Within such a community, youth's struggle for faith, fidelity, and commitment would not be viewed as a developmental task to be accomplished in one brief

period of life. Instead, in solidarity, the community itself would be living into fuller commitment to and knowledge of God. This vital, organic, open process would become a steadying force within a period of growth often characterized as extremely complex and confusing. The process would be guided and shaped by values, styles of being and relating inherent in the shalom vision.

In the final sections of this paper, we will be looking at:

1. Guiding values and styles of being within prophetic communities
2. Styles of relating to the larger community

GUIDING VALUES AND STYLES OF BEING WITHIN PROPHETIC COMMUNITIES

Experimental and Creative

A basic goal for prophetic communities should be to shape a social context in which members could experience taking control of their individual and communal lives, using their freedom and creativity to bring into existence new options and alternatives. At a time when traditional theories for social organization are bankrupt and present systems are closed and self-destructive, the idealism, enthusiasm, imagination, and creativity of youth can play a determinative role.

The present is a moment for a creativity that flows out of experience of the organic interdependence and finitude of the whole created order. It is a time for creativity which moves toward shaping new social structures that insure the full participation of all parts of the creation in movement toward shalom. As Carl Rogers has warned, without such creativity "the lights will go out." "Whether we are talking about making work or living situations more compassionate, about economic systems, issues of food, energy, or nuclear proliferation, unemployment or over-employment, boredom or alcoholism, creativity lies at the heart of relieving the pain. We need a new way of living and working if the species *homo sapiens* is to survive. And maybe we need a *new kind of homo sapiens.*"[30] An underlying dream of any prophetic community would be to work toward new patterns of socialization through which a new kind of homo sapiens may arise. To discover these new patterns, an action/reflection mode of operation would be essential so that the community could learn from their own experiences.

Justice and Compassion

Within prophetic communities the central norm for shaping and testing new ways of living together would be the biblical understanding of justice and compassion. Nurturing and action would strive toward a justice which does not "judge" what one does or does not deserve. Rather it will try to reflect God's justice which always expresses concern and love for the weak, the oppressed, those in need. Structuring for justice means creating ways of relating to one another and the earth so that all are cared for and share in meaningful life.

Recovering the meaning of compassionate living is especially needed in a period when we are forced to acknowledge limits and the web of connectedness of the whole created order. Thomas Merton reminded us that "the whole idea of compassion is based on a keen awareness of the interdependence of all living beings, which are all part of one another and all involved in one another."[31] What could be more appropriate in our world?

In summary fashion, Matthew Fox states that "To be compassionate is to incorporate one's fullest energies with cosmic ones in . . . (1) relieving the pain of fellow creatures through justice-making, and (2) celebrating the existence, time, and space that all creatures share as a gift from the only One who is fully compassionate. Compassion is our kinship with the universe and the universe's maker; it is the action we take because of that kinship."[32] Prophetic communities are called to create structures and styles of living expressing compassion and justice.

Freedom and Simplicity

Seeking to live in compassion and justice involves a radical reorientation of values and use of freedom for most persons. Prophetic communities will be trying to recover the meaning and quality of the life abundant promised by Jesus. To do so, the vision of life abundant must be extricated from linkage with quantitative, affluent life orientations. In a time when persons are often numbed by pressured existence and escape into the consumptive, passive, plastic pleasures of affluence, they may need to rediscover ways they can enjoy themselves, others, and the earth more fully. Our society as a whole needs to recover the joy of ordinary life, meaningful work, and natural ecstasies of learning, creating, and simply being and enjoying God's good creation. This is the positive side of simple living efforts which can allure youth and adults alike.

It must, however, go hand in hand with "an understanding of what we do not need, rather than one that operates out of fantasies of all the things we can or should have."[33] In a consumer economy which preys on the substitution of wants that are insatiable for needs that are necessary and satiable, this will be a difficult task—perhaps especially for youth who are denied full freedom and responsibility in the larger society and who are "educated" for a superficial, pseudo-freedom which finds expression in consumerism. The fact that youth have been given a major identity role as consumers to satisfy the needs of our economic system, points to an especially formidable task for prophetic communities. It has been estimated that by the end of high school, young people have viewed some 350,000 commercials.

This experience alone not only causes extreme confusion between wants and needs but also distorts youths' (and adults')
understanding of freedom.

Speaking of our confusion about the meaning of freedom,
Michael Novak says:

> Freedom in the U.S. too often reduces to a consumer's freedom: To
> use Crest rather than Ipana, to take social science 108 instead of
> political science 202, to work for J & L instead of LTV . . . to live in
> Rosewood rather than Rosemont. Americans have external freedoms,
> but these are not the freedoms of self-transcendence. The freedom
> which makes (persons) wonder about their identity is that which
> shakes their identity to its core . . . makes demands on them, draws
> them into the pit of nothingness in order to confront them: "now
> choose." . . . Freedom is creation out of nothingness: an act of self-
> affirmation. . . . It is in exercising such freedom, brooding over an
> inner chaos, that (persons act) in the image of the God spoken of in
> the myth of Genesis."[34]

In a day when we and our youth are manipulated by media and
our production-oriented economy as well as by world events,
institutions, structures, and prescribed identity roles, recovering
our life-forming freedom is an arduous struggle. Freedom from
these pressures will involve a sense of loss and grieving. It is
painful to let go of the enticing promises of materialistic security
and dreams of power, control, and recognition. It is fearful indeed to choose to follow one who revealed the fullness of freedom
through healing the sick, feeding the hungry, freeing the captive,
confronting the powers, and accepting the cross. The decision to
use life-forming freedom in this manner can only be made within
a nurturing community of persons who support group and personal efforts to shape destinies in the likeness of Christ. Such
radical use of human freedom will not bring success or security as
the world views it, but as Dorothy Day reminds us, "If we had an
understanding and love of poverty (simplicity) we would begin to
be as free and as joyous as St. Francis, who had a passion for Lady

Poverty, and lives on with us in joyous poverty through all the centuries since his death."[35]

For youth and adults to exercise authentic freedom, it will be necessary for communities to provide new experiences and environments in which persons experience the joy that accompanies a life of compassionate simplicity. Some of these include:

1. *The security and joy found in God's love* from which "neither death . . . nor anything else in all creation will be able to separate us" (Romans 8:37–38). The power of this love can be recovered as it is actually incarnated in the community. Then and then only will persons be able to relinquish former securities by experiencing the liberation from threat and fear envisioned in 1 John 4:18–21.

As with the early Christians (Acts 4:32ff), experiences within a compassionate community might lead members to experiment with a more just and equitable sharing of meaningful work and the "fruits" of work—both within and outside the community. Some form of economic sharing might arise to free the community from inordinate resource and service needs. These might include: equipment and clothing exchanges, cooperative farming ventures, exchange of "professional" services or responsibilities for care of children or the bedridden. It is easy to imagine all the gifts youth would have to offer, the learnings gained, and the needs met.

Some communities might even consider sharing living space and/or a redistribution of resources through income pooling. Clearly experiencing one's self to be an essential part of a trustworthy organic whole diminishes one's fear and need to establish and secure identity in terms of control, achievement, or acquisition. Such "freedom from" provides the foundation for freedom to create yet unthought possibilities.

2. *The joy of the interconnectedness of all life*. Often the simple act of being and interacting with the natural world in non-time-pressured, nonexploitative, nonviolent ways is enough to start

one on the road to recapturing the mystic experience of knowing that we *belong* to the earth. Within natural, simple settings persons are better able to name the things they do not need and do not want. Often as people experience the organic unity and wonder of all life, they realize the hollowness of much of our attempts at "entertainment." Certainly the camping and retreat resources already controlled by the church offer unlimited possibility for playing a major role in enabling persons to become more aware of:

—the demonic aspects of "the immemorial human warfare against nature"[36]

—the joys of a simple life which embrace the reciprocity of all creatures and the earth itself.

Prayer and Worship

Prophetic communities will not have the imagination for creative change or the power for just and compassionate living unless they allow their tradition of faith to lead them out of captivity. As Bonhoeffer reminded us, "Our being Christian today will be limited to two things: prayer and righteous action. . . . All Christian thinking, speaking, and organizing must be born anew out of this prayer and action."[37] All too often in the past, Christians involved in social justice concerns have allowed the very nerve of their action to be severed by neglecting nurturance in the faith. New communities will need to avoid this pitfall. Metanoia occurs only as the memory of God's past action is brought into dialectic tension with the present and persons are motivated to live toward God's vision for the future. In this dynamic interplay, perceptions and mindsets are transformed. It is by giving expression to this transformation in worship, prayer, and ritual that persons are empowered into a new identity and action. Social values are communicated and kept alive through rituals; consequently, to express different values through communal worship and prayer is to disrupt the dominant culture's chain of communicating values.[38]

Nurturance is given as communities worship, sharing struggle, pain, grief, and guilt, as well as hope, thanksgiving, praise, celebration, the breaking of bread, and the hearing of the Word.

STYLES OF RELATING TO THE LARGER COMMUNITY

Hearing the Oppressed—Listening to God

To nurture an alternative consciousness within prophetic communities, intense dialogue with persons who are among the most oppressed is critical. As Bonhoeffer observed, "There remains an experience of incomparable value... to see the great events of world history from below, from the perspective of the outcast, the suspect, the maltreated, the powerless, the oppressed, the reviled—in short, from the perspective of those who suffer."[39] Although we all, Pharoahs as well as slaves, are oppressed by contemporary powers and principalities, the majority of the white church is not fully aware of its own oppression; therefore, it cannot view radically structures of destruction and death. Until we see our global crises from the perspective of those who are most aware of their suffering under evil forces in our world, we are unlikely to be able to move far from our limiting and limited world view. We will be tempted to let go of what Segundo calls "ideological suspicion" and fall back into traditional methods of defusing and entombing God's Word. We will be tempted to return to old security gods and maintaining things as they are. This temptation is lessened as communities place themselves in a listening posture, hearing the cries of the oppressed which expose not only demonic powers but also the agony of God. It is among those who suffer most that God's will always surfaces and manifests itself in justice and compassion (Exodus 3:7–8).

It is in this arena that the oppressed affluent can join in solidarity with the poor and powerless. As we gain a more complete experience of the consequences of structuring life as it is, we also see more clearly our own complicity through collusion in those unjust systems. We are awakened to our enslavement in them and our oppression under them.

In addition to listening to the oppressed, we need to be doing Bible study and theologizing with them. Against the backdrop of the harsh conditions of our world, there is a need to wrestle with the fresh new word God is speaking through liberation theologians. Perhaps then we will know more clearly what God is doing and be liberated from our "ideological captivity."[40]

Within such a context, we can begin asking questions we have never asked before. Within such a context, we will take more seriously the radical word God speaks through the lived experience and the biblical text. This step alone will create a revolutionary change in the human community as it did in the time of Joshua, the prophets and reformers, and Vatican II. "We must continually take time and invest creativity into listening to our people, especially the poor. For it is they who, out of their frustrations, dreams, and struggles, must lead the way for all of us."[41]

Youth's Contribution in Hearing the Oppressed. Youth can bring a unique psychological and social perspective to the broader community. As previously noted, they are themselves victims of a social order which provides prescribed roles for shaping their identity and activity and which limits them to second-class citizenship. They participate in a view from below, for they are outside the power structure. Thus youth can be more objective and less defensive than many adults in hearing the oppressed by virtue of the simple fact that they have fewer years of cultural conditioning and investment in the status quo. They can be more open to seeing things as they are for persons at the bottom of our economic ladder. From their position of "underdog," children and youth have always raised "inappropriate," embarrassing, and critical social and economic observations and questions.[42] These perceptions need not be silenced within a prophetic community which would view them as valuable contributions.

As was true in the protest of the sixties, youth can still play a significant part in opening up the inconsistencies and contradictions between stated belief and practice and between cultural and biblical values. I believe that youth can return to this valuable role within a community of hope. Even though young people often tend to think that seeing and talking about a problem is equivalent to solving it, by working within a larger community, appropriate actions can be planned and implemented with heavy youth involvement.

Providing a setting in which youth of classist churches can interact with other victims of our social and economic systems places them in a space where open rapport can enliven empathy, caring, concern, and passion. Such settings provide much-needed multi-cultural education by crossing age, race, class, faith, and national barriers. Finding kinship with the broader human community, and joy and excitement in diversity, youth may experience the desire and need to break out of cliquish behavior which often characterizes youth socialized in a hierarchical thinking culture.

Dialogue with the oppressed can awaken the social conscience of youth as they begin to uncover:

1. Oppressions and needs which are as "bad" as or worse than their own
2. Connections between personal acts, attitudes and values and the way life has been structured in the community and world
3. Consequences of consumptive/affluent lifestyles on other groups of persons and the earth
4. The web of interconnectedness within all life
5. The social implications of individual and communal acts from the perspective of the Christian faith.

Understanding that can come from hearing the oppressed

places youth in a better position to do critical political analysis of their own position in society. Through such analysis, youth will recognize that many youth problems and hurts are social problems which cannot be healed by individual perseverance, escape relief, religion, education, or therapy.[43] In this posture, youth could assist adults and other young people in identifying where problems are rooted in socialization patterns and social structures. Through this process, those who are both oppressor and oppressed can experience a shared humanity with the national and international Third World, as well as with groups of feminists, homosexual persons, persons from ethnic minorities, and the elderly in this country. At this point, people are ready to work in true solidarity with the most oppressed, seeking a mutual liberation from the same sources of evil.

Although this process will open up untold pain and hurt, it need not trigger disillusionment and apathy. The experience of solidarity can generate empowerment, especially within communities assured by God's past and present action for justice and liberation. Within such communities, the proverbial idealism and enthusiasm of youth can find expression and give health to the total community.

Bonding—Justice Making

Along with listening to the oppressed, prophetic communities will want to join with them and others within our global community who struggle for justice. Although often such movements are marginal, many of them do radically address public institutions and values and engage in action for structural change. These advocacy and action movements include:

1. Those focusing on root economic issues such as some of the world hunger groups, those concerned about corporate power and transnationals, etc.
2. Victims of our society who are engaged in liberational

struggles such as those radically addressing the criminal justice systems and those exposing hierarchy and paternalism, whether in its racial, sexual, or economic expressions (nationally or internationally)

3. Those seeking to extricate themselves from consumptive/affluent/highly technological lifestyles and those experimenting with alternative ways of living in community and relating to the earth

4. Those involved in efforts related to militarism, nuclear power, the energy crises, and other related ecological and technological concerns.

5. Those alienated from the dominant culture who are seeking to expose the exile-producing power of our dominant culture, such as the Gray Panthers and the Gay Rights movements.

Instead of falling back into old traps of thinking that the church alone can do correct analysis, or instigate positive change with study groups, church pronouncements, and simplistic, peripheral "social action projects," prophetic communities need to establish close identification with some justice movements that are attacking root issues, working with them and learning from them. This means that discovering linkages and building networks with justice movements and other prophetic communities is crucially important if we are to: (1) avoid the pitfalls of fragmented social justice efforts which cannot mobilize enough energy to bring about structural change, (2) uncover the web of interconnectedness which links national problems to global crises, human problems to ecological and technological devastation, social justice to eco-justice, economic rights to social rights, black concerns to women's concerns, and intergenerational problems to intragenerational ones. Through action/reflection involvement in such movements, we can rediscover our kinship with all life and affirm what Chief Seattle knew so long ago, that "all things are connected" and that whatever people do to the web of life, they do to themselves, or as Francis Thompson reminds us:

> All things by immortal power
> Near or far
> Hiddenly
> To each other linked are,
> That thou canst not stir a flower
> Without troubling a star.[44]

Youth's Need for Bonding. Being involved with others in justice action becomes a primary channel for youth to make contact with their own abilities, power, and hidden anger (righteous indignation) which is a suppressed source of energy. Making this contact, youth will begin to move out of a powerless, apathetic posture. Through involvement with others in meaning-filled activity that benefits others as well as themselves and contributes to the larger community, they will be empowered. They will experience taking part in shaping their own destiny, as well as that of future generations. Through such a process, youth and adults alike will grow in humanness.

Significant engagement in society can also enable youth and adults to:

1. Experience cooperative work disassociated from economic gain, perhaps helping to destroy the destructiveness of our extreme association of work with drudgery and competitiveness necessary for securing one's existence. Through this experience, growth toward maturity might be viewed in a perspective larger than autonomy or gaining economic independence.
2. Recover something of the natural rhythm and interplay of learning, working, and playing.
3. Use lonely, bored, and unfilled hours which often come to

youth in spite of our entertainment boom, our media, and our hurried and harassed existence.

4. Perceive new and varied vocational possibilities by working with persons who have a variety of skills and abilities and by testing one's own gifts and abilities. Persons might also start to explore new, more human ways for scheduling work, learning, living in community, and exchanging goods and services.

5. Know that the joy of being human involves using one's gifts and abilities for and with others and receiving gifts from others—not just achieving, competing, acquiring, consuming, and being a rational creature.

6. Focus their attention on the perceptions and needs of others, developing sensitivity, empathy, and caring skills.

7. Move toward social maturity by being mutually responsible and interactive with significant others.

8. Discover a cause and a faith demanding total life-forming commitment to One who can secure our present and future life.

9. Experience a truth that is learned as it is done and witnessed—a knowledge and belief that has no reality outside the Word made flesh—a nurturance and transformation which can only occur as the church is in mission with God.

Witnessing—Deed Words

By being foolish enough to risk leaving the old order behind—

By breaking the power of the old order, refusing to play its games and bow down to its gods, thereby showing they are not necessary for human life—

By enfleshing new values and structures as faith, mission, and life are shared together—

By living a theology of relatedness to the natural world—

By being practitioners of liberation, active in exodus events—

By allowing new perceptions and values of communal life to transform interactions with the dominant church and dying order—

By calling the larger community to fresh, new forms of faithfulness—

prophetic communities may discover and demonstrate ways of structuring life together which might some day be undertaken on a larger scale.[45]

Through hearing and bonding with the poor, the powerless, the captive and the alienated, prophetic communities can help in bringing to public expression the fears and terrors, hopes and dreams that have so long been unseen, denied and suppressed. Their words and acts can blend with others prophetically announcing that even in the Twentieth Century God is doing a new thing.

> See, I am doing a new deed,
> even now it comes to light;
>   can you not see it?
> Yes, I am making a road in the wilderness,
>   paths in the wilds.
> The people I have formed for myself
>   will sing my praise.
>
> (Isaiah 43:19, 21)

REFLECTIONS: Andrew P. Grannell

This is a strong prophetic call to look without flinching at the convergent threats to our present society as represented by mainline churches . . . and what our response to these threats should be. If you have ears to hear, eyes to see, and hearts that are open, then no amount of rationalization will rid you of the conviction that indeed the threats are momentous. Some years ago, word came from the Nuclear Regulatory Commission that the Maine Yankee generating facility at Wiscasset (50 miles north of Portland on Route One along the coast), would be closed for an extended period because of the dangers posed by any possible earthquake. Reaction to this shut-down by native Mainers ranged from disbelief to outright ridicule. As local wisdom seems to have it, there had not been a significant quake in the living memory of contemporary Mainers. About the same time, the vice president of the chief utility in the State (which owns the majority share in the Wiscasset nuclear plant) was interviewed concerning the connection between the plant's shut-down and the new film just then showing in local theaters entitled, "The China Syndrome." The utility executive's words are worth remembering, "I believe in the China syndrome about as much as I believe in Japanese movie monsters!" Well, about two weeks after the shut down of the plant at the behest of the NRC, a 5+ earthquake struck the region. The epicenter of which was a mere twenty miles from the site of the plant. About one month later, we all sat back and watched in stunned silence as the China syndrome uncoiled before our eyes, very much like a Japanese movie monster, threatening the livelihood, the health, and the lives of some three hundred thousand persons in the greater Harrisburg, Pennsylvania, region. Earthquakes on the rockbound coast of Maine, you say!? The China syndrome nearly duplicated almost simultaneously on the television screens in our home while it played in fictional counterpart in neighboring movie theaters across the country.

Christians have always lived between the times, between the old order and the new, between the pragmatic and common-sensical world and the reality of God's reigning new order. We do indeed need to be continually reminded of the uncertainties of the established order and our finite abilities to ultimately control either the natural order or civilized order. How, then, should we live?

First, the reality is that we are inextricably bound up both as persons and societies in the structures of evil. We are called as Christians to grapple continually with this fact. Bring it to consciousness, identify it, admit, confess it, and then resolve again to discipline our lives so that it speaks a clear word to the personal and social realms.

Second, we are called to celebrate the wholeness, the grace, the freedom, and the community which has been given to us through the life of our Lord Jesus Christ. More than celebration, we are called to work actively and continuously on behalf of God's great cause, that is, the cause of bringing his just reign to bear fruit upon the earth.

We need to demythologize youth and stop our romanticizing, indulgent, and illusionary quest to make youth "a special time before." Youth like all of us need to be part of the established order of things, to feel a sense of belonging and responsibility. Taking seriously the potentials of calling us forth once again to live as a pilgrim community means that we can and must demythologize this cultural creation.

There is a song sung by Noel Paul Stookey, a convinced Christian (formerly Paul of the Peter, Paul, and Mary trio of the sixties). The title of the song is "And Then the Quail Came." The first band of refugees or pilgrims had made their precarious way out into the desert en route to freedom and the establishment of a more just order. But where was the sustenance to continue this journey? You will find the story in Exodus 16:1–30. This is very much a song of youth and still it is our song too.

> I tell you people this journey is crazy . . . I heard some say in his rage.
>
> How long will it be til we realize our folly and get back to where we were safe?
>
> Then the quail came, falling like dew on the ground,
> The quail came . . . each evening our food to be found.

And taking our curses, and turning 'em round and filling our ears with those ungrateful sounds.

Unworthy to stand, I bow down.[46]

Thank you Jackie Smith for this strong, clear, and resilient call to go forth once again.

NOTES

1. Rosemary Ruether, *New Woman, New Earth* (New York: Seabury, 1975), p. 183.

2. Rosemary Ruether, "Political Theologies: Biblical Roots and Social Context," *Network Quarterly*, 6, No. 4, (Fall 1978), pp. A7–A8. Used with permission of the United Society for the Propagation of the Gospel, London.

3. Robert L. Heilbroner, *An Inquiry Into the Human Prospect* (New York: W. W. Norton & Co., 1974), pp. 132–33, 138.

4. Victor Ferkiss, *The Future of Technological Civilization* (New York: George Braziller, 1974).

5. Matthew Fox, *A Spirituality Named Compassion and the Healing of the Global Village, Humpty Dumpty and Us* (Minneapolis: Winston Press, 1979), pp. 251 and 105. Used with permission.

6. Joseph R. Thomas, ed., *Young Ideas: Viewpoints on Changing the World Written by High School Students* (New York: Christopher Books, 1980), pp. 9–15. Used with permission.

7. Walter Brueggemann, *The Prophetic Imagination* (Philadelphia: Fortress Press, 1978), p. 12.

8. Ibid., p. 13.

9. Walter Brueggemann, *The Bible Makes Sense.* (Winona, Minnesota: St. Mary's College Press, 1977), p. 93.

10. Walter Brueggemann, *Living Toward A Vision* (Philadelphia: United Church Press, 1967), pp. 15ff.

11. Rosemary Ruether, "Political Theologies," p. A5.

12. Ibid., p. A4.

13. Ronald J. Sider, *Rich Christians in An Age of Hunger* (Downers Grove, Illinois: InterVarsity Press, 1977).

14. Gregory Baum, *Religion and Alienation* (New York: Paulist Press, 1975), pp. 198–201.

15. Walter Wink, "Unmasking the Powers: A Biblical View of Roman and American Economics," *Sojourners*, October, 1978.

16. Bruce C. Birch, "Shalom: Toward a Vision of Human Wholeness," *Response* (February 1980), p. 42.

17. Ibid., p. 5.

18. Fox, A *Spirituality Named Compassion*, p. 65.

19. Georgeann Wilcoxson, *Doing the Word: A Manual for Christian Education: Shared Approaches* (New York: United Church Press, 1977), p. 11.

20. Gregory Baum, "Values and Society," *The Ecumenist* 17:2, (January-February 1979), pp. 27–28. Used with permission of the Paulist Press.

21. Richard Shaull, "The Death and Resurrection of the American Dream," in Gustaro Gutierrez and Richard Shaull, *Liberation and Change* (Atlanta: John Knox Press, 1977), p. 140.

22. Brueggemann, *The Bible Makes Sense*, see p. 133.

23. Bruce C. Birch and Larry L. Rasmussen, *The Predicament of the Prosperous*. (Philadelphia: Westminster Press, 1978), see Chapter IX, "What Form for the Church?" for a thought-provoking discussion of "as if" communities.

24. David Riesman, *Individualism Reconsidered and Other Essays*. (New York: The Free Press, 1954), p. 70.

25. Ronald Enroth, *Youth Brainwashing and the Extremist Cults* (Grand Rapids: Zondervan, 1977), p. 215.

26. Morris Dickstein, *Gates of Eden* (New York: Basic Books, 1977), p. 272.

27. Arlene Skolnick, *The Intimate Environment* (Boston: Little Brown & Co., Second Edition, 1978), p. 34.

28. Thomas, *Young Ideas*, p. 20.

29. Michael Warren, "Youth Ministry in Transition," lecture at Union Theological Seminary, Richmond, 1978.

30. Fox, A *Spirituality Named Compassion*, pp. 104–105.

31. Thomas Merton, A *New Charter for Monasticism* (Notre Dame, Indiana: University of Notre Dame Press, 1970), p. 80.

32. Fox, A *Spirituality Named Compassion*, p. 34.

33. Michael J. Warren, "Spirituality for Young Adults," an address to Catholic Young Adult Conference, 1980, in Richmond, Virginia, p. 11.

34. Michael Novak, *The God Experience* (New York: Newman Press, 1971), pp. 8–9. Used with permission of the Paulist Press.

35. Dorothy Day, "Poverty and Precarity," *The Catholic Worker* 47:7 (September 1979), p. 1.

36. William James, "The Moral Equivalent of War," in *Memories and Studies* (Longmans, Green & Co., 1911, 1924), p. 291.

37. Dietrich Bonhoeffer, *Letters and Papers from Prison* (New York: Macmillan Co., Enlarged Edition, 1972), p. 300.

38. Aidan Kavanagh, see "Teaching through Liturgy," *Notre Dame Journal of Education* 5:1 (1974), pp. 35–47.

39. Bonhoeffer, *Letters and Papers from Prison*, p. 17.

40. Robert McAfee Brown, see *Theology in a New Key* (Philadelphia: The Westminster Press, 1978).

41. Catholic Committee of Appalachia, "This Land Is Home to Me," a pastoral letter on powerlessness in Appalachia by the Catholic Bishops of the Region, p. 3.

42. Robert Coles, see *Privileged Ones: The Well-Off and the Rich in America*, vol. 5 of *Children of Crises* (Boston: Little, Brown & Co., 1977).

43. Kenneth Keniston and the Carnegie Council on Children, *All Our Children* (New York: Harcourt Brace Jovanovich, 1977), pp. 214ff.

44. Birch and Rasmussen, *The Predicament of the Prosperous*, quoted on p. 179.

45. Ibid., see p. 191.

46. Michael Blanchard, "Then the Quail Came," in *Band and Body works*, sung by Noel Paul Stookey (South Blue Hill, Maine: Neworld Media, 1979). Used with permission of Michael Kelly Blanchard, Gotz Records, Harwinton, Connecticut.

Chapter 8

The Creative Process in Adolescent Development

DON RICHTER

> Create in me a clean heart, O God,
>   and renew a right spirit within me.
> Cast me not away from thy presence,
>   and take not thy Holy Spirit from me.
>
> (Psalm 51:10–11)

THE CONTEXT OF CREATIVITY

Creativity is more than that divine spark within human nature. The creative process is God at work within human history to transform lives and to give meaning and purpose to existence. It is our *heart* (lēb), our theonomous connection, that which puts us in touch with what the Holy Spirit is doing in the world to make and keep life human.[1] The process is not limited to the awareness of religious men and women, but permeates all developmental stages and growing experiences of our lives. God's love is creating, redeeming, and sustaining human life in spite of our hardness of heart.

It does make all the difference in the world, however, whether or not a person perceives (yāda) this existence in light of what God is doing. It is the difference between living the life for which we were formed and to which we are called, or partly living—

living life without a center and never really experiencing who we are meant to be.

Human life is four dimensional: the "I," the go-between self, the void, and the holy.[2] The "I" is that separate essence which I experience as being uniquely myself. This "I" is experienced in relationship, for I can say both "I have a body" and "I am my body." The dimension of the self goes both to this separate essence and to the lived world. As Kierkegaard defined it, the self relates itself to its own self and thereby relates itself to another.[3] As this *go-between self* relates the "I" to that which is beyond itself, it composes everything we experience as the world.

While everyone experiences life in these two dimensions, there are two other dimensions constituitive of human existence. The *void* is experienced as the presence of an absence, and it leads us to despair as we consider the condition of our finitude. We continually try to suppress the eruptions of the void in our lives; we do this until we can pretend no longer.

> We do not wish anything to happen.
> Seven years we have lived quietly,
> Succeeded in avoiding notice,
> Living and partly living.
> There have been oppression and luxury,
> There have been poverty and licence,
> There has been minor injustice.
> Yet we have gone on living,
> Living and partly living.
> Sometimes the corn has failed us,
> Sometimes the harvest is good,
> One year is a year of rain,
> Another a year of dryness,
> One year the apples are abundant,
> Another year the plums are lacking.
> Yet we have gone on living,
> Living and partly living.
> We have kept the feasts, heard the masses,

We have brewed beer and cyder,
Gathered wood against the winter,
Talked at the corner of the fire,
Talked at the corners of streets,
Talked not always in whispers,
Living and partly living.
We have seen births, deaths, and marriages,
We have had various scandals,
We have been afflicted with taxes,
We have had laughter and gossip,
Several girls have disappeared
Unaccountably, and some not able to.
We have all had our private terrors,
Our particular shadows, our secret fears.
But now a great fear is upon us, a fear not of
   one but of many,
A fear like birth and death, when we see birth
   and death alone
In a void apart. We
Are afraid in a fear which we cannot know,
   which we cannot face, which none
   understands,
And our hearts are torn from us, our brains
   unskinned like the layers of an onion,
   our selves are lost lost
In a final fear which none understands.[4]

The void itself is neutral, but it is the mission of evil to evoke the experience of nothingness in our lives. Tillich defines this predicament of our existence as *estrangement* from the ground of our being, from other beings, and from ourselves.[5] We construct artificial structures of transcendence, but these still do not overcome our experience of incompleteness, for "No act within the context of existential estrangement can overcome existential estrangement."[6] The only way in which the void can be faced and overcome is by encountering the true transcendent dimension of existence: the *holy*. The holy is the "numinous" (Rudolf Otto); it is the experience of the "mysterium tremendum" which draws a person toward it in fascination and yet evokes awe and dread; it is "the New Being in Jesus as the Christ as the conquest of estrangement" (Tillich).

God is made known to us now by the objective presence of his Holy Spirit in the world. Sharing inner dialogue with the Holy Spirit enables a person to confront the void and embrace it, for by faith we know that this dimension is at work transforming the other three. We can then rejoice in the knowledge that God has been composing our world all along. The life of the individual is now understood as the participation of that person in the continuum of human history from the perspective of God's history. The individual carves out a personal history which is characterized by his/her confrontation with and management of life's conflicts throughout personal development. This lifelong process of development is, as we have maintained, under the guidance of the Holy Spirit through the creative process.

The creative process involves a progression through five stages: conflict, interlude for scanning, insight, release of tension/ energy, and public expression. One can consciously enter the process at any stage, yet every stage is essential to the completion of the process. The creative process is usually initiated by (1) an unresolved and abiding conflict which is pressing toward resolution. A conflict in this sense would usually be more significant than trying to decide in the morning what color pants to wear. The conflict need not always have been foremost in one's thoughts, but it is the type of problem which will remain in the subconscious until it has been adequately resolved.

There is then (2) an interlude for scanning during which the mind consciously and subconsciously investigates various possibilities for solving the conflict. It should be mentioned that many scientific discoveries have been made in which no conscious effort or strategy was used for solving a problem. Consider

Archimedes, who discovered volume displacement as he was entering his bath, or Newton, who connected the falling of an apple with the force of gravity. Some creative thinkers, such as Einstein, make discoveries through image or visualization. Arieti describes the amorphous cognition which precedes discovery as an "endocept."

> The endocept is a primitive organization of past experiences, perceptions, memory traces, and images of things and movements. . . . The endocept cannot be shared. We may consider it as a disposition to feel, to act, to think, which occurs after simpler mental activity has been inhibited. The awareness of experiencing an endocept is also extremely vague, uncertain, or partial at best.[7]

When things suddenly fit together, when a gestalt is formed, when endocept is transformed into a conceptual cognition which can be communicated to others, this is (3) the moment of insight. There are many ways of reacting to an insight, depending on the nature of the conflict. Some may choose, like Archimedes, to go running through the streets naked, shouting "Eureka! Eureka!" Others may try to find out how they "logically/rationally" arrived at this discovery, upon which they have actually stumbled.

Regardless of how (4) tension is released and new energy expended, there is the final stage of the creative process which evaluates the integrity of the insight by a (5) public expression of its continuity. If the insight—and the process—is valid, it cannot remain a subjective gnosis but must be communicated within the public realm. This is certainly evident in the scientific disciplines, which place great emphasis on the repeatability of any experiment to verify it. Often the final stage assumes primary importance to the neglect of the four stages which have preceded it; as stated, however, every stage is essential to the completion of the process.

The creative process is evident in many areas such as developmental psychology, therapy, scientific discovery, aesthetic creativity, and social transformation. Our basic presupposition is that an awareness of the creative process as *God's* work in our lives can lead us to experience this process in a convictional way and thereby open us to a four-dimensional life. But is there a stage in life during which the individual becomes mature enough to realize that God's creative process is shaping his/her development? If we can, in some way, determine this age or stage, are there ways that we as Christian educators can help to facilitate this awareness in a person and thereby make use of a teachable moment in that person's life?

It is my thesis that the conflict-ridden transition through adolescence is the period of human development during which most individuals become mature enough to perceive the operation of God's creative process in their lives, and that this awareness makes them *reif* to experience the transforming moments of their lives with convictional force.

In support of this thesis, I wish first to describe how my participation in a production of the musical *Godspell* when I was 15 can be seen as a paradigm for experiencing the creative process convictionally at this age. Second, I will try to show developmentally why this stage makes it possible for an individual to become aware of his/her creative potential and relate it to what God is doing in the world. Third, I will point to particular methods (informed by the *Godspell* paradigm) which seem to facilitate this creative awareness in youth. The format of this presentation runs parallel to my own faith pilgrimage: experiencing, learning about, teaching, and ministering.

A PARADIGM FOR EXPERIENCING THE CREATIVE PROCESS

"The Play's the Thing"

In the fall of 1972, an off-Broadway production of the musical *Godspell* came to Huntsville, Alabama, which I attended with two other high-school friends. The three of us were captivated by the message of this play, which is a creative way of conveying the "good news" of the life and teachings of Jesus ("Godspell =

"gospel" = "good news"). We left the theatre thoroughly inspired, feeling that this musical expressed exactly what Christianity meant for our lives at that time. We also left with the feeling that *we*, too, had to convey this message to others in the same way, that they might better understand our faith. The necessity to emulate *Godspell* was met by the necessity to come up with some idea for a production which would involve the youth from the Huntsville Presbytery (UPCUSA) and from the Presbytery of North Alabama (PCUS). There was a joint retreat planned for the coming spring during which we would put together a musical for production in the various churches of our presbyteries; could we somehow do a musical based on the exciting theme of *Godspell?*

There had been two previous retreats involving the youth from both UPCUSA and PCUS churches. The first one had been unstructured and ended being a weekend beerbust. At this point it was decided that our future efforts should be project-oriented, building community and enjoying each other's fellowship as we worked together toward a common goal. For various reasons a musical production seemed to lend itself to accomplishing our objectives. Our second joint retreat provided an opportunity to put together the musical *For Heaven's Sake*, and it was as a result of this experience that I discovered that I could act and sing. I was therefore eager to be a part of our next production, especially with the possibility of self-expression afforded by *Godspell*.

Since the play had only recently made its appearance, however, we knew that the royalties would be out of our price range. There was some doubt as to whether we would be able to perform a suitable rendition of the play as it was written, and we also wanted to include more than ten youth in the acting and singing roles. Our solution was to do an adaptation of the stage show—adapting the same music to a large chorus and composing our own skits based on what we had seen in the original production, yet keeping in mind that we would be performing this in a church setting.

Bert, Tom, and I (the three who had seen the show), spent time before the retreat writing a skeletal framework for the skits. We relied on our memories of the original production to imitate the same techniques which had been used, including mime, the clown motif, and the basic juxtaposition of biblical themes and songs. Because many of the scenes revolved around the parables which Jesus told, we took parables from the gospels (especially Matthew and Luke) and rewrote them after the comical style of *Godspell.* Often, we tried to think of who would play what part and fit the lines to that person's character. For instance, one fellow in our group was an excellent debater and was nicknamed "Explicit Diction." Casting him in the role of the older son in the Parable of the Prodigal Son (Luke 15:11–32), he would complain to his father upon hearing of his younger brother's return:

> What! All my life I've worked for you like a slave, and what have you given me for my efforts? Not even a bottle of wine to celebrate with my friends. But your precious prodigy spends and squanders your property, paying for the pleasures of prostitutes and other preposterous perversions, while you purposely persist in protecting his pathetic practices and prodigality. It ain't right!

We allowed space for any additions or revisions to be made in the script once the cast had been selected and we began putting the skits together. The three of us understood that the skits would be rehearsed during the retreat weekend, but the musical numbers were given priority and our efforts were not considered. We were thoroughly offended by this, and I recall voicing my anger to the adult leader: "But you don't understand! It won't mean anything if we do the songs without these skits!" The indignation was not merely from having our contribution snubbed. We felt a desperate need to communicate ourselves through these parables, as though this was something that we *had* to do. We therefore refused to participate in any part of the show until assured that our material would be given a fair trial at a later date.

Our leaders were sensitive to our persistent pleas and selected an acting cast of ten to rehearse on weekday evenings during school. At these rehearsals, we encouraged each other to express spontaneous humor and allowed the script to evolve in this process. Through our playing together, the play became our own. In this relaxed setting, we came to experience "the child within" each of us.

Our efforts were not devoted merely to thinking of amusing one-liners, however. We spent considerable time discussing why Jesus was portrayed as a clown; why he put makeup on each disciple and then wiped it off during the Last Supper; why the Last Supper produced such a dramatic shift in mood from exuberance to somber anticipation. Linked to this was our most crucial discussion of whether we would wrap the body of the crucified Jesus in a sheet and carry him down the aisle, and, if so, whether he would rejoin the cast in the finale as the resurrected Jesus or just as an actor (without makeup and costume). The production we had seen did not attempt to portray a physical resurrection, yet we were doing this play in a church context, and so the decision was ours.

There had been an important event in our lives which now emerged as we considered the topics of death and resurrection. That previous summer, a member of our youth group had died in an automobile accident while returning home from a youth leadership training camp in Tennessee. Taylor had lived just around the corner from my home, and our parents had been friends for years. The loss of their 17-year-old son was devastating to the Coleman family. The tragic event seemed unreal to us, his peers. The shock was numbing, although we had never come together to share our feelings about this untimely death. In piecing together *Godspell*, however, we were forced to deal with our understanding of death, and of *Taylor's* death, albeit indirectly through the medium of drama. Some of us argued that a physical resurrection was not important to faith, and that our attempt to portray it would come across as phoney and contrived. We had experienced the death of a friend as an existential fact which could not be overcome in this life as we knew it. Others of us felt that we needed to present Jesus' resurrection so that people would be given hope in what was ultimately possible in Christ. Our debate over this issue was a clear indication of how each of us had been struggling to come to terms with Taylor's death.

Although there was nothing specifically mentioned at this point, I believe that we were all amazed by the role which each of us had chosen to perform in this production, particularly those of us who had been close to Taylor. There had been no question from the beginning that Bert would play the role of Jesus, even though he could not carry a tune and we had to adapt several of the songs on his account. Bert was Taylor's first cousin; they had grown up together (same age) and were in the same class in high school. Beverly, who had a strong affection for Taylor, had planned to sing the poignant "By My Side": "Where are you going, where are you going? Can you take me with you?" Steve, one of the other two fellows who was in the car accident with Taylor, was mostly involved with playing the music, but had asked to sing the "Crucifixion Song": "Oh God, I'm bleeding. . . . Oh God, I'm dying. . . . Oh God, I'm dead. . . ." Steve, of course, had been there when Taylor was dying. Taylor's younger brother, Brian, had not been a part of any of the previous musicals, but he was singing in the 50-member chorus for this one. Perhaps our dedication of *Godspell* to Taylor became clear to us when Mr. Coleman led us in prayer immediately prior to the opening performance.

As with most performances, once underway the musical seemed to run on its own momentum. The large church was packed, and the audience response generated that much more enthusiasm on our part. Those who had not performed with much confidence in rehearsals now rose to the occasion and did a magnificent job. In fact, we were feeling so joyful about the "success" of the show that the transition in mood brought about by the Last Supper scene was like being doused with cold water. While Bert was breaking the bread and passing around the jug of grape juice, there was an eternal moment of time during which the audience faded from our conscious perception. We actors experienced only the presence of one another and the presence of Christ among us as we sat there on the stage floor in a circle. Entering the characters of the disciples which we were portraying, we shared a worried anticipation for what we knew was impending: the death of the very person who had brought us so much joy and happiness. We knew all too well the sting of death as we thought of Taylor.

After the "Crucifixion Song," we carried our enshrouded friend Bert down the center aisle to a simple threnody: "Long Live God." We walked directly past Mr. and Mrs. Coleman, and the tears in their eyes produced tears in mine as I realized the painful emotion this funeral procession must have evoked for them. Upon reaching the narthex, we put Bert down and began walking, then running, up the aisle singing "Prepare Ye the Way of the Lord." After we had reached the stage, Bert came running up the aisle to rejoin us as "the Risen Lord," and this prompted a spontaneous hugging of one another and an outpouring of emotion which was by no means rehearsed. Our former joy was renewed, a meaning was given to life, and the resurrected body was reified to us through the reversal of death. We became apostles of this good news, going out into the audience and encouraging them to share our joy.

At the end of this performance of *Godspell*, we came to know that we had received far more that we could have given. That is why those of us who participated in this event regard it to this day as one of the most significant transforming faith experiences in our lives. To explore the therapeutic and convictional character of this experience, our next step is to see how the creative process was operating as the key dynamic in transforming our lives.

The Convictional Character of the Experience

It is our contention that this creative process is the work of God's Holy Spirit to make and keep life human. How does our production of *Godspell* fit this description of the creative process?

(1) The basic *conflict* in our situation was our inability to deal with the death of a friend. There was anxiety produced by our confrontation with the void, with the presence of an absence. (2) There are two phases to the stage of *scanning* in our case. The first phase occurred between Taylor's death and our insight to do *Godspell*, during which time we were struggling for an answer to our problem of understanding death. We were given "the answer" in our decision to do this musical, but we still were not consciously aware of our conflict at this point. Thus, after the insight was given we had to return to another phase of scanning to discover why performing this play was such a necessity for us. In sharing the insight with others who had been close to Taylor, we brought them into the process by letting them create roles to express their relationship to him and to express what had happened because of his death.

(3) The insight stage was the point at which we entered the process with conscious awareness. This awareness, however, was not something that we could explain rationally to someone else. It was "the eternal voice" (Jung) telling us that this was a mandatory thing to do, that is, to express ourselves as the actors in *Godspell* were doing. It was the amorphous cognition, the endoceptive awareness which had come to us through the process of scanning. We knew that we had to do this musical because we felt that we had to do it, but we could not have explained why. That is the reason we became indignant when we thought that our skits were not going to be included; we had no discernible reason for insisting that they *had* to be included.

Why is this particular insight to do *Godspell* significant for this conflict of dealing with death? Young people who have been exposed to death and have had to handle the situation maturely for a period of time will often revert to childlike behavior. They do this to assert that they are not completely ready to be "grown up" if that entails the fear of confronting one's own finitude.[8] Jung describes the archetype of the child as a fascinating symbol of wholeness and of the unity of irreconcilable opposites:

> Because the symbol of the "child" fascinates and grips the conscious mind, its *redemptive* effect passes over into consciousness and brings about that separation from the conflict-situation which the conscious mind by itself was unable to achieve. . . . The "child" is all that is abandoned and exposed and at the same time divinely powerful; the insignificant, dubious beginning, and the triumphal end. The "eternal child" in man is an indescribable experience, an incongruity, a disadvantage, and a divine prerogative; an imponderable that determines the ultimate worth or worthlessness of a personality.[9]

Godspell was the perfect vehicle for allowing us adolescents to regress back to childhood after experiencing the loss of a friend. The "clown motif" signified to us that Christianity should be a joyful and childlike faith, not a serious and morbid religion. The childlike playfulness of *Godspell* is what gave us our insight into how we could finally come to terms with our own ontological fear. This playfulness is initiated by the image of Jesus as a clown, showing his disciples that life is meant to be lived in a different way than they had been living it. In the play, Jesus comes as an insight to a yet-to-be-defined conflict. There is then an interlude during which Jesus instructs his disciples with various teachings and parables, to which they can say, "Gee, this is great stuff . . . but what is it for?" The insight and interlude make sense to them only when they understand the crucifixion as the conflict. The disciples' experience of the resurrection is concomitant with the release of tension and the push for public expression which follow.

Godspell was a powerful insight for us because the sequential flow of this musical was parallel to the outworking of the creative process in our own lives: insight, scanning, conflict, release of tension, and public expression! What this meant was that we could reexperience the full cycle of our own pilgrimage in the creative process as we accomplished the fifth stage of public expression by performing the play. We would be proclaiming, in effect, "This is what *we* have created and this is what has created *us!*" Our comprehension of the insight to do *Godspell* was hardly this profound at the time. As mentioned, it was originally an endoceptive awareness which did not lead to thoughtful reflection so much as it pushed for public expression.

(4) In our preparation for the performance, there was a feeling of amazement as we came to realize why certain persons among us (vis-à-vis the conflict) had chosen the expressive roles which they had. I have mentioned several that dealt directly with Taylor. My own expressive role had to do with forgiving God for what had happened. In one of the skits we adapted, I would say, "Lord, how many times must I forgive a person who does me wrong?" After agreeing with Jesus that I should forgive a person not only seven times, but seven times 777,777,777 times and then still once again, I was immediately struck down by a hard and painful slap from one of my friends. I would jump to my feet in a rage, grab this guy by the collar, and get ready to punch him in the face—and I really wanted to; that slap hurt! But each time that I drew back my fist, everyone else would caution me in unison: "uh-uh!" Finally, with Jesus staring over my shoulder, I would put my fist to my head and say calmly, "Hello. You want to speak to whom? Yeah, he's right here." Then, as if giving Jesus the telephone, I would say, "It's for you; I think it's your Father calling."

This skit expressed my anger with God because of Taylor's death, which had come like a slap in the face. In a rage, I wanted to strike back somehow and at someone, but I had come to see that this was both a useless and unproductive preoccupation. I had been forced to calm down and vent my anger through humor instead. This type of catharsis enabled me and the rest of the cast to relax in spite of the rough edges as we approached the performance date. There was a feeling of confidence that our efforts were being guided by God's providence.

(5) We were fortunate to have had a very affirming and supportive audience to evaluate the integrity of our creative efforts. We explained ourselves by reenacting how the Holy Spirit had been working through us by means of the creative process. Our presentation was made all the more powerful by the progression of similar stages in self-discovery between the musical and our own lives. One of the most important aspects of this stage of public expression was that the *Creator Spiritus* did not remain hidden in the process (as is often the case) but became manifest in the performance. We could make it explicitly and implicitly clear that the inspiration behind the show was not the result of merely fulfilling our human potential: the Spirit was at work through our humbled but exalted human spirits.

The brokenness of our lives was made clear to us as we broke bread and shared the cup together during the Last Supper scene. Our brokenness was met by the brokenness of Jesus in the crucifixion event, negating our negativity and restoring us to wholeness. The resurrection became, then, a powerful sign of what God has done, and is doing, to restore the brokenness of creation. Having confronted the void, and having allowed it to compose our world, we now encountered the Holy which negates the void, and in so doing, recomposes the world for us in four dimensions. We had been composing this production of *Godspell* with our own "Jesus" until the Last Supper scene. Then there was a sudden figure-ground reversal[10] as we experienced Christ among us and realized that we could no longer compose him into our world because he was now composing the world for us!

The feeling of being uplifted is not the same as lifting oneself up by the bootstraps. The feeling of accomplishment following the show was different in *kind* from the feelings that I have experienced following the successful production of other musicals and plays. This is in keeping with Tillich's criterion for "judging the Spirit" within the church:

> The criterion which must be used to decide whether an extraordinary state of mind is ecstasy, created by the Spiritual Presence, or subjective intoxication is the manifestation of creativity in the former and the lack of it in the latter.[11]

Another important criterion is that transformation by the Holy Spirit is not an isolating experience but is *community-building*. A person knows that he/she is a member of the Body of Christ, the *koinonia*, the fellowship of believers. As Barth points out to us:

> The saints of the New Testament exist only in plurality. Sanctity belongs to them, but only in their common life, not as individuals.[12]

In the love we shared as we struggled and grew together, we had a foretaste of God's kingdom in our midst. It was an experience we have sought over and over again, and yearn after still. A number of our group are presently involved in theological study and preparation for the ministry. Since continuity over time is a criterion for the validity of a convictional experience, our continued quest for God's kingdom bears out the convictional character of the *Godspell* experience. I regard this event as one of the most significant in my twenty-four years of life, and certainly one of the most meaningful for my religious development.

CREATIVE CONFLICTS OF ADOLESCENCE

The adolescent experience in America is certainly characterized as a period of conflict and turmoil for a young person. The question we are posing is this: Can this stage be viewed *constructively* as a period during which a young person can interpret life's conflicts as part of the creative process? We have already indicated an affirmative answer by the examination of the *Godspell* paradigm which functioned creatively in the lives of a number of young people. Was this an exceptional event, or are there personality qualities common to middle adolescence (15 to 18 years) which imbue this stage with creative potential?

"Although creativity may occur at any age of life . . . it seems logical to assume (although it is by no means certain) that an inclination toward creativity must be fostered in childhood and/or adolescence."[13] To move past this assumption, let us now examine six of the basic conflict-producing concerns of this stage of adolescence: physical growth and sexual awareness, identity, intellectual maturing, facing new values, reordering family relationships, and responding to God. This is not to imply that these concerns impinge only upon young people, but rather that these issues emerge as central for a majority of today's youth. Developmentally speaking, those conflicts which are not confronted at this stage must be dealt with later in a person's life.

Physical Growth and Sexual Awareness

Girls have normally matured physically during early adolescence, while boys are just beginning a period of rapid growth at this time. The result of this disparity is that girls are usually attracted to boys two-to-five years older than themselves, while the sexually maturing boys seem to be left out of the picture for awhile. The biological urges are strong and discomforting, and there are accompanying guilt feelings over masturbation, sexplay, and premarital sex. "As a result of these changes there is an increase in energy which propels teens and leaves many parents weary. Teens often act without thinking and on impulse. Increased energy also brings increased appetite, impatience, awkwardness, and accidents."[14]

To cope with their rapidly changing physical situation and

sexual awareness, young people seek to imitate the behavior of significant *models*. Teachers can have an important role as identification models in the creative learning process, particularly since many parents tend to inhibit the creativity of their adolescents by being overly anxious that these young people become properly socialized, act grown up, and think about becoming self-supporting. Teachers are not as possessive of young people as parents are, and can influence youth by the process-content of their teaching (the "hidden curriculum") as well as by the subject-content. However, no one can influence an adolescent as significantly as can another adolescent:

> With adolescents, peer group members do serve as models and may actually have a greater influence on imitative behavior than parents and teachers, partly because they share common characteristics, partly because the peer group has control over the rewards that matter to adolescents.[15]

With reference to our paradigm, we can see the creative results of a youth-initiated project in which young people serve as models for their peers.[16]

Identity

The physical changes occurring during adolescence contribute to the overall conflict in identity experienced by the young person. Erik Erikson has classified the main challenge of this stage as the conflict of identity formation versus role confusion. The adolescent begins to question how to connect the roles and skills cultivated earlier with the ideal prototypes of the day. The question is whether there is a continuity between who I have been and who I will become, and this question becomes an abiding conflict. A psychosocial moratorium is needed to facilitate the integration process. This period of interlude and scanning consists of the young person "replaying" the former conflicts of his/her life to establish that they have been adequately resolved.[17]

In attempting to resolve the crisis of identity, the young person searches for: (1) people and ideas to have faith in; (2) opportunities to decide *freely* what duty or service to become involved in; (3) peers and influential adults who will give imaginative scope to his/her aspirations: (4) a vocation which is personally rewarding. These areas provide insights for youth in establishing their identity.[18]

As we have described in the paradigm, our identity formation in *Godspell* follows the criteria set down by Erikson. We had (1) a religious solution to our identity and ideology issues. (2) There was a double leap in development: *backward* to childhood expression and innocence of the ego and *forward* in the inherent capacity to affirm life with integrity in the face of our own finitude. (3) Our identity was revealed to us by the five stages of the creative process, realizing that the Holy Spirit was helping us compose our worlds.

Intellectual Maturing

In evaluating the creative potential of adolescents, one of the most important considerations is the ability of the mind to make connections, bisociations, abstractions, and the like: the cognitive gymnastics involved in comprehending the creative process in order to experience it convictionally. While intellectual aptitude is not an indispensable ingredient in the process, as proven by the creative work of mental patients,[19] there is a stage of cognitive development which greatly enhances the creative potential. This is the stage defined by Piaget as the period of formal operations, and usually becomes a possibility for persons moving through adolescence. Not all young people, or adults even, will develop this intellectual maturity. But we should examine the characteristics of this period as it relates to our study.

"Formal operations" involve the same basic operations as the previous stage of concrete operations, but now the operations are performed on verbal descriptions and abstractions rather than on objects, and reflection on these operations can lead to the formation of hypotheses. Thinking is done independently of concrete reality; "thinking takes wings."[20] This capacity to think "abstractly" is not limited to solving math problems:

> A formal operation that is critical for the development of social perspective is the ability to stand outside of oneself and see the self and another person from a third-person viewpoint. This allows one to anticipate what another person might be thinking and feeling, and, in addition, to know that the other is also able to anticipate what the self is thinking and feeling.[21]

The relation between formal operational thought and effect is very significant for understanding the conflicts of youth:

> It is these new thoughts about what the world might be that present the challenge of adolescence to the formal-operational adolescent. Responses may range from new highs about the adolescent's strengths and the beauty of the possibilities for himself or herself and the world, to deep depressions about his or her weaknesses and faults, and the impossibility of bridging the gap between what is and what might be.[22]

The adolescent comes to believe that others are as preoccupied with his/her appearance and behavior as he or she is. This preoccupation leads to the construction of the "imaginary audience" and the "personal fable."

> This tremendous pressure of always being on stage in front of an "imaginary audience" accounts in part for adolescent self-consciousness, overreaction to self-perceived successes and failures, and to a need for privacy and seclusion, to get off stage (which, of course, everyone will notice too). The adolescent develops a "personal fable," a story he tells himself which accentuates his uniqueness, his greatness and worth, and the reactions of others to his victories, defeats, and death. In a circular way, the adolescent develops his fable out of the feeling that his thoughts and behavior are of universal and eternal importance, and then uses the fable to reinforce this.[23]

I perceive a definite connection between formal-operation thinking and creative potential. In our paradigm, the insight was produced by our ability to imagine the possibility of doing the *Godspell* musical ourselves. Much of our humor was the product of bisociation and unexpected juxtaposition. Our "imaginary audiences" and "personal fables" were replaced by a real audience and personal stories as we left our inhibitions behind and concentrated on self-expression via our characters.

Facing New Values

Kohlberg has contributed greatly to our understanding of the moral implications of a developing cognitive ability. He proposes various stages of moral development, with progress from one stage to the next resulting from the adaptation to cognitive disequilibrium.[24] The youth in middle adolescence will often be found to have conventional level Stage 3 moral reasoning, which requires some ability to handle formal operations at the cognitive level.[25]

At this stage, laws are considered by young people as guidelines for good behavior and for the prevention of chaos. Breaking the law may only be justified if one has good intentions. Something new which appears at this stage is love and relationships of affection. This is related to the development of roletaking ability and empathy: the ability to project oneself into the feelings and ideas of another. Yet this ability is limited in the young person who tries to put himself/herself in the place of another who has substantially different values or background. "The structure in stereotyping is the keyhole that shapes a Stage 3 concept of persons; the *content* of the stereotypes varies according to the culture, subculture, or significant group."[26]

Authority is external for young people in Stage 3; it lies outside of them and is usually tacitly assumed. An authority figure must have admirable personal qualities and must live consistently with these qualities, yet when an adolescent perceives a contradiction in behavior the cognitive conflict is resolved through compartmentalization. "In compartmentalization, opposing views exist side-by-side and generally are considered separately."[27] In relation to authority is the influence which the values of one's groups have in determining personal values. For the first time (developmentally), the social perspective includes a *community* of persons which heavily influences individual choice.[28] "One's own identity and faith are derived from membership in a group or groups characterized primarily by face-to-face relationships."[29]

In reference to the paradigm, we see that *Godspell* provided us young people with an excellent role model for moral behavior: The character of Jesus was very sensitive and human and was someone with whom we could empathize. As disciples we formed a "group conscience" in relation to this authority figure whom we could admire and respect. Our cognitive conflict came when this authority figure was suddenly destroyed; there was resentment against the one who had caused our authority to be usurped. Only when we realized that Jesus' authority was the power of his love, not in his love of power, could we resolve the contradiction and prepare ourselves for progression into a Stage 4 understanding: "Stage 4 is validated by internal processes and that truth has an ideological or systematic quality."[30]

Reordering Family Relationships

There are several important factors which have redefined the relationship between parents and adolescents in the past two decades. Many parents are petrified at the thought of having to deal with their teenagers in relation to some of these issues. (1) The birth control pill and other available forms of contraception have opened up the possibility of complete sexual involvement without marriage/procreation. (2) Marijuana and other drugs have become an acceptable social affair, and alcohol use among teens has dramatically increased. (3) Teenagers are having experiences today which their parents never had, and this has resulted in an "experience gap." Teens are now educating their parents about social customs and values. (4) Although adolescence has been prolonged by the educational system and by our expectations for psychosocial moratorium (noncommitment) among youth, there is so much exposure to the world that young people are forced to "grow up" faster and be mature in all situations.[31]

One of the main dynamics in this parent-teen relationship is the teen's struggle for independence and the parents' demand for responsibility. The two developmental tasks of adolescence in relation to independence are: achieving emotional independence of parents and other adults, and achieving assurance of economic independence. The former task is specifically related to middle adolescence.

In acting out *Godspell*, we were saying to our parents and other adults, "Look, we are going through a lot of things which you probably did not have to experience at our age. We respect you and your values, but we must find a different way to express our feelings and values. This play symbolizes the paradoxes we have been experiencing in our lives. We cannot explain our feelings, but we hope you can sense them through this effort."

Responding to God

In Stage 3 of cognitive development, symbols no longer have the literal correspondence quality which they had before (with concrete operations). An individual is now able to understand metaphor, allegory, parable, word plays, and various levels of symbolic meaning, although there may still be an ontological connection between the symbol and the object symbolized. The diversity of symbols used in Christian worship can now "come alive" in a new way for young people, some who enjoy participating in the liturgy of formal worship as acolytes or lay readers.[32] "Typical images of God at Stage 3 are no longer physically anthropomorphic, but are based on 'personal' qualities of the deity—for instance, God as friend, companion, 'lifeline,' comforter, guide, mind."[33] A person can now begin to grapple with the paradox of Jesus as both God and man. The humanity of Jesus can no longer be taken for granted, but becomes a cause of wonderment and confusion.

After having lived the previous years absorbed in self-concern and one's own interests, there is a welcome release of tension when a young person discovers the joy of serving and caring for others.

> Joy may take the form of quiet exuberance over the simple pleasures of living. Or it may be a shout of celebration and hope that contrasts with the despair and cynicism so often heard from twentieth-century man. It is the cry of youth whose joy is in a sense of identity and mission that centers in the person of Jesus Christ. . . . In short these youth have found a meaning system that brings order to their lives and gives answers to ultimate questions of existence.[34]

Our production of *Godspell* was our celebration of joy in the discovery of our real identity in Christ. We could rejoice in the formation of community, a community which accepted us because of who we were and not because of what we did. We did not feel that our response to God was constrained by traditional models and expectations, but rather that we had found an authentic way of expressing our faith. The open-endedness of the parables allowed for creative interpretation, and we were cognitively able to appreciate their symbolic quality. Our image of Jesus was aptly conveyed by the clown figure, who was able to express the wide range of emotions which we were experiencing in our lives at this time. More than ever, we could relate to the personal struggles of this man. More than ever, we were baffled by the mystery of incarnation: How could the almighty God assume such a fragile and vulnerable human nature? Since true knowledge is demonstrated by learning to ask the right questions in life, our raising of such questions indicates the reasonable dimension of the creative process. For us young people, *Godspell* was a point of departure in faith seeking understanding (*fides quaerens intellectum*).

Fostering Creativity in Youth

Informed by the *Godspell* paradigm and by my subsequent work with young people, I am proposing four potential areas of youth ministry which might enable young people to explore the creative presence of the Holy Spirit in their lives. The first two, music and drama, are direct implications of the paradigm experience. The other two, sacraments and pastoral care, were also integral and significant aspects of that experience. Some current and popular approaches to youth ministry have concentrated on music and drama, downplaying sacramental life and confusing pastoral care with being "a nice guy" or being "hip." It is hoped that the following discussion will provide correctives to such distortions. These are not the four miracle ingredients to a successful youth program, but they are effective methods for engaging youth in the creative process.

Music

Music is the art form which most closely expresses the temporally-conditioned existence of humanity. Melody, rhythm, and harmony are the musical components which illustrate this contiguity: *Melody* expresses the process of life moving from the past into the present with a view of the impinging future; *rhythm* expresses the pulse of life, particularly the systolic and diastolic contraction and expansion of the heart muscle; *harmony* uses the dissonance-consonance interplay to express the conflict-resolution pattern of life.[35] "Music is an acoustic medium that can approximate, objectify, convey and evoke content of endoceptual significance."[36]

Music is ideal for achieving maximum group involvement. In a musical production, at least 70 percent of the singing should include the chorus. In doing *Godspell*, we were fortunate to have music that was diversified, fun to sing, superb lyrically, and full of both contagious enthusiasm and *pathos*. In short, it was *good* music, not like the many contemporary excuses for music which are called "Christian" rock or folk:

> Among these the ratio of quantity to quality is appalling. And it is all supposed to support a so-called radicalizing gospel. Its advertising abounds with superlatives and "with it" slogans, as if to repeat back to the world in its own jargon such fallacies as that the value of a thing is determined by what it is called, not by what it intrinsically is. So we mix entertainment with the crucial task of exposing a person to the whole force and weight of the gospel.[37]

It may be difficult to get a youth group to begin singing if this has not been their tradition. While music was the main unifying bond between young people in the 1960s, this past decade has witnessed an increased tendency toward the "spectator sport" mindset, and singing has not been exempt from this trend. Music must be found and produced which expresses the hopes, fears, and passions of today's youth, and which preserves the integrity of the Christian message.

Drama

Few adolescents will be able to compose music that is suitable for performing, yet most young people can do exciting and creative work in the area of dramatics. Particularly in this stage of increased cognitive ability, role-playing and parables offer challenging new options for youth. Role-playing exercises are excellent ways to stretch youth by putting them in another person's shoes to examine an issue from this perspective. Biblical characters can be *experienced* by young people as they discover how they, themselves, would respond: as Peter, having Jesus wash his feet; or as Mary, finding the empty tomb.[38] Much encouragement is needed, for often these peer-oriented youths are still self-conscious and do not want to be embarrassed by their acting. An example of role play by the leader will be helpful in easing the situation.

Parable was the chief vehicle for our spiritual journey in *Godspell*.

> The parable is a story especially appropriate to adolescence. The parable is not simply fanciful nor simply literal, although it contains elements of both. Parables are fanciful in that they are "might have been" stories. They may also have happened, but the telling may also use fanciful elements. At the same time they undoubtedly refer to comments, events in the hearer's experience. [39]

Ths use of parable is important at this stage to help young people deal with their encroaching sense of ethical ambiguity. Lehmann acknowledges the parable as Jesus' supreme pedagogical device: "A parable . . . has to do with an imaginative juxtaposition of what is incommensurable, namely, the ways of God and the ways of man." For the Christian, the *environment* of decision, not the *rules* of decision, gives to behavior its ethical significance. The parable is that "right word" or "sign" that human relations are going on in an environment of trust. [40] The New Testament parables can be reinterpreted and retold to make them relevant to present-life situations. As stories with transforming power, they may remain latent in a young person's heart until called forth during a time of personal conflict.

Sacraments

The popularity of various para-church youth organizations has been achieved in part by attacking the institutional church, and this has resulted in the separation of Word and Sacrament for many young people who are involved in these groups. Sacraments are the visible sign of God's presence in the *communio sanctorum*. They signify our participation in the reality of God's inbreaking Holy Spirit, that is, they proclaim that our existence is indeed four dimensional.

Baptism involves *naming*, and naming is a creative act. We are named by the community of faith in worship (the intersection of sacred time and human experience); in this way we are called to *be* and empowered to *become*. We are named by our family, through the Christian nurture which teaches us what it means to be human and to love. We are named by the world, which calls us "Christian" when we go forth from our place of security to proclaim the gospel as authoritative over human history.[41]

Youth who have been baptized as infants can renew their baptismal vows, as they are now able to experience how God's grace has been shaping their lives. A correct teaching of baptism will help young people to see that the church is not an exclusive club, but a community with an *inclusive* membership policy. We have been baptized *out of* all those things which separate us from one another: race, sexuality, socio-economic standing. Although churches often behave like clubs, young people should realize that the institutional church is always repenting its failure to be the true church which it is called to be.

Whether in the sanctuary or on a retreat, young people should gather together frequently to celebrate the Eucharist: "The Eucharist, more than any other sacrament or act of worship, asserts the real objective presence of God in our midst."[42] The Eucharist is a supreme teaching instrument for Christianity; it teaches by enactment all of the essential doctrines of faith, such as creation, atonement, salvation, incarnation, and reconciliation. And yet the Eucharist is more than this: "One's whole being is enveloped in the eucharistic action, and perhaps this is how it should be if the Eucharist is meant to transform and sanctify human life in its entirety."[43] By their ability to grasp the meaning of this powerful symbol, young people can relate the brokenness of Christ to the brokenness of their own lives, experiencing transformation by his negation of their negation.

Pastoral Care

Young people are looking for significant adult role models to imitate, and many are initially attracted to the successful "well-groomed" Christians who admit no personal weaknesses and who are "nice" people to be around. While this seems to achieve the desired goal of evangelizing youth, it does not present the church authentically, and as young people mature and sense incongruities or contradictions in their models, they may also question the integrity of their faith and leave the church.

More than anything, youth want adults to be authentic and self-revealing; too many leaders try to impress youth with gimmicks. Youth leaders should be present to young people as "wounded healers:"

> This is so because a shared pain is no longer paralyzing but mobilizing, when understood as a way to liberation. When we become aware that we do not have to escape our pains, but that we can mobilize them into a common search for life, those very pains are transformed from expressions of despair into signs of hope. [44]

This does not mean that youth leaders should pour out their souls at every opportunity, but that they should recognize the creative potential of conflict situations and encourage young people to confront the eruptions of the void in their lives. Youth leaders must not be afraid of rejection when they confront young people, for pastoral care must strike a balance between comforting and confronting. The adults who worked with us in our production of *Godspell* were tremendously supportive, though most of their work was done literally behind the scenes. Without this firm guidance and selfless giving on their part, our group experience of the creative process might never have been actualized. [45]

REFLECTIONS: Andrew P. Grannell

Ezra Pound, in attempting to describe the power of metaphor, turned naturally enough to another metaphor, that is, the vortex.

Pound wrote that it is the peculiar power of metaphor to draw us into it, through it, and out of it in a continuing stream of related images.[46] The vortex of this paper is the "good news" as so rendered by the youthful retelling of the Christian story in *Godspell*. Into this vortex came a handful of troubled youth, through this vortex they were drawn with surprising ease and power, out of this vortex they were spun off as changed persons. This creative process as described here is captivating, highly motivating, terribly affecting, and finally a freeing experience. In this view, the centrifugal forces into which these young lives were cast became centrally important and powerfully meaningful. The creative process for the adolescent became a lived passion.

Whitehead describes the shifts we must suffer as our faith moves through such transforming vortices as the movement from God the void, to God the enemy, to God the companion.[47] It would appear that these shifts were evidenced in this creative process. The struggle with the meaning of Taylor's death (God the void) is characterized here very aptly as "the presence of an absence." Later, it became evident that deep-seated anger has replaced this anomie and the slap of rejection becomes its symbol. Finally, there is the centering moment of concelebration where reconciliation becomes possible with the recognition and acceptance of the "power of his love." This living reenactment of this strangely catastrophic-yet-joyfilled story became the means of a profound shift in faith consciousness.

The nurturing, supporting, and confirming adult community (for which we evidenced great yearning in our sessions) undoubtedly could not have known the shared inner meaning of this passionate retelling. Still, it is an excellent example of the intergenerational, loving, and participative experience that has emerged here as of central importance.

At the outset, Don Richter has given us what was for me an exciting preview of James Loder's book entitled, *Transforming Moment* (Harper & Row, 1981). Deeply influenced by Loder's creativity paradigm, Don has succeeded in bringing forward to us a key transforming experience of nearly a decade ago. The test for any good theory lies in its elegance, simplicity, fruitfulness, and paradigmatic power. Clearly, Loder's creativity paradigm meets all of those tests as Don has carefully shown.

There are two parts to his thesis that need our separate and careful examination for our purposes here: First, is conflict-ridden adolescence the period when most individuals become mature enough to understand the operation of God's creative process? Second, does the dawning awareness/understanding create a strong drive to want to experience the transforming moment with convictional force?

First, Don makes good use of Erikson, Piaget, Kohlberg, Elkind, Fowler, and Strommen to give us a summary look at the meaning of adolescent maturation. In each case, after this brief summary he turns to reflect upon the *Godspell* experience and finds confirmation. Although I find much benefit from this personal and varied examination of this seminal creative experience, there is little broad evidence offered here that would lend support for this thesis.

While it may well be accurate to depict the overall potential for understanding God's creative designs as presented through developmental writings, and while it certainly is clear that at least for this group of players the potential was present, we must guard against jumping too easily to the conclusion that "most individuals become mature enough to perceive the operation of God's creative process." Certainly, this is a hypothesis that merits further investigation. In this regard, it might be fruitful to examine the experiences of the Covenant Players of California over the past few decades.

Second, I must follow suit in challenging whether there is in fact an inherent drive to experience the transforming moment with "convictional force." Viktor Frankl with his understanding of the "will to meaning" and Paul Tillich with his understanding of the "courage to be" would certainly support Don Richter's thesis here, I would suggest. Yet, there are powerful forces of resistance operating in our psyche which block all potential for experiencing these moments. Adolescents are bound up in fear, loathing, self-depreciation, anxiety, and hopelessness as Strommen continues to verify. The conflict runs deeper than cognitive struggles for reconciliation of contraries. Again, as experience with psychodrama might show us, this is a terribly important and deeply freighted territory for adolescents. We are as likely to run afoul of the playing out of egocentric "personal fables" as we are the creative dramatization of the gospel story.[48]

In summary, I find this to be fine experiential and theoretical exploration of a creative resolution of a critical adolescent dilemma. Its systematic cross-referencing of experience with theory makes it most fruitful as a writing hypothesis. I would, however, find little broad support at present for either part of the author's main thesis. It is a carefully done, productive, and generous exploratory piece all the same.

NOTES

1. Paul Lehmann, *Ethics in a Christian Context* (New York: Harper & Row, 1963), pp. 344–367.

2. James Loder, *The Transforming Moment* (San Francisco: Harper & Row, 1981).

3. Søren Kierkegaard, *Fear and Trembling/Sickness Unto Death*, trans. Walter Lowrie (Princeton: Princeton University Press, 1936), pp. 49–58.

4. From *Murder in the Cathedral*, by T. S. Eliot, copyright 1935 by Harcourt Brace Jovanovich, Inc.; renewed 1963 by T. S. Eliot. Reprinted by permission of the publisher.

5. Paul Tillich, *Systematic Theology* (Chicago: University of Chicago Press, 1957), vol. 2, pp. 44–47.

6. Ibid., p. 78.

7. Silvano Arieti, *Creativity: The Magic Synthesis* (New York: Basic Books, 1976) pp. 54–55.

8. Freda Gardner, Princeton Theological Seminary.

9. C. G. Jung, *Psyche and Symbol* (Garden City, New York: Anchor Books, 1958), pp. 133, 145. Reprinted by permission of the Princeton University Press.

10. Loder, *Transforming Moment.* This is a perceptual phenomenon in which one determines how the ground might be contained within a figure rather than vice versa.

11. Tillich, *Systematic Theology*, vol. 3, p. 120.

12. Karl Barth, *Church Dogmatics*, trans. G. W. Bromiley (Edinburgh: T. & T. Clark, 1958), vol. 4:2, p. 513.

13. Arieti, *Creativity*, pp. 361–362.

14. Rex Johnson, "Middle Adolescence," in *Youth Education in the Church*, eds. Roy Zuck and Warren Benson (Chicago: Moody Press, 1968), p. 258.

15. Arieti, *Creativity*, p. 362.

16. Rolf E. Muuss, *Theories of Adolescence* (New York: Random House, 1962), p. 254.

17. Erik Erikson, *Identity: Youth and Crisis* (New York: W. W. Norton & Co., 1968), pp. 87–128.

18. Ibid., pp. 128–134.

19. Arieti, *Creativity*, pp. 180–182, 210–215.

20. Mary Wilcox, *Developmental Journey* (Nashville, Tennessee: Abingdon Press, 1979), p. 97.

21. Ibid., p. 100.

22. Guy Manaster, *Adolescent Development and the Life Tasks* (Boston: Allyn and Bacon, 1977), p. 47.

23. Ibid., p. 47.

24. Muuss, *Theories of Adolescence*, p. 227.

25. Johnson, "Middle Adolescence," p. 132.

26. Wilcox, *Developmental Journey*, p. 109.

27. Ibid., p. 110.

28. Ibid., p. 111.

29. Jim Fowler, *Life Maps*, ed. Jerome Berryman (Waco, Texas: Word Books, 1978).

30. Ibid., p. 72.

31. Roger Paine, *We Never Had Any Trouble Before* (New York: Stein & Day, 1975), pp. 15–29.

32. Youth may, in fact, feel more comfortable in a formal worship setting than in a sixties-style folk Mass, which uses music that is before their time.

33. Fowler, *Life Maps*, p. 64.

34. Merton Strommen, *Five Cries of Youth* (New York: Harper & Row, 1974), p. 92.

35. Classnotes from Philipps Universität, Marburg, West Germany (1976).

36. Arieti, *Creativity*, p. 240.

37. E. Dee Freeborn, "Youth and Music" in *Youth Education in the Church*, eds. Roy Zuck and Warren Benson (Chicago: Moody Press, 1968), p. 258.

38. Kierkegaard, in his *Philosophical Fragments* (pp. 68–88), claims that in the matter of faith, we are essentially *contemporaries* of the first disciples, to whom Jesus appeared as "God incognito." Jesus is asking us now, just as he asked people then, "Who do *you* say that I am?" Also see Walter Wink's *The Bible in Human Transformation* and Lyman Coleman's *Serendipity* series.

39. Donald Miller, "Revelation and Life Cycle, in *Process and Relationship*, eds. Iris V. Cully and Kendig Brubaker Cully (Birmingham, Alabama: Religious Education Press, 1978), p. 105.

40. Lehmann, *Ethics in a Christian Context*, p. 87fn, and p. 387.

41. David and Margaret Steward, "Naming into Personhood: the Church's Educational Ministry," in *Process and Relationship*, eds. Iris V. Cully and Kendig Brubaker Cully (Birmingham, Alabama: Religious Education Press, 1978) pp. 49–55.

42. John Macquarrie, *Paths in Spirituality*, (New York: Harper & Row, 1972), p. 59.

43. Ibid., p. 75.

44. Henri Nouwen, *The Wounded Healer* (Garden City, New York: Image Books, 1979), p. 93.

45. Credits at the end: Woody Finley, Meccy Wiley, and Marsha Reisser.

46. Ezra Pound, *Gaudier-Brzeska* (New York: New Directions, 1974), pp. 99, 102, 106.

47. Alfred North Whitehead, *Religion in the Making* (New York: World Publishing, 1972), p. 16.

48. David Elkind, *The Child and Society: Essays in Applied Child Development* (New York: Oxford University Press, 1979), pp. 95ff.

Afterword

D. Campbell Wyckoff

On what basis may the churches be challenged to recommit themselves to ministry with youth? From one point of view, the positions taken by the contributors to this book might lead to the conclusion that the confusion in the churches over an approach to youth ministry is reflected in the diversity of directions advocated by the experts in the field. There are sharp differences of opinion, often intransigently held. Dialogue is often impossible because of the ideological rigidity of those who would have to be partners in an open search. In some quarters it is difficult even to face the possibility that there is trouble afoot.

From another point of view, however, the survey of research, the positions analyzed and explained, and the critical responses provide insight on the problem, why we have the problem, and the possibilities for dealing with it.

We have three things here: First, the solid data on youth and youth ministry from which to proceed to constructive work on program renewal. Second, authentic expressions of the powerful points of view that are seeking to lure youth work in various directions. Third, a sharp critique and evaluation both of the data and the positions, that sets a perspective for the future.

The topics represent central issues, and have proven power to spark discussion, even to some extent dialogue, that may do three things: validate the issues, reveal the difficulties in dealing with

them, and lay the groundwork for dealing with some of the difficulties.

The outcomes are substantial data, insights of permanent
value, and useful suggestions on next steps.

*   *   *

From both the chapters in this book and from the discussions
of the various chapters by the contributors, a series of convictions about youth ministry emerge:

Youth ministry must recognize its cultural context.

It is important to have a community that spans all ages
in the church, and that includes youth in the total life
of the church.

We must learn to recognize and deal with conflicting
expectations for youth ministry in the different segments of
the congregation: youth, parents, clergy, lay advisers, the
Lord (and the gospel mandate).

We must become familiar with support services, resources,
and resource persons for youth ministry.

Youth ministry needs informed, authentic youth leaders
and other adults in the congregation who are willing to share
their excitement about God's activity in the world, and who
are sensitive to the teachable moments.

The church must be open and alert to God's present activity
in the world and to its mission in light of present converging
crises.

Youth ministry must discriminate between Christianity and
other faith commitments.

We must acknowledge the tension that exists between the
church as a cultural construct and the church as a people
of God.

Youth ministry cannot be confined to a narrow set of
stereotypes about who best does ministry, nor only to certain
expressions of faith or images of the church.

There is a need for front line pragmatics, basic training,
   the gathering of practical models. For example, we should
   find out how effective youth ministers are spending their
   time.
We can identify guidelines for youth ministry based on the
   New Testament *koinonia* and provide room for local autonomy within those guidelines.
We should enable youth leaders to realize what they have to
   give to young people so that they will have the confidence to
   do it.
Youth ministry involves youth in mission.

From the series of convictions listed above, an overall goal and
four priorities can be enunciated for youth ministry:

The goal is to help youth and persons in youth ministry gain
insight into self and community in relation to church and
culture, in tension with God's vision of community. This
means:

1. Evaluation of the cultural context; learning how to deal
with the "givens" that we may not even recognize in our particular corner of society. Specifically, what is involved is gaining insight in depth on youth in particular churches and communities, through training in knowing and interpreting youth
in their particular communities and cultures.

2. Identifying and articulating the biblical vision of community, in order to work out what is to be dealt with distinc-
tively in church youth work—the New Testament base; the
core concepts; the components of Christian community.

3. Recognizing, and developing skills in dealing with, attitudes and relationships.

4. Responding to God's activity in the world by basing youth
work in action for social justice. Dealing with the challenges of
an unjust and demanding world order; struggling with how to
integrate the social complexities of justice and liberation with
our personal agenda for wholeness and self-fulfillment.

On the basis of these convictions and priorities, the following practical follow-up activities are recommended for youth ministry:

Careful listening to and observation of what is *already* happening in various congregations. This would provide a rich variety of practical possibilities, by building up the component of local experience and wisdom. At the same time, and perhaps more fundamentally, it would help to answer the persistent question, "Am I even in the right world?"

Training people in the four key areas (above) and sending them into local congregations to facilitate experiences in these indigenous settings. The suggestion was as specific as "eighteen people out to eighteen places, preceded by the training process."

Bringing youth, lay leaders, and parents together in sharing-learning experiences—"energizing experiences of community." An outcome of such experiences might be replicable processes for youth ministry.

                              *   *   *

Freda Gardner, reflecting later on what she had written, put part of her conclusion in this way:

"Youth, whether three or four adolescents in a parish or thousands in a denomination, are addressed by God one by one and redeemed for life as the church. One-string bows in ministry to and with youth are not enough. I suspect that this points us in two directions: away from a too-narrow youth program to a more holistic view of the church as the context and process of ministry and, second, to ecumenical community ministry where several options of study, action, worship, and fellowship are open for any one young person or any group of young people. It also suggests that the churches cannot be satisfied with a ministry that concentrates on only one dimension of youth's life or one area of development. Redemption is a characteristic of life among lives—a person's new life nurtured and sustained by others newly alive.

Programs centered on recreation, sexual identity, achievement, acceptance, values, service activities, and all the rest do not constitute ministry except as they exist in the church and in order that the individuals who participate in them find themselves as a part of the Body of Christ.

"While I would not resist other motifs, I continue to find in *imago dei* power to shape the kind of ministry to and with youth (including denomination, congregation, parents, youth, and youth leaders) that we seem to be seeking. Whether it or any biblical-theological motif can empower us, individually or corporately, to seek and claim a ministry whose primary characteristics are faithfulness and Shalom (and to renounce all other marks of excellence) remains to be seen."

*   *   *

The individuals responsible for the project on youth ministry as reported in this book strongly believe that the work begun by both the project and this book should be continued by developing a future workshop on nurturing leadership for youth ministry. This future workshop should revolve around the following axes:

The workshop goal

To encourage persons engaged in youth ministry in major Protestant denominations to develop a more critical perspective on self and community in order to realize the redemptive possibilities and responsibilities that God calls us to claim in any given context of ministry with youth.

Perceived assumptions

Each person, youth and adult, has gifts for ministry. Effective ministry is a shared ministry of the community of faith.

There is need in youth ministry for a better understanding of the process of spiritual formation, how a youth is shaped in Christ.

There are ways to increase our awareness of what it means to live as the people of God in our particular cultural milieu.

Youth and adults, lay persons and professionals, are to be more fully integrated in nurturing leadership for youth ministry.

The norms for effective youth ministry will be determined by our response to such biblical mandates as justice and servanthood.

Integral dimensions of the educational experience

Relational factors—Guided personal reflection encouraging a new awareness of one's own youth, the relationship of one's personal needs to ministry, and the dynamics that one's personality brings to a given context of ministry.

Faith values—Direction in learning how to discover or rediscover for ourselves the biblical vision of redemptive possibilities and responsibilities, whatever the "givens" may be in our own lives and in those with whom we minister.

Lifestyle issues—Engagement in the exploration of the demands upon us and the possibilities for us, both personal and communal, as God's people in this world.

Expressive needs—Encouragement to communicate creatively and imaginatively to one another and to others what we are discovering about ourselves as each of us affirms his or her uniqueness in ministry.

Characteristics of the participants

Experienced in youth ministry.

Focused on *ministry*, with any special program as illustrative and supportive.

Intentional.

Dialogical—able to share oneself with others and vice versa.

Constructive—building on the previous findings; helping to test the present hypotheses and to generate new ones.

Design process

The participants will bring to the design process suggested methods for dealing with each of the four integral educational dimensions (above).

Worship and Bible study will be the central, integrating dynamic.

There will be a balance of concern for the self and for social issues. What is the method for coming to a constructive self-understanding that may be presented to youth by committed adults? How do we learn to perceive the critical issues in a particular community?

The basic movements of the design process are: lead, listen, dialogue, and build.

These elements will be considered throughout the process:

- A theological critique of existing models and approaches in ministry with youth.
- The institutionalization of youth ministry, both its benefits and drawbacks.
- The position of a youth minister, the title "youth minister," the single person in ministry, the adult leader of youth as adult.

The product

An experiential model of learning that will be applicable for youth and adults from diverse backgrounds and settings.

A process that can be replicated in a three-day period, perhaps during a weekend retreat.

A model that emphasizes the goals for those entering the process, that is, the goals of youth and adults engaged in ministry.

A follow-up proposal with suggestions for field testing the model.

*   *   *

For those who have participated in it, the project on youth ministry reported in this book has been an experience in recommitment to ministry with youth.

In 1964, the National Council of the Churches of Christ in the U.S.A. published a bulletin, *A View Toward Youth in the Church's Ministry.* It said:

> The church's youth ministry... *is* the church living its life and doing its work involving both youth and adults. .... What is offered is the life of faith and love in response to God's self-disclosure and his seeking love. This life means involvement in the worship and fellowship of the Christian community and shared opportunities for witness, mission, service, and the deepening of the personal life in educational groups, working groups, small informal groups, home life, civic life, and activities beyond the local community (p. 25).

Our own recommitment to youth ministry has been a rediscovery (the hard way, because when we were on the track of something new we often found that it was not new at all) that this is true. At the same time, we have become committed to seeing it anew in light of changes that have taken place in the youth situation, in the world, and in the church. Furthermore, our commitment now includes the use of better tools for ascertaining the needs we seek to meet, improved patterns of program design, recognition of the holistic character of youth ministry, and a realism born of years of decline in this aspect of the church's work.

The strategy that we propose to test is one of rediscovery by youth and leaders of youth together of their needs for and gifts in ministry, and mutual expansion of our self-awareness in relation to these needs and gifts by getting at our biblical and spiritual rootage in Christ, by exploring our styles of life in light of the demands made upon us and our own possibilities for response, and by discovering together the mediums and languages in which we may express who we are and in which we may carry on our mutual ministry.

This strategy, when used, will itself become a means for recommitment. It is also a training process that is replicable. When we are ready to do so, we hope to propose a further strategy by which recommitment to youth ministry may multiply in the churches through the use of such a process.

Index of Names

Abraham, 181
Archimedes, 211, 212
Arieti, Silvano, 212, 239, 240
Aristotle, 113, 127
Armstrong, James F., xi
Astin, Helen, 8, 9

Baer, Guy, 132
Ballenger, Sharon, 40
Bandura, Albert, 17
Barth, Karl, 163, 223, 240
Basso, Keith, 99
Baum, Gregory, 174, 179, 205, 206
Beckett, Samuel, 186
Bengtson, Vern, 7
Benson, Warren S., 32, 44, 53, 240
Berger, Peter, 37
Berryman, Jerome, 52, 240
Birch, Bruce C., 205, 206, 207
Blanchard, Michael Kelly, 207
Boehlke, Stephen F., xi
Boling, Don, 42
Bonhoeffer, Dietrich, 195, 206
Bowman, Locke Jr., 32, 45, 46, 52

Brekke, Milo L., 53
Bromiley, G. W., 240
Bronfenbrenner, Urie, 118, 150, 162
Brown, Robert McAfee, 206
Brueggemann, Walter, 172, 173, 205, 206
Burgess, Harold W., 133, 148

Caffee, Gabrielle, 99
Churchill, Winston, 119
Coleman, James S., 99, 186
Coleman, Lyman, 241
Coles, Robert, 207
Cooper, Mildred, 132
Crawford, Elizabeth, 132
Cromer, William, 41
Cully, Iris V., 241
Cully, Kendig Brubaker, 241

Day, Dorothy, 192, 206
Dickstein, Morris, 185, 206
Douvan, Elizabeth, 6, 8
Downs, Beth, 132
Dreyer, Phillip H., 2, 5, 7, 52, 99
Durka, Gloria, 40, 99

Einstein, Albert, 212
Eisenstadt, S. N., 3, 4
Eliot, T. S., 239
Elkind, David, 18, 238, 241
Elliott, Del, 102
Enroth, Ronald, 184, 206
Erikson, Erik H., 13, 14, 15, 16, 19, 52, 72, 74, 97, 98, 226, 238, 240
Evans, David, 38, 39, 40, 52

Farson, Richard, 106, 125
Ferkiss, Victor, 169, 205
Finley, Woody, 241
Fleck, J. Roland, 44
Fletcher, Kenneth R., 32, 46, 52
Foley, Lynn, 132
Forbes, William, 132
Fowler, James W., 22, 23, 24, 52, 97, 99, 164, 165, 238, 240
Fox, Matthew, 169, 175, 178, 190, 205, 206
Francis of Assisi, 192
Frankl, Victor, 238
Freeborn, E. Dee, 44, 240
Freud, Sigmund, 15
Fuller, Buckminster, 169

Gall, John, 113
Gallup, George, 148
Gardner, Freda A., ix, xi, 239, 245
Geertz, Clifford, 87, 99
Getz, Gene A., 21, 53
Ginsberg, Allen, 115
Glasser, William, 111, 112, 123, 124
Goodman, Paul, 20
Goslin, David A., 99
Graham, Richard, 6, 7

Grannell, Andrew P., x
Guggenheim, Benjamin, 126
Gutierrez, Gustavo, 206

Haley, Jay, 102
Hall, G. Stanley, 84, 99
Harp, Richard, 132
Hartman, Warren, 132
Havighurst, Robert J., 2, 5, 7, 17, 52, 98, 99
Hay, Susan, 132
Hayes, Kenneth, 132
Heilbroner, Robert L., 169, 171, 205
Hepburn, Katherine, 122
Hoffman, M. L., 98
Hoge, Dean R., x, 163, 165
Holderness, Ginny Ward, 32, 47, 52
Hostetler, John, 99
Huebner, Dwayne, 68
Hulmes, Edward, 53
Hunt, Richard A., 145, 148
Huntington, Gertrude Enders, 99
Hymes, Dell, 98

Isaiah, 171, 185, 202

James, William, 206
Jeremiah, 167, 168
John, Saint, 150, 193
Johnson, Arthur L., 53
Johnson, David W., 52
Johnson, Rex, 44, 240
Joshua, 196
Joy, Donald, 44
Jung, Carl G., 7, 219, 220, 240

Kavanagh, Aidan, 206
Keen, Sam, 22, 23, 52

Kellman, Herbert C., 151, 165
Keniston, Kenneth, 5, 82, 85, 98,
    99, 207
Kierkegaard, Søren, 41, 209, 239,
    241
Kight, William N., xi
Kilgore, Lois, 32, 47, 52
Kimball, Solon T., 98
King, Morton B., 145, 148
Klever, Gerald L., 21, 22, 28, 53
Kohlberg, Lawrence, 6, 16, 19,
    22, 24, 96, 97, 98, 99, 228,
    238

LeFever, Marlene, 44, 45
Lehmann, Paul, 234, 239, 241
Lifton, Robert Jay, 4
Little, Sara, xi, 32, 33, 34, 52
Loder, James E., xi, 237, 238,
    239, 240
Luckmann, Thomas, 37
Luke, Saint, 215
Lundgreen, Joann, 112, 114
Luther, Martin, 182
Lynn, Robert Wood, x

Macquarrie, John, 241
Manaster, Guy J., 13, 17, 18, 19,
    20, 21, 52, 240
Manning, Peter K., 2, 3, 52
Marcia, James, 16
Mary, 233
Matthew, Saint, 175, 215
Maupassant, Guy de, 116
McClellan, James T. Jr., 98
McCord, James I., xi
McFarland, Jean, 102
Merton, Thomas, 190, 206
Miller, Donald, 241
Miller, Keith, 154

Modgil, Celia, 99
Modgil, Sohan, 99
Moon, Sun Myung, 89
Moore, Alexander, 99
Muuss, Rolf E., 13, 15, 16, 17,
    52, 240

Newton, Isaac, 212
Neville, Gwen Kennedy, ix, 2, 9,
    10, 11, 12, 53, 95, 96, 99
Niebuhr, Reinhold, 122
Nouwen, Henri, 241
Novak, Michael, 7, 192, 206

Osborne, Cecil, 154
Otto, Rudolf, 211

Paine, Roger W. III, ix, 2, 12, 41,
    52, 240
Parsons, Talcott, 98
Paul, Saint, 150, 156
Perry, David, 132
Peter, Saint, 233
Pound, Ezra, 236, 237, 241
Piaget, Jean, 16, 18, 22, 24, 96,
    97, 98, 226, 238
Poerschke, Robert, 40
Proteus, 4
Pugh, Donald, 44

Raines, Robert, 154
Rapson, Richard, 99
Rasmussen, Larry L., 206, 207
Reisser, Marsha, 241
Rest, James, 24
Richards, Lawrence O., x, 43, 44,
    53, 165
Richter, Don, x, xi
Riesman, David, 183, 206
Rogers, Carl, 189

Ruether, Rosemary, 205
Rummery, R. M., 133, 148

Sarah, 181
Sawin, Margaret, 40
Schneider, David, 99
Schwartz, Pepper, 104
Seattle, Chief, 199
Segundo, J., 195
Selby, Henry, 99
Selman, Robert, 22, 24
Shaull, Richard, 206
Sherif, Carolyn W., 2. 53
Sherif, Muzafer, 2, 53
Sholund, Milford, 44
Sider, Ronald J., 174, 205
Skolnick, Arlene, 206
Smith, Ella, 132
Smith, Ernest A., 1, 2, 53
Smith, Jackie M., x, 205
Smith, Joanmarie, 99
Snyder, Ross, 69
Sparkman, G. Temp, 32, 40, 41, 53
Starr, Jerold, 7
Steward, David, 241
Steward, Margaret, 241
Stookey, Noel Paul, 204, 207
Strommen, Merton P., 21, 22, 25, 26, 27, 53, 73, 74, 238, 240

Taylor, Bob, 132
Tillich, Paul, 210, 211, 223, 238, 239, 240
Thomas, Joseph R., 205, 206
Thompson, Francis, 200
Truzzi, Marcello, 2, 3, 52
Turner, Victor, 88, 89, 99

Uittenbogaard, Roger W., ix
Underwager, Ralph C., 52, 53

Van Gennep, Arnold, 88, 99
Vizedon, Monika, 99
Vonnegut, Kurt, 109

Warren, Michael, 32, 35, 36, 37, 53, 186, 206
Weber, Max, 98, 170
Westerhoff, John, 2, 9, 10, 11, 53, 64, 75, 99, 132, 164, 165
Whitehead, Alfred North, 241
Wilcox, Mary, 22, 23, 24, 53, 240
Wilcoxson, Georgeann, 206
Wiley, Meccy, 241
Wink, Walter, 205, 241
Wolfe, Scott, 132
Woods, Ray T., 21, 22, 28, 53

Zuck, Roy, 21, 32, 44, 53, 240

Index of Subjects

Achievement, need for, 7
Alienation, 25, 64–66, 211
Altruism, 29
Anthropology, relation to church
    tradition, 79
Archetypal patterns of youth, 3
Authenticity, 69
Autonomy, 20
    I-me stage, 20
    I-them stage, 20
    They-me stage, 20

Birth control, 6
Boys Town Center for the Study
    of Youth Development,
    132–133

Catechesis, 9–10
Charismatic experience, 140–
    141, 148
Charismatic leader, 69–70
Church-ins, 47
Clergy, 31
Commitment to doctrine in
    youth, 21
    evangelical growth, 21
    mainline backsliding, 21

Community, 35, 63, 137, 150,
    155, 156, 158, 163, 173,
    223, 229, 234, 243
Consensual religion, 28
Conversion, 138, 141, 145, 150,
    179–180
Corporateness, 179–180
Council on Anthropology and
    Education, 80
Creativity, 189–190, 208–239
    and adolescent conflicts, 223–
    231
        family relationships, reorder-
        ing of, 229–230
        intellectual maturation,
        226–228
        new values, and, 228–229
        physical growth, 224–225
        response to God, 230–231
        sexual awareness, 224–225
    context of, 208–213
        estrangement in, 210–211
        four dimensionality in,
        209–211
        process of, 211–213
            conflict, initial, 211
            continuity, public expres-
            sion of, 212

insight, moment of, 212
    scanning, interlude for,
    211–212
    tension, release of, 212
convictional characteristics of,
    219–223
experiencing creative process,
    213–219
fostering creativity, 232–236
    drama, 233–234
    music, 232–233
    pastoral care, and, 235–236
    sacraments, 234–235
Cultural determinism, 79
Cultural relativism, 79
Culture, definition of, 82
Cults, 13, 186
Cursillo, 154

Delayed gratification, 25
Development versus/with gospel,
    63
Developmental task, 17
Divorce, 58
Drugs, 13, 32, 67, 89, 121, 147,
    169, 186, 229

Ecclesiology, 154
Economic upheaval, 169–170
Ecumenism, 33
Emotions, 24
Enculturation, see Socialization
Endocept, 212
Eriksonian theory, 14–15, 18–19,
    97, 225–226
Eschatology, apocalyptic, 13
Estrangement, see Alienation
Ethnicity, 7, 10–11
Evangelization, 35–36, 60
Extra-church movements, 63

Family, 2–3, 8, 10–11, 21, 24,
    29, 48–49, 57–58, 60, 65,
    102, 112–115, 118, 120–
    121, 137, 141, 148–151,
    153, 156, 161–163, 229–230
Family clusters, 40
Five cries of youth, 27–28, 73
    cry of joy, 28
    cry of prejudice, 28
    cry of psychological orphans,
        28
    cry of self-hatred, 27–28
    cry of social protest, 28
Formal cognitive operations,
    18–19, 226–227
Fowlerian theory, 22–23, 97
Friendship, 20, 35, 50

Generation gap, 25, 27–28, 49
Gestalt patterning, 95–96
Gray Panthers, 55

Hare Krishna, 89
Hero worship, 6
Hidden curriculum, 10, 90, 225
Hierarchical mentality, 177–178
Home Base groups, 47
Home communities, 40

Identification, 3, 6, 8, 63, 151–
    152
    factors in enhancing, 152
    sex-role, 6, 8
Identity, 14–16, 47, 49, 62, 67,
    78–79, 136–137, 191, 225–
    226, 231
    models of, 14–16
Imago Dei, 66–68, 70, 73
Indigenization, 36
Informal institutions of youth, 2

Intergenerational relationships, 3, 72, 162
Internalization, 151–152

Kairos, 171–173, 180–181
Kohlbergian theory, 16, 19, 96–97, 148, 228–229

Life-stage theories, 76–81
Lilly Youth Ministry Project, summary of, 246–249
    assumptions of, 246–247
    design process of, 247–248
    dimensions of, 247
        expressive needs, 247
        faith values, 247
        lifestyle issues, 247
        relational factors, 247
    goal of, 246
    participants, characteristics of, 247
    product of, 248
    recommitment and, 248–249
Liminality, 88–91, 97
Liturgy, 30, 32, 41–42, 69, 90, 157, 194–195, *see also* Ritual
Luther League, 76

Maturation, physiological, 17–18
Mission, 27, 42–43, 244
Modeling, 6, 152, 159, 225
Mysterium tremendum, 211
Myth, 9

National Council of Churches, 61, 70
National Society for the Study of Education, 81
Numinosum, 211

Objective of Christian Education for Senior High Young People, 61–62
Outcomes of Religious Education and Youth Ministry, 132–148
Overpopulation, 169

Parents, *see* Family
Peer-group, 26, 36, 86, 137
Personality inconsistency, 19
Piagetian theory, 18–19, 96–97, 226–227
Proclamation, 42
Project Youth, 46–47
Prophetic communities, 180–202
    enactment of, 180–181
    focus of, 180
    larger community, relation to, 195–202
    need for, 180–181, 184–186
    shape of, 186–189
    style of, 189–195
        experimental and creative, 189–190
        freedom and simplicity in, 191–194
        justice and compassion in, 190–191
        prayer and workship in, 194–195
    theological reasons for, 183–184
Prophetic ministry, 172
Protean Man, 4–5
Psychological moratorium, 49
Psychosocial moratorium, 20
Psychotherapy, 101, 114–115, 118
Puberty, 59, 83

Public School Establishment, 77
Pyramid of Snofru, *see* Snofru's
    Pyramid

Reference group, 2–3, 8, 48
Religious experience, 13–32,
    49–50
Renewal, 153–160
Responsibility, 13, 123
Retreats, 32, 34, 37–38, 47
Rites of passage, 88–89
Ritual, 9, 11–12, 63, 83, 89, 97
    phases of, 11
Role-playing, 45

Sacraments, 139
School, 2–3, 6–7, 11, 16, 58, 71,
    77, 80–81, 84
Security, contrasted to Shalom,
    173–174
Self-concept, 136, 139
Self-process, 4
Selflessness, 23
Sex education, 104–105
Shalom of God, 62, 64, 173–178,
    184, 246
Sin, 64–65, 68, 70, 73
Situation ethics, 13
Snofru's pyramid, 113–114
Social-learning theory, 17
    and modeling, 17
Socialization, 2, 4, 6, 9–12, 48,
    58, 71, 79, 85–88, 91–92
    contrasted to education, 10
    definition of, 10
    sexuality and, 11–12
Spiritual counterfeits, 184
Stage of life, youth as, 5
Stasis, 5

Structural-functionalist adoles-
    cence, 2
Sun Myung Moon Church, 89
Sunday School, 77, 134
Symbol, 3–5, 24, 49–50, 79, 84,
    86, 230–231

Values clarification, 11, 24, 47

Wesley Foundation, 76
Westminster Fellowship, 76
White church, 167
White House Conference on
    Children, 151
Withdrawal from culture, 2
Witnessing, 42, 201–202
World of Youth, 28–32
    areas of, 29–30
        culture, 29
        family, 29
        institution, 30
        psychology, 29
        religion, 29–30
    effective ministry in, 31–32
    God and youth, 31
        reasons for belief in God, 31
            authoritative, 31
            empirical, 31
            rational, 31
            utilitarian, 31
Worship, *see* Liturgy

Young Life, 60
Youth, 5, 55–56, 75–76, 81–86
    as cultural construct, 81–86
    definitions of, 5, 55–56, 75–76,
        81–82, 84
Youth movements. 21
Youth Research Center, 46–47
Youth Research Survey, 27–28

Other Important Books from Religious Education Press

RELIGIOUS EDUCATION, CATECHESIS, AND FREEDOM
by *Kenneth Barker*
A fine examination of the different responses given by religious educationists and catechetical leaders to the call to freedom issued by the church and by the world. A helpful book for educational ministers seriously concerned with providing learners with religious education and with catechesis in and for freedom.
ISBN 0-89135-028-4

RELIGIOUS EDUCATION AND THEOLOGY
edited by *Norma H. Thompson*
Provides a wide spectrum of contrasting views on the intrinsic connection of religious education with theology. ISBN 0-89135-029-2

THE THEORY OF CHRISTIAN EDUCATION PRACTICE
by *Randolph Crump Miller*
An elaboration on the way in which theology affects religious education in a determinative fashion, and on the manner in which religious education enfleshes theology. ISBN 0-89135-049-7

WHO ARE WE?: THE QUEST FOR A RELIGIOUS EDUCATION
edited by *John H. Westerhoff III*
An exploration into the identity and special calling of the religious educator as seen by many of the most important religious education leaders of the twentieth century. Many of the most important issues facing religious education are treated in this book. ISBN 0-89135-014-4

THE SHAPE OF RELIGIOUS EDUCATION
by *James Michael Lee*
No one can discuss contemporary religious education meaningfully unless he or she has read this book. Widely acclaimed as a classic in the field. ISBN 0-89135-000-4

THE FLOW OF RELIGIOUS EDUCATION
by *James Michael Lee*
A serious in-depth look at the nature and structure of the religion teaching process. This volume provides that kind of solid and systematic framework so necessary for the effective *teaching* of religion. A major work. ISBN 0-89135-001-2

THE RELIGIOUS EDUCATION WE NEED
edited by *James Michael Lee*
A prophetic volume presenting Catholic and Protestant proposals on a viable future for religious education. Exciting chapters by Alfred McBride, Randolph Crump Miller, Carl F. H. Henry, John Westerhoff III, Gloria Durka, and James Michael Lee. This book has as its axis the renewal of Christian education. ISBN 0-89135-005-5

AN INVITATION TO RELIGIOUS EDUCATION
by *Harold William Burgess*
A careful examination of the most influential Protestant and Catholic theories of religious education proposed in our time. An essential book for understanding the foundational issues in religious education. ISBN 0-89135-019-5

ABOVE OR WITHIN?: THE SUPERNATURAL IN RELIGIOUS EDUCATION
by *Ian P. Knox*
An illuminating survey of the basic theological issue permeating all religious education activity, namely: "How can the religious educator help learners of all ages meet God in their own lives?" A book centering on God's revelation in religious education. ISBN 0-89135-006-3

CREATIVE CONFLICT IN RELIGIOUS EDUCATION AND CHURCH ADMINISTRATION
by *Donald E. Bossart*
A stimulating volume centering around two major themes: the myriad possibilities for growth inherent in all conflict, and the specific procedures which can be used in religious settings to bring out the productive potential in conflict. This interdisciplinary volume deals with the theological dynamics, psychological dynamics, sociological dynamics, and educational dynamics of conflict. ISBN 0-89135-048-9

MORAL DEVELOPMENT, MORAL EDUCATION, AND KOHLBERG
edited by *Brenda Munsey*
A seminal volume on the interrelated topics of moral development, moral education, and religious education. An interdisciplinary treatment from the perspectives of religious education, philosophy, psychology, and general education. These original essays bring together some of the most important scholars in North America, Europe, and Israel. ISBN 0-89135-020-9

RELIGIOUS EDUCATION IN A PSYCHOLOGICAL KEY
by *John H. Peatling*
A perceptive look at religious education from a psychological perspective. This volume shows how psychology can empower religious education to enrich the spiritual lives of learners. A major feature of this book is the penetrating way in which it reveals the religious dimension of psychology and the psychological dimension of religion. ISBN 0-89135-027-6